N. C. Wilson

March 1922.

THE
FUNDAMENTALS OF CHRISTIANITY
A Study of the Teaching of Jesus and Paul

THE MACMILLAN COMPANY
NEW YORK · BOSTON · CHICAGO · DALLAS
ATLANTA · SAN FRANCISCO

MACMILLAN & CO., Limited
LONDON · BOMBAY · CALCUTTA
MELBOURNE

THE MACMILLAN CO. OF CANADA, Ltd.
TORONTO

THE FUNDAMENTALS
OF CHRISTIANITY

A STUDY OF THE TEACHING OF JESUS AND PAUL

BY

HENRY C. VEDDER

PROFESSOR OF CHURCH HISTORY IN CROZER
THEOLOGICAL SEMINARY

New York

THE MACMILLAN COMPANY

1922

TO

MY TEACHER IN THEOLOGY

AUGUSTUS HOPKINS STRONG, D.D., LL.D.

READER, IF YOU FIND HERE AUGHT GOOD AND TRUE

THANK HIM.

IF YOU FIND UNTRUTH AND HERESY

BLAME ME!

CONTENTS

PROLEGOMENA

I

THE specific sources for the writing of such a book as this are, of course, the Gospels, for the teaching of Jesus, and the Epistles of Paul, for the teaching of the apostle. But we cannot understand these without taking into account the whole literature of the Hebrew people, of which these writings are an inseparable part. Though the modern Jew refuses to recognize the later collection of writings known to us as the New Testament, he cannot deny that it is as Jewish as the older collection. The apostles may have been apostate Jews, but they were certainly Jews. Only a single gentile writer, so far as we know, contributed aught to the New Testament; and even Luke was Jew by conviction, if not Jew by birth.

These writings are, without exception, deeply imbued with the spirit of the people who produced them and of the times in which they were composed. Jew and Christian are agreed in regarding them as a divine revelation (though the Jew, of course, would deny this character to the later collection), but all intelligent people of both religions have come to recognize in these books a human element, as well as a divine. They were not handed down from heaven, or even dictated by God to human amenuenses, but composed under the guidance of the divine Spirit by men who had the limitations of other men. The writers were not of a uniform grade of mentality or spiritual insight, and so great differences are discernible in the writings; in particular, the older books give us a different ideal of God and teach different ethics, from the later. Men can no longer shut their eyes to this fact; the wonder is that for ages they were able so completely to ignore it. No candid

reader of the Scriptures can now fail to see that they
many times flatly contradict each other, and none of the
processes of mechanical "reconciliation" that satisfied our
fathers will remove this difficulty for us. There is but one
honest method of reconciliation available: to recognize
these collections of writings as the record of a progressive
revelation; to admit frankly that the earlier writers "saw
through a glass darkly," and that even some of the later can
hardly be said to have seen "face to face." In other words,
God revealed himself by degrees to men, as they were able
to receive knowledge of him; and the revelations of earlier
time were of necessity fragmentary and imperfect.

It inevitably follows from this understanding of the
nature of the Bible that religious teachers can no longer
be suffered to quote the words of Scripture, on the assumption that all are of equal value and authority. The old
method of citing "proof texts" indifferently anywhere from
the first chapter of Genesis to the last of Revelation is as
dead as Julius Caesar. It follows also that the later revelation is clearer, higher, truer than the earlier; and where
the two conflict, as they so often do, the later supersedes
the earlier. And for the Christian, at least, the highest
revelation of all is contained in the teachings of Jesus.

It should seem that one who calls himself a Christian
might be safely assumed to be pledged by his chosen name
to accept Jesus the Christ as his highest authority in
religion. It might justly be assumed, one would think,
that he is bound to evaluate all other religious teaching in
accordance with the words of his avowed Master and
Teacher. Whoever and whatever accords with His words
is to be accepted. Whoever or whatever differs irreconcil-
ably from His words is to be rejected. Why, indeed,
should any man who refuses to abide by this principle as
the touchstone of truth wish to call himself a Christian?
Surely, if he refuses to bow to the supreme authority of

Jesus, he might choose some other appellation than Christian that would better fit him.

This book will not attempt formal proof of the foregoing propositions. They will only incidentally, and almost accidentally, furnish subject of discussion. They are the fundamental data on which the entire discussion proceeds; so nearly axiomatic, in the author's view, that the mere statement of them should secure hearty assent from the thoughtful Christian reader. Indeed, his fear is that more readers will pronounce them truisms than untruths. But it is only fair to give warning that any reader who seriously dissents from them will do well to lay the book aside at this point, as it would probably be pure waste of time and mental energy for him to read further. For if these fundamentals are untrue, or even doubtful, the following pages are worthless.

II

Evangelists and preachers of a certain type are very fond of saying in public that "they believe the Bible from cover to cover," that they "believe every word in the Bible, from Genesis to Revelation" (only, that type usually says "Revelations"). Even theologians educated enough to be reasonably intelligent, and so to know better, profess and teach belief in the absolute inerrancy and infallibility of the Bible. Nay more, they wage open and bitter warfare on all who will not pronounce their shibboleths. Nearly all the so-called "Bible Schools" are given over to this heresy, which they proclaim to be the only orthodoxy. One very prominent religious newspaper (at least, it makes high pretensions to religion) loses no opportunity to defame every theological institution in which it thinks this doctrine is not taught. What's in a name? especially in religious parties. There are "Evangelicals" utterly destitute of the gospel spirit; "Catholics" who are in mind and temper hopeless sectarians; "Liberals" who are the perfection of illiberality; and "Orthodox" who hold fast what is not, never was, and never can be Christianity.

All signs show that a determined and systematic propaganda of this view of the Bible has been undertaken, with the explicitly avowed purpose of branding as heretics all men and institutions that fail to conform to this standard of orthodoxy, and the more than hinted purpose of establishing some new form of organization, if that prove necessary to the attainment of the leaders' ends. In these days when the majority of Christians are thinking and talking much about Christian unity, we are seriously threatened with a new schism.

It is a time therefore for plain speech. In this age of the world no man can avow belief in "the whole Bible, from cover to cover," without casting painful suspicion upon either his sincerity or his intelligence. Nobody needs to accuse him of such defect; he accuses himself when he so speaks. No man who makes public proclamation of this belief could stand cross-examination for five minutes in the presence of the very audience that unthinkingly applauds his words. Before half a dozen questions had been asked, he would be hedging and explaining and retracting. There is no educated man living who really believes the Bible from cover to cover. There is no half educated man who believes the Bible in that wholesale way. No man can make such profession sincerely unless he has escaped education altogether. Men who say such things are talking buncombe, playing to the galleries.

There are few people of any age or any schooling who have read their Bibles with any degree of intelligence or care, without finding statements that have perplexed them, and in some parts ethics that have astonished and revolted them, as well as contradictions and inconsistencies that they could neither deny nor explain. Only an inherited reverence for the Book, or, better still, personal experience of the high spiritual worth of large portions of it, have kept many from refusing to read further. Others may have refused to read further because of just these difficulties.

Those who know how shallow and false is this dogma of Biblical infallibility, those who have learned from Christian history how and why it came to be held, those who know how unscrupulous are some of its advocates and how ignorant others, those who realize how it contradicts the hard-won results of Biblical study through the centuries, those who appreciate how damaging such a dogma is to the cause of true religion, how impossible it is to build an edifice of Truth on a foundation of lies— these must have the courage of their knowledge and convictions, must accept the challenge proffered them, must begin without delay to teach the plain Christian people the truth about the Bible, the whole truth and nothing but the truth. If they hesitate, if they listen to the counsels of their timid and half-hearted fellows, the churches will fall a prey to vociferous ignorance, and true religion will be betrayed in the house of its friends. The path of boldness, of utter frankness, of rugged honesty, is the path of safety.

III

Many of the clergy, who have been adequately instructed in a good modern theological seminary, and consequently know the facts about the Bible, are afraid to take their people into their confidence and tell them the truth. Some fear that if they should tell the truth, their people would regard them as heretics and turn against them; and they cannot bring themselves to quarrel with their bread and butter. Others excuse themselves from the duty of fearless truth-speaking, on the plausible plea that the pulpit is no place for discussing such matters, which should be left for class rooms and learned periodicals to thresh out. As to this, it may be said that of course it would be unwise to carry into the pulpit technical discussions, and expect the ordinary congregation to act as a jury and decide questions about which competent scholars differ.

But this is not at all what is meant by telling people the truth about the Bible. There is no important truth about religion that cannot be made clear to the ordinary believer. No one who has had experience in teaching in a Sunday school doubts that even minds of children are capable of taking in any important truth, when a properly trained teacher puts it before them. The average Christian congregation is fully competent to understand the general results that have been reached, within the last century especially, by historical, exegetical and literary study of the Bible. The results can be stated in untechnical language that the reader of any daily newspaper will comprehend without undue mental effort. And every preacher, when he takes a text of Scripture as subject of his discourse, or even as a mere motto, by so doing attests the traditional theory of his office: that his chief function is to expound the Scriptures to his people. How shall he honestly discharge this function, while he leaves them in ignorance of fundamental truth about the Bible? Truth that it much imports them to know, truth that would greatly alter their way of looking at all other religious truth, truth so vitally important that if they remain ignorant of it they cannot be intelligent Christians? There can be no excuse for such dereliction of duty that will stand slightest examination.

At the present moment no duty makes a more imperious call on the Christian minister than the duty of telling his people all the truth about the Bible. Claims have been made for the Bible, and are now made with fresh insistence, that the Bible does not make for itself. The validity of the Christian religion is staked by many noisy champions of it on impossible theories of the Bible's origin, meaning and authority. If those who know this, and also know what is the truth, preserve a prudent silence, how shall they excuse themselves for their failure to speak out?

Oh, but they fear they may unsettle men's minds and wreck the faith of some of Christ's little ones, if they should speak! That is a coward's plea. No man's faith was ever wrecked by truth, who had a faith worth saving. One lacks trust in God, the author of all truth, who fears to speak it. It was our Lord himself who assured us "The truth will make you free"—falsehood can make only slaves and dastards. Speak, my brothers in the ministry of the grace of God; speak, as you are called to be God's prophets; speak the truth without dilution or camouflage; and with God be the rest!

IV

What, then, should the people be taught about the Bible? They should be taught first of all its proper place in the Christian religion and warned against a cheap and harmful, even a superstitious, bibliolatry. Christianity and Mohammedanism are often said to be alike in this, that both are religions of a Book. This is far from the truth. Mohammedanism may be the religion of a Book; Christianity is the religion of a Person. Jesus the Christ is its corner-stone, not the Bible; He, not it, is the "author and perfecter of our faith." With Paul, every believer says, "I know whom I have believed"—whom, not what. Once let people get it firmly into their minds that the essence of the Christian religion is a personal experience of God's love, through Jesus who has revealed him to us as our Father in Heaven, and their faith will be built on a Rock and nothing thenceforth can shake it. Until they have this experience and comprehend its significance, they are at the mercy of every wind of doctrine that blows. "The Bible, and the Bible only the religion of Protestants" was never true, and it has lost what semblance of truth it might have had when Chillingworth said it.

Next to this, people should be taught that the authority of the Bible does not depend on men's theories and doctrines about the Bible. The inspiration of the Bible is a fact, not a dogma. A hundred generations have been finding in it something unique in spiritual quality. Nowhere else have they been able to discover such light and life, such comfort and strength and peace. For centuries men have resorted to it for sorely needed help in their struggle to escape from sin and attain goodness, and have had their spiritual energies renewed and their wills braced for further contest. The authority of the Bible does not depend on what ecclesiastical Powers have decreed, or on what theologians may have taught about it, but on what it is. It authenticates itself as God's word to the soul that is reaching out after the Most High, as a father's call in the dark authenticates itself to a frightened child. In the Bible we hear and recognize our Heavenly Father's voice and our spirits joyfully respond. This is the fact of inspiration—a personal experience of the highest validity, which is totally unaffected by this theory or that about the Bible. What matters it to us who wrote the various books, or how, or when, or why, if we thus recognize in them the voice of our God?

People should be taught the facts about the historical origin of the Bible. They should learn that the Bible is not one book, but two separate collections of books— not one book, but a library. The very name embodies this historic fact; it was originally τὰ βιβλία, the books, or, as we so often say, the Scriptures. These two collections are the best of the surviving writings of an extraordinary race during more than a thousand years. They contain, as we might expect, many different types of literature: history, drama, lyric poetry, orations, essays, apothegms. Books whose composition extends over a thousand years, and that touch men's lives at so many points, could hardly fail to be of different degrees of value, according to the intelligence and spiritual insight of their authors. Ten centuries must show progress in religious ideas—or else retrogression; in any event, change. That apparently innocent mutation of name from bibles to Bible, has done much to encourage the unhistorical notion of One Book, entirely homogeneous in character and contents, coming perfect from the mind of the Holy Spirit, without admixture of error, every part necessarily the equal of every other part, and teaching the same ideas of God and man from earliest composition to latest. This notion about the Bible, which may be called the popular theory, is such a perversion of facts lying on the very surface of the writings, that any person of intelligence and education ought to be heartily ashamed of being its advocate or defender.

People should be taught that the making of these two collections was a slow process, and that the result was long in doubt. The Jews in the time of Christ, and for long after, were not agreed as to what books should be admitted to and what excluded from their sacred writings. Ten generations of Christians lived and died before our New Testament assumed its present form. What was the determining principle in the formation of the two canons? Study of the facts discloses a common principle in the making of both: a winnowing process gradually separated the present books of the Bible from a much larger collection of similar books, because these were found, in the religious experience of successive generations, to have a superior spiritual quality. After virtual unanimity had been thus arrived at, ecclesiastical authority formally decreed that these books and no others should thenceforth be regarded as Holy Scripture. The

Bible is thus one of the most striking illustrations in history of the law of survival of the fittest. The experience that made the Bible a whole has kept it such to this day.

People should be taught that, while infallibility of the Bible is a doctrine of the Roman Catholic Church,* it has never been the official Protestant doctrine. Infallibility of the Bible has been so strenuously advocated by some Protestant theologians, however, and accepted by so considerable a part of clergy and laity, that it may be called unofficial Protestant doctrine, but it has never been declared in any Protestant creed or confession of faith. What has been the result of this attempt to make this doctrine Protestant orthodoxy? For several generations the clergy have been influenced by every bribe this world can offer—hope, honors, wealth, social consideration—and by every threat this world can devise—disgrace, persecution, stripes, chains, death—to maintain the infallible correctness of every word contained in the Bible; and as a net result faith in the Bible has been steadily weakening. Is it not about time to try another policy?

V

It is an extraordinary fact, yet fact indubitable, that the very persons who make loudest professions of belief in the inspiration and infallibility of the Bible, and insist most strenuously on the reverent treatment of the book, are the very persons who treat the Bible with least reverence. They show their faith by their works less than

---

*"For all the books that the Church receives as sacred and canonical are written wholly and entirely, with all their parts, at the dictation of the Holy Ghost; and so far is it from being possible that any error can coexist with inspiration, that inspiration not only is incompatible with error, but excludes and rejects it as absolutely and necessarily, as it is impossible that God himself, the supreme Truth, can utter that which is not true." Encyclical *Providentissimus Deus*, of Pope Leo XIII, November 18, 1893.

any other Christians. The men now posing before the public as the special champions of the Bible and almost the sole defenders of its authority, are nearly all Pre-millennarians. But the doctrine of the speedy coming of the Son of Man to reign with his saints a thousand years can be made to appear a doctrine derived from the Bible only by the most careless, not to say dishonest, exegesis. Under pretext of extreme devotion to the Bible, Premillennarians distort and falsify the Bible in the most barefaced manner. Therefore, people should be taught the truth, namely, that there is no teaching in the Bible about a millennium in connection with the second coming of Christ. There is not so much as a hint of such doctrine. Premillennial doctrine is a manufacture "out of whole cloth" of a doctrine that has not the slightest support in the Bible.

There is but a single passage, a very brief one, in the whole Bible that speaks of a reign of Christ for a thousand years. That passage is in the Revelation, a book of impassioned poetry, of profuse symbolism, the interpretation of which has caused more difference of opinion among Christian scholars for centuries than any other part of the Bible. Here are the words:

> And I saw thrones, and they sat on them,
> And authority to judge was given them.
> And I saw the souls of those who had been beheaded because of the testimony of Jesus and the word of God,
> And whosoever did not pay homage to the Beast nor his image,
> And received not the mark upon their foreheads and upon their hand;
> And they lived and reigned with Christ a thousand years.
> The rest of the dead did not live till the thousand years were completed.

Several things are distinctly stated in this vision: it is before the general resurrection, and the reign of Christ

is with a strictly limited portion of his saints: such as
had lost their lives in a great persecution, and such others
as had refused to do homage to the Beast.   However
the vision may be interpreted, these limitations cannot be
disregarded.   The persecution in the writer's mind may
have been that under Nero, or that under Domitian, or
some other.   This is a question of little importance,
because in any persecution in the Roman Empire a great
part, probably the greater part, of the Christians were
not molested at all.   Many who were arrested, and openly
avowed their faith, and steadfastly refused to sacrifice
to the gods or the Emperor, were subsequently released
when the fervor of persecution declined; others were put
to death.   Only these two classes, the martyrs and the
confessors, are seen by John as sharing with the Lord
this millennial reign.   And this is absolutely the only
reference in the whole Bible to a reign of Christ of a
thousand years.   Hence, the statement above that the
Bible does not contain a doctrine of the reign of Christ
with *all* his saints for a thousand years—which is the
"millennial" doctrine—is not only warranted but compelled by the facts.

How then do the Premillennarians, with their loudly
proclaimed devotion to the Bible, contrive to make their
self-invented doctrine appear to be the teaching of Scripture?   Why, very simply.   They first read the doctrine
into the Bible and then read it out again.   They quietly
assume, to begin with, that this passage in the Revelation teaches a reign of Christ with *all* his saints, instead
of with *some*—a meaning that, as we have seen, the text
will not bear.   Then they combine with this perverted
passage all that Jesus and his apostles have said about the
second coming of Christ; and all that Hebrew prophets
have said about Messiah's kingdom; and anything else
anywhere in the Bible that their ingenuity can bend to
their use.   And out of this hodge-podge of unrelated texts,

wrested violently from their connection and made to bear meanings of which their authors never dreamed, they make a doctrine of the millennium. And they have the colossal impudence to call this doctrine Scriptural!

This method Premillennarians fatuously suppose is showing great reverence for the Bible! And the men who do this, cap their lying exegetics with a charge of heresy against all who refuse to interpret the Bible in this scandalous fashion. For it is really nothing less than a scandal, a great scandal and outrage, against which those who truly love and reverence the Bible should delay no longer to make public and emphatic protest. The men who tear the Bible to bits, in order to piece together a crazy-quilt of unrelated texts, and publish this to the world as "the fundamentals of Christianity," must not be suffered a day longer to pose as the champions of the Bible, the only Christians who to-day are standing between Holy Scripture and the forces of infidelity.

It would be a little different if these men possessed any real knowledge of the Bible, any Biblical scholarship worthy of respect. But it would be difficult to single out a man in their ranks whose opinions on questions of scholarship are respected by other scholars. Most of the party are men who have either had no theological training, or have taken a course in some "Bible School" that gives no instruction in the original Scriptures. The greater part of their "knowledge" of the Bible is knowledge of things that aren't so. And, as usually happens, their dogmatic assurance is in inverse ratio to their sound scholarship. We hear of the pride of knowledge; there is such a thing, without doubt, but the pride of knowledge is humility itself compared with the pride of ignorance. God save the Bible from some of its professed friends!

It is strange indeed that men will learn so little from the history of this doctrine. The records of the Christian centuries may be called a museum of millenniums. The

millennium has come—and gone—more times than one
can easily count. In spite of our Lord's declaration that
not even the angels in heaven know the hour of his
coming, deluded disciples have again and again ciphered
out the exact day for the beginning of his millennial
reign. Some have learned enough from experience not
to commit themselves to a specific date and content themselves with the pronouncement that the reign is to begin
"very soon." Their cheerful hardihood is not so wonderful, perhaps, as that there should be found in every
generation a multitude that no man can number of silly
souls, incapable of receiving truth but avid of falsehood,
always waiting anxiously to be hoaxed, the predestined
prey of every crack-brained fanatic, credulous above all
regarding any error that is proclaimed with a tone of
authority and made plausible by juggled texts of Scripture. The great showman was right: one is born every
minute.

VI

One or two personal words in closing these prefatory
remarks: Attentive readers will not fail to note that
some of the words of Jesus are cited in the following
pages more than once; and that certain ideas appear and
reappear in the discussion, sometimes with no great variation of form. Such readers, one hopes, will not attribute these repetitions to slovenly thinking or careless
writing. There is good reason (as the author judges)
for such repetitions; and, at any rate, each case has been
carefully considered, and the text as it stands represents
the best effort of which the writer is capable to convey
his thought to others. He may have failed in judgment,
but he protests that he has not failed in labor. The entire
book has been rewritten thrice, and much of it a fourth
time, in the attempt to achieve clarity and brevity.

The author has not the slightest claim to speak for the theological schools, beyond the fact that he has been a teacher in one of them for more than a quarter-century. He makes no pretense of being their official spokesman, nor should they be held responsible for anything herein said. The notions here expressed are probably more radical than seminaries are prepared to avow. The author is fairly certain that one at least of his own colleagues would repudiate a considerable part of the book, and it is doubtful if a single one would approve the whole of it. But whatever they may think of this performance, the seminaries stand for modern scholarship, for fearless inquiry, for candid discussion. They hold that a Christian's attitude toward religion and church should be expressed by the maxim of Decatur—with a difference. "My country! May she ever be right, but, right or wrong, my country!" was that gallant sailor's celebrated toast. The Christian's watchword is, "My religion and my Church! if right, to keep them right; if wrong, to make them right." It is wholly in that spirit that the chapters following have been written.

THE
FUNDAMENTALS OF CHRISTIANITY
A Study of the Teaching of Jesus and Paul

CHAPTER I

JESUS THE PEASANT-POET OF GALILEE

I

JESUS wrote nothing. He was content to follow the
method traditional among his people, the method of oral
instruction to a few disciples, varied by occasional discourses to larger assemblies, fearlessly hazarding his golden
precepts upon the memories of his hearers. In this he
was by no means unique. Of the world's paramount
religious teachers, Siddhartha, Zoroaster and Socrates also
left their disciples to gather up and commit to writing
the maxims of their Masters. Only Confucius and Mohammed left behind them a written word for which they
were personally responsible.

We do not know, in the case of Jesus, if this method
was matter of choice or of necessity. He may have been
unable to write, as Mohammed seems to have been. The
incident of the Pericope, where he is described as writing
on the ground(¹) is indecisive, for he may only have appeared to spectators to be writing words: and it is not in
harmony with another passage of undoubted genuineness
in the same Gospel, "How does this fellow know letters,

(¹) John 8:6, 8. But the entire Pericope (John 7:53-8:11) is
now recognized as an interpolation in this Gospel of an incident
doubtless true, but belonging originally to some other book. This
makes such a detail of the story as the alleged writing of Jesus less
convincing. By a decision of the Holy Office, February 13, 1897,
confirmed two days later by the Pope, Catholic exegetes are required
to believe that the Pericope is genuine and an integral part of the
Fourth Gospel.

1

having never learned?"([1])   It is true that "letters" γράμματα may not be used here in the classic Greek sense of "rudiments," for we know from Josephus that it was a common word for "sacred learning." The only literature to a Jew was the Old Testament Scriptures. But the speakers at least intended to suggest that Jesus had been trained in no rabbinic school and we believed therefore to be practically illiterate.

The frequent quotations from the Old Testament in the sayings of Jesus have often been cited as evidencing a thorough acquaintance with the sacred writings of his people, so thorough as to presuppose both ability to read and much study.   But a critical weighing of those quotations fairly warrants us in inferring only that Jesus attended regularly the synagogue, and perhaps a synagogue school at Nazareth, and that he had a good memory. He presumably received the usual instruction of a Galilean youth of his day, but just what that was we do not know. That it included oral instruction in the Law is as certain as it is uncertain whether it included anything else. Galilee of the year 1 A. D. was as much gentile as Jewish, and the common language of gentile Galilee was Greek; but what opportunities a youth like Jesus would have of acquiring a speaking knowledge of Greek is matter, not of evidence, but of unprofitable speculation. Even if Jesus spoke any language other than the vernacular of Galilee, that he was acquainted with any literature but that of his own people is most improbable.   No re-

---

([1]) John 7:15. Those who accept the story of Luke 4:16-30 as entirely historical cannot well deny the ability of Jesus to read the Hebrew rolls of the synagogue. Many have pointed out that it was already in his time esteemed a religious duty to teach every Jewish child to read the Law. The boast of Josephus is well known: "If anyone asked one of his nation a question respecting the Law, he could answer it more readily than give his own name; for he learns every part of it from the first dawn of intelligence, till it is graven into his very soul." C. Apion, ii 18. But this may mean *memoriter* instruction, not learning to read.

ligious teacher ever owed less to instruction, we may safely conclude, or was more utterly thrown back upon himself for his religious ideas. Therefore, of all choice spirits of the past to whom we of the present look for light and leading, Jesus was most original. His schooling was of the slightest; God and nature were his teachers; and he became deeply learned in the lore of sky and field and flower, not in the lore of books.

In the case of any teacher who pursues the oral method exclusively, whose words are for an indefinite period handed on from lip to lip, and not published for a generation or more after his death, it becomes a question as inevitable as it is serious. How nearly do these reports of his teaching correspond to his actual words? How far were these misunderstood by those who heard, distorted by memory and travestied by tradition, before they were committed to writing? How many recensions of the words of Jesus have we, and just what authority is to be attributed to each? What proportion of the sayings truly represent his own personality, and what should be credited to the personalities of the various reporters?

The doctrine of inspiration grew up in the second century largely to answer these questions. Its aim was to give unequivocal assurance to Christians that the Gospels were at once authentic and authoritative. This met the difficulty for the time, and for some centuries there was no questioning of the authenticity of the words of Jesus, save on the part of a few bold spirits that from time to time questioned everything, and mostly got themselves burned for their enterprise. But when, during the Renaissance, the knowledge of Greek and Hebrew was revived, and critical study of the original Scriptures began anew, the doubts and questionings reappeared. It was noted that not one of the Gospels gives the slightest hint that its author supposed himself to have received any unusual, not to say supernatural, assistance in the composition of his book; while the author of the third Gospel distinctly claims to have made use of the ordinary methods of research employed by other historians, in order to discover the facts and set them forth in fuller and better form than his predecessors.

The great leaders of the Reformation were not without some comprehension of facts like these. Erasmus, Luther and Calvin, differing about almost everything else, were agreed in doubting the inspiration and authority of some books of the New Testament canon. But this first tendency towards a free handling of the New Testament documents was quickly checked by the controversial necessity, which all Protestants realized, of having an infallible Bible to cite in opposition to an infallible Church. The result was a tightening of the doctrine of inspiration, an assertion by Protestants generally of a more extreme view of the inerrancy of Scripture than had ever been held by the Roman Church.

But it was perceived after a little that this was but a falsidic solution—that a doctrine of the verbal inspiration of the New Testament made the difficulties much worse than they were before the doctrine was promulgated. There were patent and grave differences between the discourses of Jesus as reported in the fourth Gospel and those of the other three, the so-called Synoptic Gospels—differences that might perhaps be successfully accounted for, but that in any case demanded explanation. Not only so, but the same discourse was often variously reported in the Synoptics. True, these variations did not often affect the substance of a discourse, but they often did affect the form much; and sometimes form is important, not seldom it is vital. For example, take the two versions of the Beatitudes. Luke gives them as follows:

Happy you poor!
　For yours is the Kingdom of God.
Happy you that hunger now!
　For you will be satisfied.
Happy you that weep now!
　For you will laugh.
Happy you when men hate you,
　And expel you, and insult you,
　And reject your Name as an evil thing,
　On account of the Son of Man!
Rejoice at such time and leap for joy.
　For see! great is your reward in Heaven.
For in that same way their fathers used to treat the
　Prophets.([1])

That is the address of the prophet of the proletariat
to the toiling and hopeless masses, holding out to them
the prospect of an immediate coming of the Kingdom of
God, in which existing inequalities and injustices will
be righted. It was such words as these that gave unpardonable offence to the vested wrongs of his day, and
led the corrupt interests to demand the death of Jesus.
And in the Gospel bearing Matthew's name, published
in the second generation after the crucifixion, these Beatitudes assume this form:

Happy the poor in spirit!
　For theirs is the Kingdom of Heaven.
Happy they that mourn!
　For they will be comforted.
Happy the meek!
　For they will inherit the earth.
Happy they that hunger after righteousness!
　For they will be satisfied.
Happy the merciful!
　For they will obtain mercy.
Happy the sincere in heart!
　For they will see God.

([1]) Luke 6:20-22

Happy the peacemakers!
  For they will be called sons of God.
Happy they that have been persecuted for righteousness'
      sake,
  For theirs is the Kingdom of Heaven.
Happy are you when they reproach you and persecute you,
  And say all evil against you, for my sake;
  Rejoice and be exceedingly glad,
  Because great is your reward in Heaven,
  For so persecuted they the Prophets that were before
      you.([1])

The four Beatitudes of Luke have been expanded into
nine (really but eight, for the ninth is but a repetition
of the eighth) but this is not the most significant change:
the proletarian element has been spiritualized away, and
the promises for this world have been given an otherworld-
ly application.   The two versions of the Beatitudes are
therefore as different in substance as they are in form.
Which did Jesus actually teach?   That he taught both
can be believed only by a mind utterly flaccid and un-
critical, by those persons who have retained the naïve
habit of childhood, of receiving as true anything that
may be told them.

It will help us to decide this question, if we turn
again to Luke and read the converse teaching there attributed to Jesus, the Woes that follow the Beatitudes:

But woe to you rich!
  For you have received your consolation.
Woe to you who are satisfied now!
  For you will hunger.
Woe to you that laugh now!
  For you will mourn and weep.
Woe to you when all men speak well of you!
  For in that same way their fathers used to treat the false
      prophets. ([2])

_____

([1]) Matt. 5:3-12.
([2]) Luke 6:24-26.

The entire suppression of this passage by Matthew constitutes a more serious discrepancy than his alteration of the Beatitudes. These "Woes" could by no ingenuity be softened down and spiritualized as were the Beatitudes, and so the composer of the first Gospel dealt with his problem in the obvious way, by omitting the inconvenient teachings. Critical study has established that this is true, rather than the alternative that Luke composed and added the "Woes," by making it evident that the authors of the first and third Gospels used the same collection of the sayings of Jesus as their chief authority for his discourses. Before the first century had closed, we thus see the process well begun of trimming down and smoothing over the words of Jesus, to make them more palatable to the new generation of Christians. There can be no reasonable doubt that we have in Luke's version, if not the exact words of Jesus, at least a much closer approximation to them than is given by Matthew.

It is quite certain, therefore, that we cannot receive as the indubitable words of Jesus everything attributed to him in the Gospels. We have as yet got little further than recognition of this fact by a fraction of the Christian world, the greater part still refusing to admit that this is fact. The critical study of the discourses of Jesus that will give measurably assured results is only well begun, and therefore such appreciation as is here attempted must be more or less tentative and experimental. Much of what has purported to be critical study, by German scholars especially, is invalidated by lack of spiritual insight, by false philosophical assumptions and by adoption of a pseudo-scientific method.

Of these defects the first is gravest. A large part of the sayings of Jesus were received as authoritative by his original hearers, because of their resistless appeal to the religious consciousness; and that they still make the same appeal is the best proof we could have of their authenticity. The words are self-evidencing. Nobody else could possibly have uttered them. There is not another man of that generation, or of the generation following, whom we have the slightest ground for investing with the peculiar spiritual quality that these words disclose. To suppose them the invention of any disciple, or the gradual accretion of the religious thinking of many, is equally preposterous. Disciples of Jesus proved themselves capable of denaturing his teachings, but not of originating them. And in scores of cases we may be reasonably confident that we have the exact form of his words, for many of his most pregnant utterances were not so much easy to remember as impossible to forget.

It is plain, however, that such considerations as these apply only to those sayings that evince superior ethical and spiritual insight. Discourses of the apocalyptic type, and sayings of an ecclesiastical sort, may easily have been, and probably were, the invention of others, fathered on Jesus by a later age. Not all the external corroboration of texts and versions can make credible some of these alleged sayings. Of this character is part of the celebrated dialogue between Jesus and his disciples, related in Matt. 16:13-19:

Jesus.	Who do people say that the Son of Man is?
Disciples.	Some say John the Baptist, others Elijah, others Jeremiah, or one of the Prophets.
Jesus.	But who do *you* say that I am?
Peter.	You are the Messiah, the Son of the Living God.
Jesus.	Happy are you Simon, son of Jonah! For flesh and blood have not revealed it to you, But my Father who is in Heaven. [And I tell you, You are Peter, And on this Rock I will build my Church,

> And the gates of Hades will not prevail
> against it.
> I will give you the keys of the Kingdom of
> Heaven;
> And whatever you prohibit in earth will be
> prohibited in Heaven,
> And whatever you permit on earth will be
> permitted in Heaven.]

The first part of this dialogue is probably authentic, but the words enclosed in brackets could be authenticated to us only by the most positive direct testimony. They are utterly foreign to the spirit of Jesus, as his teaching in general makes him known to us. As we shall see later, there is much wit and humor in all the discourses, public and private, but nowhere does Jesus condescend to the feeble punning([1]) that some later ecclesiastical writer here puts into his mouth. The ideas and method of this "saying" cannot be rationally supposed to have occurred to anybody during the first hundred years of Christian history. Only after the tradition of Peter's Roman episcopate and primacy in the Church came to be generally circulated and widely believed—say about the time of Irenæus—would such words have had any force or acceptance. Their interpolation into the first Gospel toward the end of the second century, or early in the third, is the most plausible explanation of their presence in all our earliest texts and versions. For there is no more question that the words are canonical, than that they are not authentic.

II

Many expounders of the teaching of Jesus have attempted to show that he was philosopher, theologian, moralist, but he was none of these—he was poet. The greater

---

([1]) "Leave the dead to bury their own dead" (Matt. 8:22) is the nearest approach to a pun in any of the undoubted words of Jesus.

part of his instruction found expression in the rhythmic
forms of Hebrew prophets and psalmists. This is so apparent, even in the Greek version in which alone his sayings have come down to us, that it is a marvel how the
fact could have escaped notice for centuries. Only that
a supposed reverence for the words of Jesus prevented
men from studying them as literature can account for
such prolonged failure of perception. Among men of
"serious" mind and "religious" temperament there used
to be, and perhaps still lingers, a scarcely concealed dis-
trust and contempt of all forms of artistry. To such,
"poet" is little more than synonym for "fool." Men are
still living who can remember when reading of "Paradise
Lost" was just tolerated among pious people, because the
poem had a "sacred" theme. Even so, the "Pilgrim's
Progress," as plain prose, was much more favored; while
to read Wordsworth was to be looked at askance, and to
read Byron or Shelley was to be anathema. People so
constituted would have received almost with horror the
suggestion that Jesus was a poet; it would have seemed to
them near kin to blasphemy.

And yet, how can it be denied or doubted that such
sayings as these have all the characteristics of Hebrew
poetry?

> Again, you have heard that it was said by the ancients,
>   "Thou shalt not swear falsely,
>   But shalt perform to the Lord thine oaths."
> But I say to you,
>   Swear not at all.
> Not by the Heaven,
>   For it is God's throne;
> Nor by the earth,
>   For it is the footstool of his feet;
> Nor by Jerusalem,
>   For it is the Great King's city;
> Nor shall you swear by your head,
>   For you cannot make one hair white or black.

> But let your word be Yes or No;
>   What is more than these is of the Evil One.([1])

Or again, what could be more nicely balanced, after the parallelism of the Hebrew poetry, than these triplets:

> Ask and it will be given you,
> Seek and you will find,
> Knock and the door will open to you.
>   For every one that asks, receives,
>   And he that seeks, finds,
>   And to him that knocks the door is opened.([2])

The discourses of Jesus are not poetic in form merely; his style is a poet's. It has the qualities of imagination, elegance, elevation, repose, power, that we demand in all poets and find only in the great. Equally at home with things high and low, with themes homely and themes sublime, his mind pours forth a rich variety of thought. And his diction as well repays study as his thought: it is always beautiful in its simplicity, wholly without ornature, often illumined by a delicate play of fancy. In the case of Jesus, speech is perfect in adaptation to occasion and circumstance, and consequently rich in variety and charm. If any doubt what has been said, let him ask himself, Could any but a poet have spoken these words?

> Observe the lilies, how they grow;
>   They toil not, they spin not,
> Yet not even Solomon in all his splendor
>   Was robed like one of these.
> Now if God so clothes grass,
>   Which to-day is in the field,
>   And to-morrow is cast into the oven,
> How much more you, men of little trust!([3])

Speaking once more of form, every attentive reader of the Gospels must have noted sayings of Jesus that fall

---

([1]) Matt. 5:33-37.
([2]) Matt. 7:7, 8.
([3]) Matt. 6:28-30; cf. Luke 12:27, 28.

into the couplets of the Proverbs, sententious, crisp, pithy, argute.   Instances are:

> He that finds his life will lose it,
> And he that loses his life for my sake will find it. ([1])

> He that is not with me is against me,
> And he that does not gather with me, scatters. ([2])

> Every one that exalts himself will be humbled,
> But he that humbles himself will be exalted. ([3])

> So the last will be first,
> And the first, last. ([4])

> The Sabbath was made for man,
> Not man for the Sabbath. ([5])

> What I tell you in the dark, speak in the light;
> And what you hear in whispers, shout on housetops. ([6])

> I am sending you out like sheep in the midst of wolves,
> So become wise as serpents and guileless as doves. ([7])

Because he is poet and speaks in the vocabulary of poetry—language "thrown out at an idea," as Matthew Arnold calls it, not formal scientific definition—it requires imagination to understand and interpret the teaching of Jesus.   There is nothing fixed and stereotyped about his words; they are fluid, almost volatile; "they are spirit." ([8])   This is why his interpreters have in so many cases made a sad mess of their work: they have persisted in treating his poetry as prose, in regarding his airy dic-

---

([1])   Matt. 16:25; Mk. 8:35; Luke 9:24; 17-33.
([2])   Matt. 12:30.
([3])   Matt. 23:12.
([4])   Matt. 20:16; Mk. 10:31; Luke 13:30.
([5])   Mk. 2:27.
([6])   Matt. 10:27; Luke 12:3.
([7])   Matt. 10:16.
([8])   Jn. 6:63.

tion as exact statement or accurate exposition. And so exegetes have made hay of his delicate flowers and fresh grass. They have treated his poetic mirrorings of truth as if he were a mathematician or a professor of ethics, giving us rigid formulae or precise statement of abstract principles. So to understand Jesus is to misunderstand him. So to interpret him is to read out of his words all life and vigor, and make of them jejune and spiritless things.

III

Jesus was not only poet, but he was the people's poet. By birth, breeding and deepest instincts he was the mouth-piece of the world's workers. Everywhere we find him the Galilean peasant, artisan rather than farmer, none poorer or more obscure, none knowing better the life of those who toil patiently and hard for daily bread. Sympathy with the poor was the very stuff of life in one who spent all his days among them, shared their lot, gave his life to them and for them.([1]) It is true that in his days of public ministration, Jesus was patronizingly invited to the houses of a few rich, since he was the "lion" of the day. But he was among the rich, not of them. Sometimes he seems to have been treated with scant courtesy by these conde-scending patrons of the higher circle, where he was tol-erated at all only because he was reputed to be a prophet. On one occasion he rather pointedly rebuked his enter-tainer for failing in attentions that any host was then expected to show a guest:

([1]) Jesus offers as one of the chief proofs of his Messianic work the fact that "the poor have the Good News proclaimed to them" (Matt. 11:5; Luke 7:22). "It is a new thing that the poor, whom the Greek despised and the Roman trampled on, and whom the priest and the Levite left on one side, should be invited into the Kingdom of God." Plummer, Commentary on Luke, p. 203.

When I came into your house,
Water for my feet you gave me not,
    But she has bathed my feet with her tears,
    And wiped them with her hair.
A kiss you gave me not,
But she, ever since I came in, has not left off tenderly
        kissing my feet.
With oil you did not anoint my head,
    But she with perfume has anointed my feet.([1])

Such recognition of Jesus by "society" doubtless did not at all surprise or flatter him, since it was a tradition of his race that "the word of Jehovah" might come to the lowliest. Revelations from God were no special privilege of the high and mighty among the Jews. Almost the reverse had ever been true. Amos and Micah were peasants, and probably Isaiah also; Samuel was the son of peasants; Moses was a slave by birth, and David was a tender of sheep in youth. It was quite in harmony with Jewish ideas and Jewish history that "the carpenter's son" of Nazareth should be prophet of God and teacher of his people. The chief reason why his peasant birth and artisan training should be emphasized is that they so deeply colored every sentence that fell from the lips of Jesus. No plainer marks of heredity and environment are found in the words of any religious teacher. He was not ashamed to be known as a man of the common people. Racy of the soil, instinct with the spirit and life of the Syrian folk, are all his sayings.

Very striking is the interest shown by Jesus in the world about him. His love of nature was inborn and deep, as we might expect of a child of the fields and the open air. His teaching is redolent of earth and sky. He does not seek painfully for illustrations in nature, they spring spontaneously to his lips. The peasant-poet has an infallible eye for the picturesque and dramatic, and equally

([1]) Luke 7:44-46.

for the homely event that will send a ray of light into the heart of some great truth or so illumine a phase of the Kingdom that the dullest will be able to visualize it. With sound instinct he avoids the besetting sin of so many preachers and teachers—he never tells a story for its own sake or to ornament his discourse; his illustrations really illustrate.

And so, not a feature of the Palestinian landscape, not a scene in the Palestinian life, fails to impress him and sooner or later to suggest some spiritual application: mountain and plain, lake and river; the trees, sycamine and fig, good and bad, green and dry; the mustard plant, growing to be almost a tree; the fields at springtime, as the farmer plows and scatters seed, and anon white for harvest; the grass flourishing to-day and to-morrow fuel for the baker; the lily in her glory and the humbler herb of the house-garden; the roads wandering whitely through the land, some bordered by hedges, picturesque and broad and traveled by many, others narrow and steep, with thorns and brambles on either hand, trodden by few—even the flat stones by the wayside do not succeed in hiding from him!

For the larger phenomena of nature Jesus has a vision equally keen and comprehensive. He lays tribute on all: the splendor of the Oriental sun and the glory of the unmatched Syrian heavens by night; light and darkness, summer and winter, seedtime and harvest, growth of plant and fruitage of tree and vine; the varying qualities of soils and the vexation of weeds among the farmer's crops; signs of the weather, wind, rain, lightning; natural disasters, flood, drought, earthquake, famine and pestilence. All nature was to him an open book, of which he was a most attentive reader.

Many of the sayings that make good these general remarks will be cited hereafter for other purposes, so only a few examples can be given here, but the memory of every Gospel student will supply numberless others. Mark has preserved a unique parable that grew 'out of this observation of nature's ways:

> So is the Kingdom of God, as if a man should cast seed
>   on the ground,
>   And should sleep and rise night and day,
>   And the seed should spring up and grow, he knows
>   not how.
> The ground bears fruit of itself,
>   First the blade, then the ear, then the ripe grain in
>   the ear.
> But when, the grain is ripe, he sends forth the sickle
>   at once,
>   Because the harvest is come.([1])

One of the most pungent reproaches of the Pharisees was inspired by ordinary weather maxims of his day, which are those of our day as well, because they are founded on universal experience:

> In the evening you say, "Fair weather!"
>   For the sky is red.
> And in the morning, "Stormy to-day!"
>   For the sky is red and threatening.
> You know how to judge the sky's appearance,
>   But the signs of the times you cannot judge.([2])

Other representative instances are these:

> As the lightning-flash shines from sky to sky,
> So will be the [coming of the] Son of Man.([3])

> For he makes his sun to rise on evil and good,
> And sends rain on just and unjust.([4])

> From the fig tree learn its parable:
> When its branches become soft and burst into leaf
>   You know that summer is near;

([1]) Mark 4:26-29.
([2]) Matt. 16: 2, 3.
([3]) Luke 17:24; Matt. 24:27.
([4]) Matt. 5:45.

So, when you see all this,
   Know that He is near—at your doors!([1])

No man having put his hand to the plow and looking
      back,
Is fit for the Kingdom of God.([2])

   Enter in by the narrow gate,
Because wide is the gate and broad the road that leads
      to destruction,
   And many are they that enter in by it;
Because narrow is the gate and contracted the road that
      leads to life,
   And few are they that find it!([3])

Listen: the sower went forth to sow,
And it chanced that in his sowing some seed fell along-
      side the road,
   And the birds came and ate it up. . . .
And other seed fell among the thorns
   And the thorns sprang up and choked it
   And it bore no fruit.([4])

The Kingdom of heaven is like a grain of mustard seed,
   Which a man took and sowed in his field—
Which indeed is the smallest of all seeds,
   But when it has grown it is larger than the herbs, and
      becomes a tree,
So that the birds of the air come and roost in its
      branches.([5])

Why, what man is there of you, who, if his son ask a
      loaf, will give him a stone?
   Or, if he ask a fish, will give him a serpent?

([1]) Mark 13:28, 29.
([2]) Luke 9:62.
([3]) Matt. 7:13, 14.
([4]) Matt. 13:4, 7.
([5]) Matt. 13:31, 32.

> If you then, wicked as you are, know how to give good
>   gifts to your children,
> How much more will your Father who is in Heaven give
>   good gifts to those that ask him! ([1])

But let us not fail to note that as Jesus looked upon
Nature, he did not see merely a collection of beautiful objects, or a succession of interesting events, or a thesaurus
of illustrations, but almost a living Thing, radiant with
the glory of an immanent God. He saw everywhere his
Father's hand; in the smallest things he read proofs of his
Father's love:

> Observe the ravens, that they neither sow nor reap,
>   No storehouse nor granary have they,
>   And God feeds them.
> How much more are you worth than birds! ([2])

> Two sparrows are sold for a farthing, are they not?
> And not one of them falls to the ground without your
>   Father. ([3])

Rarely does Jesus go outside of his personal experience
for an illustration. In one case he is thought by some to
have done so; but, though we have no account of such a
thing, it is by no means impossible that at some time of
his life he had stood on the shore of the Mediterranean in
a storm:

> There will be signs in sun and moon and stars,
> And upon the earth distress of nations,
> In perplexity for the roaring of the sea and its billows. ([4])

Equally broad and precise was Jesus in his observation
of animate nature. The fauna of Palestine, great and
small, wild and domestic, are used by him with much effectiveness in his teaching. He speaks most frequently

---

([1]) Matt. 7:9-11.
([2]) Luke 12:24.
([3]) Matt. 10:29; Luke 12:6, 7.
([4]) Luke 21:25.

of the domesticated animals: the ox, the ass, the sheep,
the fatted calf, the goat, the swine, the cock, and even of
those snarling curs that infest Oriental towns, where they
serve as scavengers, not as companions, and are called dogs
by Western visitors, merely because they cannot be called
anything else. Song-birds are rare in Syria, but the spar-
row and the raven are plentiful and are often mentioned:

> The foxes have dens,
> And the birds have roosts,
> But the Son of Man has not where to lay his head.([1])

> Where the carcass is,
> There the vultures will be gathered.([2])

> O Jerusalem, Jerusalem! that kills the prophets
> And stones those that have been sent to you,
> How often would I have gathered your children,
> As a hen gathers her brood under her wings,
> And you were not willing!([3])

IV

All human interests were the interests of Jesus; nothing pertaining to man was foreign to him. One of the most
illuminating incidents in his career was when he sat by the
wellside one day, adust, athirst, aweary, and, forgetting
self utterly, taught a poor Samaritan woman to whom the
ordinary Jew would have disdained even to speak. To
her he uttered some of the deepest truths that ever fell
from his lips, concerning the Water of Life and the spiritual nature of worship. It followed that there are no
"sacred places," but every place is sacred where the spirit
of man rises above the restraints of time and place and
circumstance into fellowship with the Divine Spirit.([4])

([1]) Matt. 8:20; Luke 9:58.
([2]) Matt. 24:28; Luke 17:37.
([3]) Matt. 23:37.
([4]) John 4:6-24.

Neither the teaching nor the incident can have been invented by the author of the fourth Gospel, or by anybody else; each corresponds too closely to the nature of Jesus to admit of a doubt as to its substantial accuracy.

While all classes of men appealed to Jesus, the poor from whom he sprang were always closest to his heart He was not one of those who, so soon as they attain some small measure of fame and social vogue, promptly and completely forget former associates and associations.   He speaks much more often and more tenderly of the poor, the maimed, the halt, the blind, the sick, the beggars, than of the rich.   Perhaps the highest words of praise that he even uttered were about a certain unnamed, poor widow, who out of her great love put into the Lord's treasury all that she had;(¹) and next to hers, he praised the act of another woman who sacrificed in his honor her dearest, her costliest treasure, an alabaster vase of nard.(²)

It was the common complaint against Jesus by his enemies that he made companions and friends of tax-gatherers and sinners, as if a modern evangelist should single out "bootleggers" and women of the street for his best ministrations.   Fancy the Billy Sundays doing that!   Yet Jesus did not shun the rich, as we have seen; he dined with them on occasion; even so he did not permit courtesies to seal his lips, but spoke his message to them as others, with utter plainness, albeit with kindness.   He now and then in his discourses refers to rich men, nobles, kings, to give point to a precept; and he cites their ways in parable or sermon to make plain some spiritual truth. But it is the ordinary peasant folk whom he knows best, of whose life he is an intimate part, whom he always has in mind whatever the subject of his discourse.   They are his "little ones," whom it is worse than death to "offend," or cause to stumble.

(¹) Mark 12:41-44; Luke 21:1-4.
(²) Matt. 26:6-13; Mark 14:3-9

> And whoso puts a snare in the way of these little ones
>   that trust in me,
> Better were it for him to have a great millstone hung
>   around his neck
> And be thrown into the sea.([1])

As we listen to Jesus we catch pictures of the villages of Galilee, with their flat-topped houses([2]) and adobe walls,([3]) through which robbers could so easily dig. We see their streets and lanes, thronged by the busy people.([4]) We see the well by the house, into which ox or ass might accidentally fall, in which case he is to be drawn out even on the holy Sabbath.([5]) We see the barns([6]) of the richer and the dunghills([7]) beside them, and in the adjoining yard the plow, the threshing-floor and the great stone for threshing and grinding grain, turned by ox or ass. Within the house we see the lamp and its stand, the beds and couches, the table, cup and platter, and the key to the great door or gate.([8]) The marvel is, however, not that Jesus mentions so many of these things, but that he makes every one of them illustrate some vital spiritual truth. The lamp he uses many times and it affords one of the best instances of his method:

> The body's lamp is the eye:
> So, if your eye is clear-sighted,
>   Your whole body will be light;
> But if your eye is diseased,
>   Your whole body will be dark.
> If then the light in you is darkness,
>   How great the darkness!([9])

([1]) Mark 9:42; Matt. 18:6; Luke 17:2.
([2]) Mark 2:4; 13-15.
([3]) Matt. 6:19.
([4]) Luke 14:21.
([5]) Luke 14:5.
([6]) Matt. 6:26; Luke 12:18.
([7]) Luke 14:35.
([8]) Matt. 5:15; Mark 4:21; Luke 16:20; Matt. 23:25, 26; Matt. 16:19.
([9]) Matt. 6:22, 23.

And again:

> I am the Light of the world!
> He that follows me will not walk in the dark,
>> But will have the light of life.([1])

Other effective illustrations from the daily affairs of the household are:

> I am the Bread of life.
> He that comes to me will by no means hunger,
> And he that puts his trust in me will never thirst.([2])

> Now salt is good,
> But if the salt becomes tasteless,
>> With what will you season it?
> It is not fit for soil or dunghill—
>> Men throw it away.
> He that has ears to hear, let him hear!([3])

We are not surprised to find that his own trade furnishes Jesus with some of his most impressive illustrations. The ox-yokes, clumsy and heavy as they seem to us of the West, he likens to his way of salvation, which he commends as less burdensome than the requirements of the Pharisees:

> Come to me, all you that labor and are heavy laden,
>> And I will give you rest.
> Take my yoke upon you and learn of me,
>> For I am meek and lowly in heart,
> And you will find rest for your souls.
>> For my yoke is easy,
>> And my burden light.([4])

The importance of a good foundation for a house suggests the eloquent peroration of the Sermon on the Mount:

([1]) John 8:12.
([2]) John 6:35.
([3]) Luke 14:34, 35; Matt. 5:13; Mark 9:50.
([4]) Matt. 11:28-30.

So, then, everyone that hears these words and does them,
Will be likened to a prudent man, who built his house
    on the rock.
  And the rain came down,
  And the floods rose,
  And the winds blew,
And beat upon that house, and it did not fall,
  For it was founded on the rock!

And everyone that hears these words of mine and does
    them not,
  Will be likened to a silly man, who built his house on
    the sand.
  And the rain came down,
  And the floods rose,
  And the winds blew,
  And smote upon that house, and it fell,
  And great was its fall! [1]

Hardly less effective, though less poetic, is the reference
to the man who began to build with so little consideration
of the cost of the enterprise and the extent of his own re-
sources, that he was unable to finish and so became the
mark for the jeers of all the town. [2] Hardly a town in
Galilee, or anywhere else, would fail to furnish forth an
apposite case.

The social relations of the time supply Jesus with no
small part of his material: king and subjects, neighbor
and friend, host and guest, owner and tenant, employer
and worker, borrower and lender, judge and suitor, sheriff
and prisoner, robbers and their victim, and, oftenest of
all, master and slave. How often these social incidents
are made the basis of parable or wise saying could hardly
be effectively set forth without quoting the larger part of
the words of Jesus. Any reader of the Gospels can call
on his memory for instances or easily find them for him-

[1] Matt. 7:24-27.
[2] Luke 14:27-30.

self.   He can hardly read anywhere, indeed, without finding them.   But it may perhaps be allowable to cite a few
instances of the use made of the relation of master and
slave:

> No house-servant can be a slave to two masters,
>   For either he will hate the one and love the other,
>   Or he will cling to one and scorn the other.
> You cannot be slave to God *and* Mammon.(¹)

> Every one that lives in sin is sin's slave.
> Now the slave does not always remain in the house,
>   But the son remains always;
> So, if the Son sets you free,
>   You will be freemen indeed.(²)

> Keep your loins girt,
> And your lamps lit,
> And be like men waiting for their master,
> Until he shall return from a wedding-feast,
> That, when he comes, they may admit him at once.
> Happy those slaves whom the master finds awake when
>   he comes!(³)

Occupations of men in the fields about Nazareth are
likewise often drawn upon for illustrative material: working in the vineyards, plowing and sowing and reaping,
winnowing the wheat, watering the cattle, the fisherman
casting his nets.   The hills round about were grazed by
many sheep, and caring for them was an important part
of life in Nazareth.   The shepherd's work suggested several parables, and is the basis for an elaborate allegory in
the fourth Gospel:

> My sheep hear my voice,
>   And I know them and they follow me;

(¹) Luke 16:13.
(²) John 8:34-36.
(³) Luke 12:35, 36.

And I give them eternal life,
  And they will not be lost—no, never!
  And no one will snatch them out of my hand.([1])

I am the Good Shepherd:
  The Good Shepherd lays down his life for the sheep.
He that is a hired man and not the shepherd,
  Who does not own the sheep,
  Sees the wolf coming and leaves the sheep and runs away
    (And the wolf makes them his prey and scatters them)
  Because he is a hired man and cares nothing for the
    sheep.([2])

Not only agriculture but "business" furnishes its fair share of illustrative instances: the merchantman seeking goodly pearls,([3]) bankers and interest,([4]), as well as the coins in which all transactions took place—"talent," "pound" (*mina*), "penny" or "shilling" (*denary*), "farthing" or "mite" (*lepta*).([5])

Nothing seems too insignificant to merit the attention of Jesus, or too homely or too familiar to serve his purpose. He shows us the housewife mending the family clothes, or spinning flax or wool to make new garments; sweeping the house with lighted lamp to find her lost coin; or putting yeast in her meal to make bread, as well as the small, flat loaves into which she bakes it, the oven in which it is baked and the rude stone hand-mill in which she grinds her meal. He shows us the store-room or "treasury" out of which the householder brings things new and old; and the "treasure" or hoard of every family in the East, generally a sum of money buried in the dirt floor or under the pavement:

([1]) John 10:27, 28.
([2]) John 10:11-13.
([3]) Matt. 13:45, 46.
([4]) Luke 19:13.
([5]) Matt. 18:24; Luke 19:13; Mark 12:42, etc.

Treasure not for yourselves treasures on earth,
   Where moth and rust destroy,
   And where thieves dig through and steal;
But treasure for yourselves treasures in Heaven,
   Where neither moth nor rust destroys,
   And where thieves do not dig through and steal.
      For where your treasure is,
      There will be your heart also.[1]

Clothing, that for every day and that for special occasions, often figures in the discourses of Jesus; the cloak and tunic,[2] girdle, sandals, staff, purse, scrip[3] (or, as we say, "grip"), and for more formal occasions the robe, "long robes," "wedding garment."[4]. In short, from the parables and sayings of Jesus a whole volume on Jewish archaeology might easily be compiled.

Popular customs not infrequently furnish an apt simile or other illustration, especially the religious: the habits of prayer, the interior of the synagogue and its form of service. The chief events of life—birth, marriage, death— which have not only an individual but a social significance, are very prominent in the teachings. The marriage-feast, in particular, everywhere in the East one of the chief social functions, is a favorite subject, the main theme of several parables and an object of frequent allusion. The music and dancing by hired entertainers that are usual accompaniments of Oriental social occasions, are by no means forgotten.[5] Even the street games of the village urchins are levied upon for illustration.[6]

On everything included in the broad term "politics," public events and policies, Jesus is significantly silent. Things military, war and weapons, so prominent in ancient times and especially under Roman rule, he mentions spar-

---

[1] Matt. 6:19-21.
[2] Matt. 5:40.
[3] Matt. 10:10.
[4] Luke 15:22; Matt. 22:11.
[5] Luke 15:25.
[6] Matt. 11:16-19; Luke 7:31-34.

ingly, and more because they are things generally familiar to his hearers than because they filled any large place in his own thinking.

> "Or what king sets out to encounter another king in battle, without first sitting down and considering whether he is able to meet with ten thousand the one advancing against him with twenty thousand. And if not, while the other is still a long way off, he sends envoys and asks terms of peace."([1])

If we did not positively know that Jesus was country-bred, we could with absolute certainty infer it from his words; for everywhere it is the processes of nature and the life of country-folk that suggest to him spiritual analogies, not the life of camp or city.

([1]) Luke 14:31, 32.

CHAPTER II

JESUS THE PROPHET AND TEACHER

I

Our Gospels warrant us in concluding that his prophetic function bulked largest in the consciousness of Jesus. His mission, as he conceived it, was to make God known to men, that he might bring men back to God—made especially clear in the Fourth Gospel, but by no means obscure in the others. But to realize this purpose, to make God known effectively, Jesus must be teacher, no less than prophet. Among the greatest teachers he was, if we consider his method merely; while he was the great Teacher of the ages, if we consider also his message. In this chapter we are to consider the method chiefly, while the two chapters to follow will be concerned mainly with the message. It may not prove possible in all cases to preserve this distinction with exactitude, but as a general description it should pass muster.

To his own generation, the chief pedagogic trait of Jesus seemed to be his tone of authority. Frequent in the Gospels are passages like this: "The multitudes were astonished at his teaching, for he taught as one having authority, and not as their scribes."[1] How did their scribes teach? Just as a modern preacher teaches: they took a text from the Law and then expounded and enforced it. They sheltered themselves behind the authority of Moses and the Prophets: they claimed no authority of their own.

[1] Matt. 7:28, 29; 13:54; 22:33; Mark 11:18; Luke 4:32; John 7:46.

But Jesus differed sharply from them in that he claimed independent, essential authority:

> You have heard that it was said,
>   "Eye for eye,
>   And tooth for tooth."
> But *I* say to you,
>   Resist not the evil man.

> You have heard that it was said,
>   "Thou shalt love thy neighbor
>   And thou shalt hate thine enemy."
> But *I* say to you,
>   Love your enemies,
>   And pray for those that persecute you.[1]

Many of the words of Jesus are redeemed from insufferable conceit, from wicked arrogance and pretension, only if we concede to him what he claimed, unique authority as Teacher. The Pharisees continually revolted against this claim; his own disciples often protested and grumbled among themselves;[2] but he went on calmly announcing his great truths, mostly to dull ears and unbelieving hearts. He never bated one jot of his claims; in no case did he soften his teachings to make them more palatable. To the end, his tone was that of one born to command speaking to those born to obey. Not that he was imperious, overbearing, haughty—every reader of the Gospels knows that he was the reverse of this, but every reader also knows that he was authoritative.

Why do not teachings of such character jar our sensibilities? Why did they not expose Jesus when he spoke to the scoffs and jeers of the multitude? The record shows that men might reject his teaching, they might hate him with deadly hatred, they might conspire to put him to death; the one thing they might not do was to laugh at

---

[1] Matt. 5:38, 39, 43, 44.
[2] *e.g.* John 6:60, 66.

him. True or false, he spoke with an authority that separates his teaching from all other teaching.

The secret of this authority of Jesus as Teacher can of course be sought in nothing else than in his character. When a Marcus Aurelius speaks, the imperial purple may dazzle men and make them see in his commonplaces profound wisdom; but there was no rank, no adventitious circumstance, to give undeserved weight to what Jesus said. To all appearances he was nothing but an ordinary peasant of Galilee. But he was more: so much more that men hung on his words and treasured them in memory. What he was determined what he spoke and feathered the arrows of truth that he sent always into the gold. Because Jesus surpassed all men in the depth and reality of his life with God, he was God's prophet as none other. Because he and the Father were one, he speaks with the calm, deep certitude of one who knows spiritual things, not guesses them.

The method of Jesus was the intuitional. He relied on the religious intuitions, his own first of all, but next on those of his hearers. The method of most teachers is the logical; they aim to prove religious truth by reasoning. But all reasoning goes back ultimately to a few principles that are intuitively perceived and are themselves incapable of proof. They are deliverances of consciousness, which we must take on faith solely. No amount of argument or proof can make these fundamentals more credible to us than they are in themselves. If a man is not convinced, on a mere statement of the proposition, that things equal to the same thing are equal to each other, or that two and two make four, or that right is right and wrong is wrong, then no testimony, no syllogisms, can ever clear the matter up for him. So Jesus ignored the logical process and appealed straight to the intuitions. Jesus never argued. Jesus never proved. Open the Gospels where you will, and you shall find him simply announcing truth, leaving those who have ears to hear, to hear.

It is therefore to wisdom and experience, the intuitive element in knowledge, that Jesus appeals for confirmation of teaching, when he cites any corroborative authority, not to scholarship and criticism, knowledge painfully acquired by study. Yet he could on occasion worst the scribes in their own rabbinic dialetic. A good example is his retort after they had tried to trip him by asking subtle questions of legalism:

> How do the scribes say that the Messiah is David's Son? David himself said, in the Holy Spirit,
>> *Jehovah said to my Lord,*
>> *"Sit on my right hand,*
>> *Till I put thine enemies underneath thy feet."*
> David himself calls him "Lord"; and whence is he his Son?(¹)

The question was unanswerable, so long as they refused to accept Jesus as the Messiah, and it reduced his critics to silence. A similar case was his reply to Sadducees who quibbled about the resurrection, and propounded to him the problem of the woman who had been married successively to seven brothers, and as climax demanding, "In the resurrection whose wife shall she be of the seven?" Jesus in reply accused them of misinterpretation of their own standard of authority, the Books of Moses, and used against them their own methods of exegesis; quoting the words of God to Moses at the burning bush, "I am the God of Abraham, and the God of Isaac and the God of Jacob," from which he drew the inference, which they were unable to dispute, "He is not the God of dead men, but of living. You greatly err."(²)

The much maligned Friends have come nearer than any other modern Christians to understanding the spirit of Jesus and imitating his method. Unfortunately for the

(¹) Matt. 22:41-46; Mark 12:35-37; Luke 20:41-44.
(²) Matt. 22:23-32; Mark 12:18-27; Luke 20:27-40.

reception of their truth, they mingled with it much foolish exegesis of Scripture, and taught with equal emphasis error with truth, so that the world has rejected both. But George Fox was quite in line with his Master in urging that the religion of the letter, of the printed book, of rites and ceremonies, is by comparison nothing. But the life of the spirit is difficult; to profess a complicated creed, to practice a florid cult, is easy. Yet Jesus did his best to make the spiritual life the simple life. His teaching, though profound as ocean, is always sane, convincing. Our inmost souls respond to his word; deep calls to deep. For to Jesus truth was not something written in books, or something handed down on the lips of wise men of old; it was something living, throbbing with reality, something autoptic, indisputable, indestructible. But every man must see it for himself, or it cannot be truth for him. The Master's teaching was described by Peter as "words of eternal life," spiritual truth that must be received by every disciple on its own self-evidencing power, and consequently meaningless to any man until by so receiving it he makes it his own. Then it is his inalienable possession forever.

And so, only on a single occasion, and then because the occasion itself required it, did Jesus ever formally expound the Scriptures of his people, or cite them as his authority. Often he cited them as the authority of his hearers, as an *argumentum ad hominem,* to prove to them that, from their own point of view, their criticisms and objections were groundless. But he never claimed them as the source of his teachings, or as giving his words higher value. In his treatment of tradition and Scripture, he gave his followers a lesson for all time—a lesson little to the profit of the greater number in all the centuries, because they have refused to heed. Jesus dealt with the substance of truth, not the form, with eternal realities rather than with transitory and imperfect attempts to express eternal verities. Which is the same as saying that he ignored the Jewish theology of his day.

We do not heed this lesson, because theology seems so important that we have come to identify theology with truth. Our minds are so anaesthetized by doctrines said to be drawn from inspired sources that our moral intuitions do not function when we read the words of Jesus. To the man who believes that anything must be accepted as true, just because it may be plausibly deduced from something that somebody (often an unknown person) wrote in a book two thousand years ago, one appeals in vain to trust his intuitions or to exercise his reason. His intuitions are atrophied by disuse; his reason has abdicated and turned his soul over to authority. He cannot perceive truth, he dare not reason about truth—he might be damned if he did!

There are several possible (and actual) theories about divine revelation. There is the orthodox Protestant theory: that God spoke often two or three thousand years ago, mostly to a few peasant folk, and then shut himself up in his Heaven and has ever since refused to speak to anybody. And then there is the orthodox Catholic theory: that God has remained shut up in his Heaven most of the time and for most people, but has now and then opened a window and spoken to a saint here and a saint there. If one had to choose between the Protestant theory and the Catholic, one would choose the latter, as the one that honors God most and insults common sense least. But fortunately there is another theory: that God never shut himself up in his Heaven, but has always remained in his world and among the men he has made, too often unrecognized by those who boasted of being on most familiar terms with him, but ready ever to speak to any who cared enough about his word to listen. As that is the most sensible theory, the most God-honoring theory, the only theory that accords with the facts of religious experience, naturally both Protestants and Catholics with one voice shout at anybody who mentions it, "Heresy! Heresy! Put him out!"

Inspiration meant among the Hebrews that all their great men and women—kings, warriors, lawgivers, no less than poets and prophets—were believed to receive communications and direction from Jehovah. Among early Christians inspiration meant that the Spirit of God was given to all believers as guide and teacher, while he bestowed special gifts on some, who in the aggregate were many. Only at a relatively late period did the idea emerge that inspiration was restricted to the small group who produced the surviving literature, whether Hebrew or Greek; or that this inspiration was of a special quality, unshared by others; or that it entirely ceased at a given time. These notions of inspiration have nothing to commend them to this generation but their supposed antiquity, and on examination that turns out to be a sham. The commonly prevailing concept of "inspiration" was originally invented by the Fathers of the early Catholic Church, as a weapon against the numerous heretics of the first three centuries. An infallible Bible furnished an inexhaustible arsenal of texts against those who defied the authority of the Church. But heretics could cite texts, too, and the Church soon found herself so embarrassed by her own doctrine of inspiration that it was suffered quietly to slip into the background, while emphasis was laid more and more on the authority of the organization itself and of the Fathers who buttressed it.

This demand for infallibility seems instinctive; at any rate it is universal. What a pity it cannot be satisfied! There is authority in religion, but not infallible authority —it is the authority of truth alone. Every other authority on which man has leaned for infallible guidance has showed itself to be no better than a broken reed. Men have found by bitter experience that the Pope is not infallible, that the Church is not infallible, that the Bible

is not infallible, that the human reason is not infallible,
that the Christian consciousness is not infallible.   Falli-
bility, we must conclude, is an inescapable limitation of
humanity, inseparable from the possession of finite powers.   Even divine inspiration cannot infuse infallibility
into a finite mind and spirit; or, if that be open to debate
as an abstract proposition, it is demonstrable fact that
inspiration has never yet produced infallibility in man.
"For now we know in part" must forever continue to be
our confession.   Absolute truth is known to God alone;
to us the search for truth, with, we may hope, an approximation to the goal that increases from age to age.

> When he, the Spirit of Truth, is come
> He will guide you into all the truth—[1]

guide you, gradually, ultimately, not reveal to you truth
in its fulness all at once and once for all.   The Christian
world would be delivered from intolerable bondage if it
could, in some happy hour, learn that its cherished "doctrines" are not absolute and final truths, but guesses at
truth, working hypotheses regarding the Kingdom of God,
from their very nature subject to constant modification
and revision in the light of advancing knowledge and enlarged experience.

II

In form, the teaching of Jesus was no less remarkable
than in substance, though possibly less unique.   All Oriental teachers deal much in metaphor, the literary expression of poetry rather than of prose.   Jesus abounds in
metaphor.   He describes his disciples after this fashion:
Peter is "a Rock," James and John are "Sons of Thunder,"[2] and all are "fishers of men," "sheep in the midst
of wolves," "little children," "the salt of the earth," "the

---

[1] John 16:13.

[2] But perhaps this name was given by their fellow-disciples,
not by Jesus.

light of the world," and some are "eunuchs." To be his disciple is to "take my yoke upon you," or "take up the cross and follow me," or "drink the cup that I am about to drink." The Pharisees are a "generation of vipers," "whited sepulchers," "actors wearing masks" (the exact sense of "hypocrites"), "wolves in sheep's clothing," and their teaching is "yeast." The relation between character and conduct is not defined with careful precision of words, as a Western teacher would attempt, but expressed in a double metaphor:

> Either make the tree good and its fruit good,
> Or else make the tree rotten and its fruit rotten.[1]

Or, again, this time with a touch of scorn:

> Do men gather grapes from thorns,
> Or figs from thistles?[2]

Truth and error are many times expressed in terms of light and darkness, while both death and life are symbolized in the growth of a kernel of wheat. Himself, his character and mission, are most frequently set forth in metaphor—he is the Light of the World, the Bread of Life, the Water of Life. Once his metaphor was wittily turned against him, when he seemed to reject the plea of the Syro-Phenecian mother, with the word, "It is not fitting to take the children's loaf and throw it to the dogs." In a flash she replied, "True, sir, but even the dogs eat of the crumbs that fall from their master's table." Deeply moved and pleased, Jesus responded, "Madam, great is your trust! Be it done to you as you desire."[3]

Sometimes the metaphors were so extraordinary that they seemed to his hearers extravagant or meaningless. Nicodemus could not comprehend the saying:

[1] Matt. 12:33.
[2] Matt. 7:16.
[3] Matt. 15:22-28; Mark 7:25-29.

> Except one be born from above
> He cannot see the Kingdom of God.([1])

And some who had followed him until then, turned their backs on him when he declared:

> Unless you eat the flesh of the Son of Man
>   And drink his blood,
> You have not life in yourselves.([2])

To this day many of his most characteristic and important words are stumbling-blocks to his professed disciples, because they persist in applying to his Oriental metaphors a principle of literal interpretation that they by no means always apply to the formal definitions of councils and the statements of creeds. Such a case, for example, as this:

> If any man come to me,
>   And hate not his father or mother,
>   And wife and children,
>   And brothers and sisters,
>   Yea, even his own life,
>   He cannot be disciple of mine.
> And whoso does not carry his own cross and come after me,
>   He cannot be disciple of mine.([3])

III

Renan is quite justified in his assertion that the wit and humor of Jesus constitute one of the most impressive features of the Gospels. Certainly, they are the most distinctive feature. Most amazing, therefore, is the failure, the total failure, of interpreters in all ages to recognize what is by all odds the most shining quality of Jesus among the great religious teachers of the world, the faculty

([1]) John 3:3.
([2]) John 6:53.
([3]) Luke 14:26, 27.

that sets him head and shoulders above all others. The reason for this failure is, no doubt, the fact that even now to speak of Jesus as a humorist will strike the majority of pious Christians as a shocking irreverence. And this again is because people in general have come to entertain a low and degrading idea about wit and humor. It is quite true that much of that humor" of which the American people are the proud and sole possessors is nothing better than a feeble jocosity alternating with dull buffoonery. We are in danger of becoming a nation of clowns and patrons of clowns. We never do anything by halves, but our labors to be funny are our hardest work. We are fond of quoting:

A merry heart doeth good like medicine,(¹)

but not so fond of another saying of the Wise Man:

For as the crackling of thorns under a pot,
So is the laughter of the fool.(²)

As a people we have little appreciation of the happy medium between sobs and smiles, grins and groans. We have never learned that to be cheerful it is not necessary to giggle, nor that to be serious one need not weep. "Quips and cranks and wanton wiles" abound in our conversation, in our newspapers, in our books, to such an extent as to suggest national lack of discrimination between condiments and foods. A dash of tabasco in soup or gravy is appetizing, but a spoonful is torture. Too much fun is worse than none. A continuous round of pleasure ends in complete boredom—as that wise man understood who said, "Life would be quite tolerable but for its amusements."

The suggestion that Jesus used wit and humor freely in his discourses will give a distinct shock to many readers, in whose minds still lingers the Puritan superstition

(¹) Prov. 17:22.
(²) Eccl. 7:6.

that a deep gravity of word and demeanor is alone suitable to the discussion of religious themes. But the Puritans and their descendants have shown themselves quite unable to appreciate either the nature of Jesus or the nature of wit and humor. For wit and humor are by no means restricted to that volatile jesting whose chief function is to conceal absence of thought. They do not consist in sheer boisterous banalities. Their purpose is not merely to provoke laughter of light-minded folk. They have their serious use also, and this is by far their most important function in literature and life.

Jesus always spoke with deep inner seriousness, yet much of the time with wit that gives his teachings point and keenness, nearly always with lambent humor that makes his sayings tender and appealing. He at least comprehended, if some of his followers do not, that a sense of humor is imperatively needed for the attainment of true moral values, and is an indispensable part of the equipment of a great religious teacher.

It is precisely this trait that makes the Synoptic Jesus so human a figure. Other great religious teachers—Confucius, Buddha, Moses, Mohammed—have taken their message and themselves with that deadly seriousness which tends to defeat its own purpose. The ethical sobriety of Jesus is wholly consistent with an intellectual gayety of the sort that the French call *esprit,* and not a little of his power is distinctly traceable to this element, which the Christian sages have so persistently ignored—possibly because the saving gift of humor has been withheld from so many of them, but more probably because they felt that to attribute humor to Jesus would be almost like accusing him of sinfulness. The truest reverence for the Master is to see Him as he was.

Wit, it is commonly agreed, consists in putting together objects or ideas not usually associated, so as to produce a pleasing sensation of surprise. But the quick flash of wit is like an electric spark, in that it not only surprises but illumines. Jesus uses wit not so much to give pleasure as to give light. His sayings never provoke a laugh, but often they make one see truth with a vividness not otherwise possible. Perhaps oftenest his wit takes the form of apothegm, neat, terse, pregnant sayings, frequently paradoxical, that, once heard, fix themselves in memory forever. Familiar cases are:

> A house divided against itself cannot stand. [1]
> The Kingdom of God does not come with watching for it. [2]
> A man's life does not consist in the extent of his possessions. [3]
> To him that has will be given,
> And from him that has not will be taken even what he has. [4]
> Every one that exalts himself will be humbled,
> And he that humbles himself will be exalted. [5]
> Whoever would be first among you will be your slave. [6]
> I came to cast fire upon the earth,
>> Would that it were already kindled!
> So I have a baptism to undergo,
>> And how am I distressed till it is accomplished!
> Think you I have come to give peace in the earth?
>> No, I assure you, but rather dissension. [7]

Sometimes the wit takes the form of epigram:

> Give then to Caesar what belongs to Caesar,
> And to God what belongs to God. [8]

On a few occasions Jesus seems actually to banter his adversaries, the Pharisees. Thus, when they demanded of him, "By what authority do you do these things?" such as driving the traders out of the Temple, he replied:

---

[1] Mark 3:25.
[2] Luke 17:20.
[3] Luke 12:15.
[4] Matt. 13:12.
[5] Luke 14:11 (repeated several times).
[6] Matt. 20:27.
[7] Luke 12:49-51.
[8] Mark 12:17, etc.

> I will also ask you a question:
> The baptism of John—
> Was it from Heaven or from men?

His nonplussed critics dared say neither the one nor the other, and so replied, "We don't know." So Jesus closed the matter by saying, "Neither do I tell you by what authority I do these things."([1]) At another time, when messengers came from the Baptist, asking for a clear declaration whether he was the Messiah or not, after answering them Jesus spoke to the crowd in this bantering way:

> What went you out into the wilderness to see?
> A reed swayed by the wind?
> But what went you out to see?
> A man robed in soft garments?
> Lo, people who wear gorgeous clothing and live in
> luxury are in palaces.
> But what went you out to see? A prophet?
> Yes, I assure you, and more than a prophet.([2])

The truth is of course that we have been so long preoccupied with the profound spiritual truth in the words of Jesus that we have failed to note their pungency. Few teachers have been so signal masters of the art of packing a great thought into a few simple words. But as we read further in the Gospels we discover that epigram and paradox not infrequently pass over into hyperbole. With some persons, exaggerated statement of fact or truth is unconscious, the result of over-eagerness to make a strong impression on hearer or reader; but with others, as with Jesus, exaggeration is deliberate, in which case it is almost invariably humorous. Only hopeless intellectual dulness could take literally such sayings as:

> If your right eye causes you to stumble,
> Pluck it out and cast it from you.([3])

([1]) Matt. 21:25, etc.
([2]) Matt. 11:7; Luke 7:24.
(³) Matt. 5:29.

The very hairs of your head are numbered.([1])

If these shall hold their peace,
The very stones will cry out.([2])

Easier might heaven and earth pass away
Than for one dot of an *i* to lapse from the Law.([3])

If you have faith as a grain of mustard seed, you
    will say to this mountain,
  "Remove hence to yonder place,"
And it will remove.([4])

It is easier for a camel to go through a needle's eye,
Than for a rich man to enter into the Kingdom of God.([5])

These are examples of that method of overstatement for the sake of vividness, or with intentional humor, which is a fundamental characteristic of American speech and writing. We, if any Western people, ought to be able to comprehend and rightly evaluate this Oriental element in the teaching of Jesus. To some sober-minded persons even among us, however, all exaggeration seems nothing else than a form of lying; and to such it will therefore appear to be a shocking and irreverent thing to say of Jesus that on any occasion he exaggerated. They could never comprehend the principle on which exaggeration may be ethically justifiable, which has been stated (the statement is itself a good example of humorous exaggeration) in this fashion: "When you tell a lie, tell it so big that nobody will believe it, and then it isn't a lie."

([1]) Matt. 10:30.
([2]) Luke 19:40.
([3]) Luke 16:17, etc.
([4]) Matt. 17:20. How persistently in all the ages men have misunderstood and misapplied that saying, as a literal promise of wonder-working powers, and have refused to see the grim warning that lurks under the kindly humor of the saying. Jesus would convey to us, that the great thing is not to move mountains but to have faith, and the man who desires faith in order that he may move mountains puts himself on the level of Simon Magus, and will never come within seeing distance of the faith.

([5]) Matt. 19:24.

What interpreters of the Puritan temperament have done with the sayings of Jesus is matter of history. See the average commentary or sermon on texts like the following:

> Whoever smites you on one cheek,
> Turn to him the other also.[1]
> Why do you behold the splinter in your brother's eye,
> And consider not the beam in your own eye?[2]
> I say not to you, Until seven times,
> But, Until seventy-times seven.[3]
> For every idle word that men shall speak
> They will give account in the Day of Judgment.
> For by your words you will be acquitted,
> And by your words you will be condemned.[4]

Yet let not those of us who clearly see the humor in such words make the opposite mistake from that of those who are blind to the humor: they have been overliteral in interpretation; let us not evacuate such words of all serious meaning. Take the last saying above quoted as a test: hyperbole, no doubt, but that should not be an excuse for lightly dismissing it from our minds as of no consequence. For, though a humorous saying, it has a serious and profound meaning, that justifies itself to every man of sound moral sense. Men will be judged, men are daily judged, on the basis of character, and character is the net result of word and deed. Every act, every word, contributes something to the result. A man is never again just the same man after he speaks or does. Each deed and word automatically reacts, leaving its mark, great or infinitesimal, helping to fashion character.

To those unfortunates who lack the sixth sense, the wit and humor of Jesus cannot be other than a stumbling-

---

[1] Matt. 5:38.
[2] Matt. 7:3.
[3] Matt. 18:22.
[4] Matt. 12:36, 37.

block. They will to the end of time be no more able to comprehend him than was Nicodemus. Insisting on taking the words of Jesus, as the French say, "to the bottom of the letter," they will always turn into foolishness the wisdom of the Wisest. Understanding of humor, like the use of it in teaching, is possible only to one who has something of the equipment of the philosopher: it demands vision broad enough to take in the incongruities between aspiration and achievement, the contrasts of joy and sorrow, the facts of success and failure, of sin and righteousness, that make up human life and constitute not only its humor but its pathos. For true humor is never far from tears.

Even more characteristic of the teaching of Jesus than the humor of hyperbole is a delicate irony, never absent long from his discourses in the Gospels, that makes his words glow and warm. Of this character is the entire passage in the Sermon on the Mount on human worries:

> Wherefore I say to you:
> Do not worry about your life,
>   What you will eat and what you will drink;
> Nor for your body, what you will wear.
>   Is not life more than food,
>   And the body than clothing?
>
> Look at the birds of the air:
>   They sow not, they reap not,
>   They gather not into barns;
> Yet your Heavenly Father feeds them.
>   Are not you worth much more than they?
>
> And which of you, by worrying, can add to his life a
>   single inch?
>   Then why do you worry about clothing?
> Consider well the lilies of the field, how they grow;
>   They toil not, nor do they spin,
> But I tell you, not even Solomon in all his splendor was
>   robed like one of these.

Now if God so clothes the grass of the field,
　Which to-day is and to-morrow is cast into an oven,
Will he not much more clothe you?
O men of little trust![1]

Briefer passages, perhaps less familiar, will illustrate the quality quite as well. What, for example, could appeal to a popular audience more effectively than this little reminder of those family jars that were doubtless quite as common then as now:

For I am come . . . to set the daughter-in-law against
　the mother-in-law.[2]

Cases of this gentle satiric humor abound everywhere:

Is it lawful on the Sabbath to do good or harm,
　To save life or kill?[3]

They that are healthy have no need of a doctor
　But they that are sick.
I am not come to call the righteous to repentance,
　But sinners.[4]

He that is without sin among you,
　Let him throw the first stone at her.[5]

How unanswerable, how wakening of somnolent conscience, how utterly abashing, that ironic thrust! In many of the parables, this gentle play of humor adds greatly to their force. For example:

Nobody sews a piece of unshrunk cloth on an old cloak,
　For the patch will tear away from the cloak,
　　And a worse rent follows.
Nor do they put new wine into old skins;
　If they do, the skins burst and the wine runs out,
　　And the skins are spoiled;

---

[1] Matt. 6:19-34; cf. the somewhat different version in Luke 12:22-34, the latter thought by some to be nearer to the original form of the discourse.
[2] Matt. 10:35.
[3] Mark 3:4.
[4] Luke 5:31, 32.
[5] John 8:7.

> But they put new wine into fresh skins,
> And both are preserved together.([1])

The parable of the two slaves, in which one is represented as refusing to his fellow the mercy that his master has just shown him;([2]) and that of the wedding guests and their frivolous excuses,([3]) are other familiar instances. Sometimes the irony is a little less playful, becomes rather sharp pointed, just a pinch of bitter with the sweet, yet without losing its kindliness. As:

> If you were blind, you would have no sin;
> But now you say, "We see"—
>   Your sin remains!([4])
> If I by Beelzebub cast out demons,
> By whom do your sons cast them out?([5])
> How much more then is a man of more value than
>   a sheep!([6])
> Will you lay down your life for me!
>   Truly, I tell you truly, The cock will not crow
>   Before you have thrice disowned me!([7])
> Have I been so long time with you,
> And you do not know me, Philip!([8])

Socrates taught the world for all time the effectiveness of irony in controversy, but no more effectively than Jesus. How could the Pharisaic opposition to his teachings be more neatly satirized than by this comparison of his adversaries to the sulky children whom nothing can please and who "won't play" whatever their companions do?

> To what shall I compare this generation?
>   It is like children sitting in the market-places,
>   Who call to their fellows and say,

([1]) Matt. 9:16, 17.
([2]) Matt. 18:23-25.
([3]) Luke 14:15-24.
([4]) John 9:4.
([5]) Matt. 12:27.
([6]) Matt. 12:12.
([7]) John 13:38.
([8]) John 14:9.

"We piped to you and you did not dance;
 We wailed and you did not beat the breast."
For John came neither eating nor drinking,
 And you say, "He has a demon."
The Son of Man came eating and drinking,
 And you say, "See! a glutton and a drunkard,
 A friend of tax-gatherers and outcasts."[1]

One should be charitable and gentle in judgment of modern interpreters who have so completely overlooked this side of the Master's teaching, when we note that the delicate point of his humor so often missed its mark with his original hearers. Accustomed as Oriental people are to this method, the average Galilean peasant does not appear to have been a very humorsome person, and the average Pharisee was quite destitute of humor—or he could never have been a Pharisee! Most of those to whom Jesus spoke seem to have belonged to the class, still by far the larger part of mankind, who can never understand a humorous saying, unless with it they were handed a diagram and mathematical proof of the proposition. Even the Twelve were, as a Scotchman would say, "verra slow on the uptake." When Jesus warned them to "beware of the Pharisees' yeast," it required an elaborate explanation to make them comprehend that their Master was talking about doctrine, not bread. An incident of the last days affords a fine illustration, both of the irony of Jesus and the dourness of spirit that made his hearers so incomprehensive. The throngs and acclamation of Palm Sunday, the crowds of eager hearers in the Temple on several succeeding days, have blinded the disciples to the actual situation. So Jesus says to them, in effect: "This is the hour, not of triumph, but of danger; our enemies are upon us; this is a time for swords; if your own safety is paramount, provide yourselves with money and weapons." As usual,

---

[1] Matt. 11:16-19; Luke 7:31-34.

when quick comprehension of a nice thought was required,
the disciples entirely misunderstood. They took his irony
literally, as stupid people always do, and replied, "Here
are two swords." Jesus saw that it was vain to attempt to
penetrate solid ivory and gave it up, saying, "It is
enough!"—what is the use of my talking any longer.(¹)

Although Jesus could always be patient with stupidity,
bad faith sometimes provoked him to sharper words. The
button then comes off the foil, and a deadly thrust is made
at evil. Irony becomes sarcasm, keen, biting, lethal. Of
many examples these will suffice:

> They bind heavy burdens and grievous to be borne,
>   And lay them on men's shoulders,
> But themselves will not touch them with their finger.(²)
> You seek me, not because you beheld signs,
> But because you ate the loaves and were filled.(³)
> Give not a sacred thing to dogs,
>   Nor cast your pearls before swine,
> Lest they trample them under foot
>   And turn and bite you!(⁴)
> Can the blind lead the blind?
> Will not both fall into a pit?(⁵)
>   Why do you call me Master, Master
>   And do not the things that I say?(⁶)

Yet even in his bitterest denunciations there is a saving
touch of humor—no hardihood of evil could make his
words other than severely kind:

>   Woe to you Chorazin!
>   Woe to you Bethsaida!
> For had the mighty works been done in Tyre and Sidon
>   That have been done in you,

(¹) Luke 22:35-38.
(²) Matt. 23:4.
(³) John 6:26.
(⁴) Matt. 7:6.
(⁵) Luke 6:39.
(⁶) Luke 6:46.

Long ago would they have repented in sackcloth and ashes.([1])

Woe to you, teachers of the Law and Pharisees, hypocrites!
Because you scour sea and land to make a single proselyte,
> And when it is done,
You make him tenfold more a son of Gehenna than your-
> selves!([2])

Woe to you, teachers of the Law and Pharisees, hypocrites!
Because you pay tithe of mint and dill and cumin,
And have neglected the weightier matters of the Law:
> Justice and mercy and faith.
> The former you should have done,
> And not left the other undone.
> Blind leaders! who strain out the gnat
> And swallow the camel!([3])

The sting of such words helps us to understand whence
came those shouts of "Crucify him! Crucify him!" on that
fateful Friday morning in Jerusalem.

IV

The instinct of the Galilean people was sound when
they recognized Jesus, from the very beginning of his
ministry, as the successor of the prophets.([4]) His disciples repeated to him on one occasion the gossip current
among the people: many besides Herod([5]) believed him to
be John the Baptist risen from the dead: others said he
was Elijah or Jeremiah reborn in the flesh: generally he
was held to be "one of the prophets."([6]) But he was more
than successor, he was fruition, he was culmination. In
him prophetism reaches its climax, delivers its message in
its fulness. As God's prophet, Jesus did more than all

([1]) Matt. 11:21.
([2]) Matt. 23:15.
([3]) Matt. 23:23, 24.
([4]) Mark 6:15, Luke 7:16; Matt. 14:5; 21:11; John 7:40.
([5]) Mark 6:14.
([6]) Matt. 6:14; Mark 8:28; Luke 9:10.

who preceded him to make God known, understandable, lovable. If we have dwelt long on the unique form of his teaching, we must not let this prevent our appreciation of the far greater import of the substance.

The history of religions is the record of an age-long contest between prophet and priest, and the priest has nearly always had the better of it. The reason he that runs may read: the prophet seeks to move us by the ravishment of high ideals; the priest subtly appeals to us with a set of plain rules. The prophet is a mystic, the priest a realist. The prophet is the man of vision, an intuitionalist; the priest a man of precedent, a legalist. Prophetic religion makes a heavy draft on the best on man; priest religion is content to accept man's average—or even a little less. The prophet sets before men a rough and thorny road leading to the heights; the priest opens to men the way of least resistance along the plain. Prophetic religion is only for the thoughtful, the earnest, the aspiring; priest religion is for the idle, the careless, the selfish. The prophet calls for renunciation, so few heed his words; the priest permits indulgence, and therefore has a large following.

So it was ever in Judaism. The prophets enjoined a new life of justice, mercy, righteousness; the priests sought to establish a cult, with machinery for obtaining on easy terms God's pardon for failure to do what the stern prophet exacted. Piety was to be accepted for righteousness, sacrifice for mercy, tithes for justice. The prophets said that God required of his worshipers a pure heart; the priests said that he required clean linen. The one sort of religion cherished as its ideal social justice, the welfare of the people; the other was content with rites scrupulously performed by the rich. One stood for democracy, the other for aristocracy.

The prophets had always insisted that the relation of man to God is personal; the bond between them is an ethical bond. God is holy; man must be righteous. The priests had always declared that the relation between man and God is mechanical, not vital; that it is established and maintained by rites and sacraments mediated by appointed persons. The prophets taught that every man has direct approach to God, and so is privileged at any time or place to come into intimate relations with him. This doctrine was ruination to a priesthood, which was under professional obligation to insist that approach to God and forgiveness of sins can be had only through Temple and priests. Priestly intercession was therefore a necessity; God would not hear the cries for mercy of laymen, however penitent, but must first be appeased by offerings and sacrifices made through a priest, who thus held the Keys of Heaven.

Against this theory of priesthood and practice of ceremonial religion, Jesus contended as he contended against no other thing. He maintained that it was a perversion of the character of God and of religion, the sin of all sins. The great burden of his teaching was the nearness of God to men, his readiness to pardon sin, his impartial love for all his creatures; and it was upon this basis of the character of God as Father of all mankind that he founded his practical work as institutor of the Kingdom of God. The Sermon on the Mount is nothing else than variations in many keys upon this one theme.([1]) For priesthood and all its pretentions, for its fruits as incarnated in the Pharisees, Jesus manifests utmost contempt and detestation. For purely formal and ceremonial religion he reserves his severest censures; he does everything possible to make plain that the prophetic type of religion is to him the only religion. It would be superfluous to quote passages in support of this summary characterization of the teaching of Jesus; any reader who cannot recognize its accuracy, and instantly call to mind a score of sayings

([1]) See esp. Matt. 5:45; 6:4, 14; 7:11; cf. Mark 11:25, 26.

that justify it, convicts himself either of unfamiliarity with the teaching or of failure to comprehend it.

His own work finished, Jesus sends forth his disciples into the world to proclaim this prophetic religion, as the most precious truth he has to leave with them, the one truth that the world needs to learn. And what do these disciples? They instantly, with one accord, abandon prophetic religion and devote themselves to establishing a new cult—excusing themselves, no doubt, on the plea that they were making Jesus the centre of that cult. They failed to see that at the very time they were deifying Jesus they were defying him. They began a process at Jerusalem that went on as Christianity advanced, by which the idea of holiness again became ceremonial and Christian prophets were transformed into Catholic priests. Followers of the Christ deserted the Jewish cult only to devise another still more outrageous in pretensions and sterner in spiritual tyranny. They began the greatest apostasy in history; they helped to revive and make permanent as orthodoxy of the ages the gravest and most pernicious of all heresies: that God is well pleased by being worshiped with *things* instead of with *hearts*. Hence, to this day, the splendor of Christian churches and the emptiness of Christian lives.

It lessens the emphasis of this condemnation but little to urge that the disciples of Jesus merely did what the disciples of Buddha and other great religious leaders and teachers have invariably done: that an irresistible tendency of human nature leads men always to supplement religious and ethical teachings with a church and a cult. Even Comte, who hoped that he had demolished all previous religions, felt himself compelled to invent a new cult, which he called the worship of humanity. True this is, no doubt, but its truth neither explains nor excuses the immediacy or the completeness of the apostasy of the disciples of Jesus. Their one excuse, such as it is, must be that they never really understood their Master, and that the temporary ascendancy he had obtained over their minds gave place to the renewed ideas of their race and religion, so soon as the power of his personality no longer controlled them. Only on such a hypothesis can we account for their naïve belief that their cries of "Lord, Lord" were an equivalent for doing what he had commanded.

CHAPTER III

JESUS THE REVEALER OF GOD

No trait in the personality of Jesus is more arresting than the greatness of his claims. Both implicit and explicit in his teachings are assertions of right to direct the lives of men that, in the case of any other, would be pronounced presumptuous, extravagant or ridiculous. He is the one person in all history who could make such claims without being laughed out of consideration by all serious persons. Why?

We have already noted the tone of authority in his teaching that astonished his hearers, but we have not analyzed it, nor even considered it more than casually. Among his injunctions to his disciples was this:

> Be not called Rabbi,
> For One is your Teacher,
> And you are all brothers.([1])

Such words can escape accusation of conceit or arrogance only if Jesus was, and knew himself to be, the supreme Teacher of his time and of all time. Nothing but his possession of such knowledge can explain or justify his assertion for himself and his words of a higher sanction than could be ascribed to the prophets and teachers of Israel:

> The Queen of the South will rise up in the Judgment
> with the men of this generation and condemn
> them,
> Because she came from the ends of the earth to hear the
> wisdom of Solomon,

([1]) Matt. 23:8.

And see! One greater than Solomon is here!

Men of Nineveh will rise up in the Judgment with this
       generation and condemn it,
Because they repented at the proclamation of Jonah,
And see! One greater than Jonah is here!([1])

And so, whenever he saw fit, Jesus asserted and exercised
the right to set aside tradition. In the Sermon on the
Mount he repeatedly contrasts his own teaching with Jewish tradition, and even with the Law:

      You have heard that it has been said...
      But *I* say to you . . .

recurs again and again, and the "I" is very emphatic.
Jesus refused to admit the validity of the cut-and-dried
Pharasaic piety; their parvitudes regarding observance of
the Sabbath he annulled in a single phrase:

    The Son of Man is Master of the Sabbath also.([3])

The punctilious pedantry of rule that ignored the state of
affections and will from which all true obedience springs,
and concentrated attention and effort on the mere outward
act, was an abomination to Jesus. In like manner he set
aside the precepts regarding fasting, begun in the Law
and greatly elaborated by tradition, sweeping away the
whole system:

Now, when you fast, be not like the hypocrites;
    For they put on gloomy looks,
    So as to let men see they are fasting.
I tell you truly, They have received their reward.
But when you fast, anoint your head and wash your face,
    So as not to seem to men to fast,
    But to your Father who is in secret;
And your Father, who sees in secret, will reward you.([4])

([1]) Matt. 12:41, 42.
([2]) Matt. 5:27, 28; 33, 34; 38, 39; 43, 44.
([3]) Mark 2:28; Luke 6:5.
([4]) Matt. 6:16-18.

He even warmly approved the practice of his disciples, in the face of criticism by the Pharisees, and made feast days of the fasts of his people.([1])   The mass of accumulated tradition, so dear to the teachers of his people, could not stand before his profoundly spiritual intuition.   This was especially true of those tribal taboos, coming down from a past of superstition and priestly imposture, that claimed all the sanctions of the Law, but never had the slightest title to a divine origin.   At one swoop he made null and void the whole elaborate rules of "clean" and "unclean," when he said:

> Not that which enters into the mouth defiles men,
> But that which comes out of the mouth.([2])

And yet even this was not the sum of his offending, in the eyes of Pharisees; he deliberately set aside, on his own authority solely, positive precepts of the Law that they regarded as indubitably of Mosaic origin.   And by so doing, he of course virtually claimed to be superior as religious teacher and lawgiver to Moses, who was believed to have received the Law directly from God.   Thus Jesus said,

> Moses for the hardness of your hearts suffered . . .
> But *I* say to you . . .([3])

and thereupon laid down a new principle regarding divorce—or reaffirmed a principle yet more ancient than Moses, as others believe.

Some moderns have been inclined partially to excuse the Pharisees, if not boldly defend them, on the ground that their fault was after all only that they were too religious, as Paul said the Athenians were.   But this exculpation ignores the chief clause in the indictment: Jesus denied that the Pharisees were religious at all.   In modern

---

([1]) Luke 5:33-39.

([2]) Matt. 15: 18-20; Mark 7:15, 18-23

([3]) Matt. 19:3-12; Mark 10:2-12.

phrase, they did not practice religion, but religiosity. They had a semblance of piety, but were strangers to the real thing. They were full of bounce and bluff. They were "long" on promise, "short" on performance. So Jesus called them "hypocrites," actors of a part, pretenders to religion under whose mask was an essentially irreligious character. The case against Pharisaism did not rest chiefly on its officious and offensive priggishness, as so many readers of the Gospels infer, but on its confusion of ethical values. Pharisaism not merely made the unimportant important, which is vexatious, but not serious; it made the important unimportant, which is often vexatious and always serious. The weighty accusation of Jesus was,

> You leave the commandment of God
> And hold the tradition of men.(¹)

In proof of his charge he specified their traditions regarding "Corban," or dedication of property to Jehovah, the chicane by which Pharisees nullified the fifth commandment and evaded obligations to parents. On another occasion, he reproached Pharisees for nullifying the obligation of oaths by traditional glosses on the Law:

> Woe to you, blind leaders! Who say,
>   "Whosoever swears by the Temple,
>   It is naught;
>   But whosoever swears by the gold of the Temple,
>   He is bound."
> Senseless and blind!
>   For which is greater, the gold,
>   Or the Temple that makes the gold sacred?
>
> And (you say) "Whosoever swears by the altar,
>   It is naught;
>   But whosoever swears by the gift on the altar,
>   He is bound."
> Blind! For which is greater, the gift,
>   Or the altar that makes the gift sacred?

(¹) Mark 7:8, 9, 13; Matt. 15:3, 6.

He who swears by the altar,
  Swears by it and by everything on it;
And he who swears by the Temple,
  Swears by it and by Him who dwells in it.
And he who swears by Heaven,
  Swears by the throne of God
  And by Him who sits upon it.(¹)

Modern Pharisaism is a worthy lineal descendant of
the ancient, malefic, vulpine, ophidian. It also nullifies
the Law under pretext of greater piety. To do this, it
has invented a Pentalogue of its own: Thou shalt not
drink alcoholic liquors; Thou shalt not use tobacco; Thou
shalt not go to the theatre; Thou shalt not play cards;
Thou shalt not dance. And in most of our highly "Christian" circles, if a man but flaunts his obedience of these
five words of man he may with impunity flout all Ten
Commandments of God.

If Jesus precisely appreciated the spiritual condition of
the ancient Pharisees, what shall be said of the modern?
Shall we say, as he said, that the outcasts of society are
entering into the Kingdom, while the sons of the Kingdom
are shut into the outer darkness? Certainly it is a fact
that the lives of a great part of those who flatter themselves
that they are "saved" are sordid and selfish and unutter-
ably small and mean. Willingness to renounce self, to
give life for others, is quite as often found among "sinners" as among "saints." Of our friends and neighbors,
how often the stingiest, crossest, most annoying, least oblig-
ing, are members of churches "in good standing," while
some of the finest people we have ever known make no
particular boast of having any religion. Is a "salvation"
that does so little for men and women in this world, that
so palpably fails to make them better members of the
family, better neighbors, better in business relations, a
thing really worth while? Does the character of the average "Christian" afford good ground for hope that he will

(¹) Matt. 23:16-22.

fare better in the next world than an "unsaved" man of average decency? When the sheep come to be divided from the goats there will be great surprises, for that line of division will not run along conventional ecclesiastical lines.

II

Not only some but all the words of Jesus, not his words merely but his deeds also, imply possession of this unique character and authority. He never sought honor of men, but he accepted as his due their homage and their recognition of his singular and transcendent personality, when these were spontaneously offered him. Instances that will at once suggest themselves to readers of the Gospels are:

> You are God's Son,
> You are Israel's King;[1]

> You are the Messiah, the Son of the living God;[2]

and the exclamation of the hitherto doubting Thomas,

> My Master and my God![3]

Of the same order were the acclamations of the multitudes at his entry into Jerusalem:

> Hosannah to the Son of David!
> Happy he that comes in Jehovah's name.[4]

Jesus was not content, however, with merely accepting such tributes: he explicitly avowed himself to be Son of God, in some exceptional and extraordinary sense, that other men could not claim for themselves:

> Before Abraham was born, I am.[5]

---

[1] John 1:49.
[2] Matt. 16:16.
[3] John 20:28.
[4] Matt. 21:9.
[5] John 8:58.

> I and the Father are one.[1]
> He that has seen me has seen the Father.[2]

It is true that the most explicit of these declarations are found in the fourth Gospel, on the historical accuracy of which more doubt has been thrown by modern criticism than on the Synoptics: yet the words in John are little more precise in assertion than these in Matthew:

> All things have been delivered to me by my Father,
> And no one knows the Son, save the Father;
> Nor does any know the Father, save the Son,
> And he to whomsoever the Son wills to reveal him.[3]

And at the trial before the Sanhedrin, according to the first Gospel, the high priest demanded of Jesus on his oath the truth about his mission: "I adjure you, by the living God, to tell us whether you are the Messiah, the Son of God." And under the sanctity of that oath, well knowing that he was condemning himself to death, Jesus made reply, "You have said"—a strong affirmative in the idiom of his people.[4]   There is no real difference, therefore, between the fourth Gospel and the first or third in this recognition of the unique Sonship of Jesus.

And therefore, especially in the case of critics unwilling to accept this idea of the unique Sonship, serious doubt has been suggested whether in any of these accounts we have trustworthy words of Jesus—some have even gone so far as to deny that anything more than a few detached sayings can with certainty be attributed to him.   Even the most destructive of critics have not ventured to question the authenticity of a baker's dozen or so of the words ascribed to Jesus in the Synoptics; on the ground, as they admit, that these are of such character that they cannot be

---

[1] John 10:29; cf. 10:35, 36.
[2] John 14:9.
[3] Matt. 11:27; cf. Luke 10:22.
[4] Matt. 26:64.

rationally supposed to have been invented and fathered on Jesus by his contemporaries or by a later generation. That is a sound critical principle; and a just application of it will be found to validate the greater part of the reported sayings of Jesus, not a few merely.

The words of Jesus must be accepted as his, because of most it may be fairly said that we cannot rationally suppose them to have been invented by men who believed precisely the contrary, as practically all his generation did. And more: with certain few exceptions, men have gone on believing the contrary to the present moment. The disciples of Jesus were devoted to his person, but his gospel never penetrated their minds. They heard, they remembered, they recorded, but they never understood, much less believed. One of the plainest things in the Gospels is that there was no intellectual contact between Jesus and those who heard his message. Even the Twelve failed to comprehend: to the last he had no real disciples. Nineteen centuries before Hegel he might have uttered that philosopher's plaintive words: "Only one living man understands me—and he misunderstands!" This may well be our ground of confidence in the substantial accuracy of the reports: it would have been manifestly out of the question for the followers of Jesus to have originated sayings that they never understood and on which they promptly turned their backs.

But if the discourses of Jesus in the main must be accepted as his, for the conclusive reason that the invention of them by his disciples is an intellectual and moral impossibility, there is, as has already been noted, one important exception: the apocalyptic discourses attributed to him. The principal discourse of this character belongs to the last teachings in the Temple, and is said to have been given in response to questions that his disciples were led to ask by a prediction of Jesus that a time was soon coming in which not one stone of that building, the pride of all

Jews, would be left upon another. The simplest form of this discourse is in Mark, chapter thirteen, but it is re-edited and much enlarged by Matthew and Luke. Some parts of the Marcan discourse may have been uttered by Jesus, in relation to the destruction of Jerusalem, to foresee which required no supernatural prophetic gift. Judea was seething with disaffection toward the Roman rule, and a re-bellion was morally certain to come; and one who had an idea of the irresistible power of Rome in that age could not be doubtful of the result of such a clash. But the rest of the discourse so exactly corresponds to the ideas of the age, has so many features in common with Jewish apocalypses, is so in harmony with the later preaching of the apostles, that we have here the only part of the teaching of Jesus that his disciples were competent to invent and send forth to the world under the authority of his name. We cannot doubt, when we compare this discourse with those that we have such solid reasons for accepting as genuine, and noting the wide difference in tone and viewpoint, that it is mainly the work of the disciples, who were inspired to undertake it by a few words of Jesus that they misinterpreted.[1] This conclusion is strengthened when we find on turning back to the earlier teaching and studying it again with this thought in mind, we find occasional evidences that the first Gospel especially apocalyptizes some of these earlier teachings.([2])

Before passing on, one other thing is worthy of note. Some of the modern interpreters of Jesus insist that he

[1] My critics have a bad habit of accusing me of ignorance of every book or idea that I do not choose to mention in my writings. May I then enter here this *caveat*, as a lawyer would say: I am *not* ignorant of the books of Schweitzer, Bousset and others, which maintain the eschatological discourses of Jesus to be his best authenticated words and his most characteristic teachings. From which follows logically enough their theory of *Interimsethik*. To discuss adequately the reasons for rejecting this view would require the writing of another volume, at least as large as this.

[2] For example, compare Matt. 16:28 with Luke 9:27 and Mark 9:1.

did not put into his utterances the fulness of meaning that the present generation thinks it finds there. In other words, we idealize Jesus too much. But if this were true, were it not sufficiently wonderful that a religious teacher gave the world a mould into which twenty centuries have been pouring their spiritual ideas, without either over-flowing or breaking it? If we have new religious thoughts, we do not need for their adequate expression other words than Jesus has given us. Surely this sets him apart as the unapproachable Teacher of the world. Yet, is not rather this the truth: so far from reading into the words of Jesus spiritual wealth undreamt of by him, we have not yet plumbed the depths of meaning that are really there?

III

Just as the form of his teaching was shaped by his life among the peasants of Galilee, so its substance was the product of the religious experience of Jesus. From early childhood he would no doubt be instructed in the Law and Prophets, like every Jewish child. The quickness with which he was able, on occasion, to cite an apposite passage from these writings is convincing testimony to the thoroughness of his instruction. A writer may think out and look up citations at his leisure, but they must come instantly to a speaker's mind or not at all. Jesus seems also to have acquired in some way considerable knowledge of rabbinic tradition, though never under formal instruction, but its only effect on him was to produce disgust and revulsion. His progress in religious knowledge was normal and regular, and he was never compelled in later years to unlearn what he had learned earlier, as all his disciples more or less had to do.

And yet we may be sure that what Jesus learned was the least part of his religious knowledge. The really significant and valuable part he obtained from no human teacher, but from private meditation, and from prayer, through which he entered into fellowship with God such as no other man had ever known. The story in Luke's Gospel of his visit to the Temple at the age of twelve is something more than the instance of religious precocity for which it is usually taken: it is a hint of the early dawning of that consciousness of unique relationship to God which he afterwards expressed in "Father" and "Son." This sense of intimate and unbroken fellowship with God, of complete harmony with God's will, became the fundamental fact of his consciousness. Out of the deeps of that experience he spoke to men of the Father in Heaven, in hope of bringing them also into fellowship with him—

> We speak what we know,
> And bear testimony of what we have seen,
> And you do not receive our testimony.[1]

All that Jesus said about God came from the heart of his personal experience. To him God was never a Monarch, ruling over subjects whose only right is the right to obey; nor yet a Judge, before whom sinful man is arraigned to answer for his misdeeds, meting out punishment in proportion to transgression; but a Father, whose love for his children is as immeasurable as his Being, whose mercy is therefore everlasting. "This is the heart of the Gospel of Jesus, that Man and every man is the child of God, that the spirit which we are is one with the Spirit whose we are."[2] This is beyond compare the greatest gift of Jesus to the world, this new conception of the character of God and his relation to all mankind. His relation to the world, and his immutable righteousness, the Hebrew prophets had taught clearly enough. Even the enlightened heathen were not ignorant on this point. Socrates maintained strenuously that God is not the author

---

[1] John 3:11, 32.
[2] Francis A. Henry, "Jesus and the Christian Religion," p. 58, New York, 1916.

of evil, but only of the good. ([1]) What the world was hungering to hear was this assurance of the universal Fatherhood of God.

Reader, can you think back far enough into your childhood days to realize for a little what the name "father" once meant to you? Why, father was the greatest man in the world—you pitied other boys who had to get on somehow with the kind of fathers they had! Father knew everything, father could do anything, father would always take care of his boy and see that he came to no harm. And father was always bringing home the most marvelous things, he could make the most surprising contrivances, he could teach the most amusing games and tell the most fascinating stories. O father was a wonder!

And what Jesus meant to teach us children of a larger growth was to look up to Our Father in Heaven, and think of him in like terms. The fountain of all wisdom, the source of all power, tenderly caring for his little ones, showering gifts upon even the ungrateful, forbearing towards the sinful, merciful towards the penitent—such, said Jesus, is your Father-God. He wished to reawaken the trust of which advancing years and what we call worldly wisdom have bereft us; he urged us to "receive the Kingdom of Heaven as a little child," as the only way by which we can possibly enter in and possess its glories. Jesus did not repudiate or deny or belittle any truth regarding God that the Jews had attained: he enriched their knowledge, he "revealed the whole truth, opened the wholeness of truth." ([2])

The worst foes of Jesus have ever been, as he himself phrased it, "they of his own household." Worse than all attacks on his teaching by unbelievers have been misrepresentations of it by professed believers. To this day

---

([1]) Plato's "Republic," bk ii, §379.
([2]) George Harris, "A Century's Change in Religion," p. 71, Boston, 1914.

many Christian theologians and preachers vehemently
deny that Jesus ever intended to teach the universal fatherhood of God. In this they become the allies of a destructive school of criticism, which maintains that Paul and not
Jesus was the true founder of Christianity, the first to
teach universalism in religion. But if the historic interpretation of Paul is correct, he taught no real universalism: his is a limited universalism of races and nations,
while as to individuals he taught the narrowest sort of
particularism, an election of a few to salvation and condemnation of the greater number to perdition.

As we shall see later, this interpretation does Paul great
injustice; he is fairly entitled to the praise of being the
most powerful advocate of universalism among the first
generation of Christians. The Twelve, if left to themselves, would never have taught or practiced universalism,
and would have made of the religion of Jesus nothing
more than an obscure Jewish sect. This is the clear testimony of the Christian documents. But this merely es-
tablishes the fact that Paul, who probably never saw the
face of Jesus, understood him better in this fundamental
matter than his most intimate companions. But the documents also make the fact indisputable that Jesus first
taught what Paul afterwards so successfully championed,
and that our religion is rightly named Christianity and
not Paulinism. Our theology is another question altogether.

It is quite possible to quote some words of Jesus that
seem inconsistent with the view here adopted, such as his
address to the Twelve when he sent them out to proclaim
the Good News of the Kingdom:

Into a way of the heathen go not,
And a town of the Samaritans enter not;
But go rather to the lost sheep of Israel's house.([1])

But this was a special mission, necessarily confined to a

([1]) Matt. 10:6.

limited sphere, and the injunction merely indicates that
the time for larger proclamation of the Good News of the
Kingdom had not yet come, and does not imply purpose
to restrict the Kingdom to Jews.   It may also be conceded that other words of Jesus, sometimes cited to prove
a larger aim than a mere national and racial gospel, are
not altogether decisive: such as,

> The Sabbath was made for man.([1])
> The tax-gatherers and harlots go into the Kingdom of
>   God before you.([2])

But there are declarations not at all reconcilable with
the notion that Jesus taught the Jewish religion of exclusiveness:

> Many will come from the east and the west,
> And will sit down with Abraham and Isaac and Jacob in
>   the Kingdom of Heaven,
> But the Sons of the Kingdom will be cast forth into the
>   outer darkness.([3])

> You are the salt of the earth,
> You are the light of the world.([4])

More than once Jesus recognized the superior receptiveness
of the gentiles, as when he declared to the nobleman, "I
have not found so great faith, no, not in Israel."([5])   If
we may not plead as evidence, because of their doubtful
authenticity, Matthew's words of the Great Commission,
"Go and make disciples of all the nations" (or gentiles),([6]) we are not so enjoined from citing the words
preserved by Luke, essentially identical in meaning:

([1]) Mark 2:27.
([2]) Matt. 21:31.
([3]) Matt. 8:11, 12.
([4]) Matt. 5:13, 14.
([5]) Matt. 8:10; Luke 7:9.
([6]) Matt. 28:19.

> You will be my witnesses,
>   Both in Jerusalem,
>   And in all Judea and Samaria,
> And to the uttermost part of the earth.([1])

And most significant of all, perhaps, is the fact that the universalism of Jesus is the reason assigned by Luke for his rejection at his own home, Nazareth. As the third Gospel relates the story, Jesus told the Jews plainly that they were not God's "chosen" people, in any such sense as to exclude other peoples from his love and mercy. And the worst of it was, that he proved his point from their own Scriptures. He cited the instance, familiar to every one of them, of Elisha's lodging with a poor widow of Zarephath, and followed this with the equally familiar story of the cure of Naaman of leprosy.([2])

Yet, after all, our reliance should be on the general drift and spirit of the teachings, rather than on any isolated "proof-texts" that can be made to mean pretty much anything we desire them to mean. The significance of most of the parables is unmistakable. If we might pervert into a narrow sense such as those in the fifteenth chapter of Luke—the Lost Sheep, the Lost Coin, the Lost Son—we cannot so easily limit the Sower and the Tares, with the interpretation of Jesus himself, "The field is the words."([3]) The Sheep and the Goats, the Talents, the Wise and Foolish Virgins,([4]) and above all the Good Samaritan,([5]) are incapable of perversion to Jewish exclusiveness. In the last named parable, Jesus makes a

---

([1]) Acts 1:8.

([2]) Luke 4:16-30.

([3]) Matt. 13:3 sq. 18 sq. 24 sq. and the parallel passages.

([4]) Matt. 13:38. There can be little doubt that the author or final editor of the first Gospel was not a hearty universalist. He shows in many cases a disposition to edit the sayings in a particularistic sense. Compare, for example, his story of the Syro-Phenecian woman, with the version of Mark, as given in any Harmony, and likewise his version and Luke's of the sermon at Nazareth. Yet Matthew gives most of the parables that have a universal trend.

([5]) Luke 10:30 sq.

member of a despised and hated race a better exemplar of
true religion than the most pious Jews, priests and Levites.
This must indeed have been gall and bitterness:

The fourth Gospel is so outspoken in its universality
that not a few critics have made this an objection to its
authenticity:

> For God so loved the world that he gave his only-begotten
> Son,
> That whosoever trusts in him should not perish,
> But have eternal life.([1])

"Whosoever" is a word very prominent in the Johannine
writings, and its content is as large as humanity. So when
certain Greeks sought the disciples in the Temple, wishing
to see Jesus, the Master hailed this as the climax of his
career:

> The hour is come that the Son of Man should be honored.([2])

It may, of course, be argued by the champions of Paul
or others that the fourth Gospel was not written until many
years after the great apostle to the gentiles had made universalism part and parcel of the Gospel. No one will
question the historic fact that it was through Paul mainly
that the principle of universalism gained general acceptance; but that is quite a different proposition from asserting that he invented the principle. He never claimed
to do so, but in this, as in all his preaching, asserted that
he was the interpreter and ambassador of Jesus. The
fourth Gospel at least shows how Christians had come, by
the close of the first century, to understand the teachings
of Jesus—that they were by that time unanimous in at-
tributing the universalism of their message to Jesus and
not to Paul.

([1]) John 3:16.
([2]) John 12:23.

IV

As life with God was the secret of the character of Jesus, so love of God is the foundation-stone of his teaching. To love his Father in Heaven was the spontaneous impulse of his pure soul, which found in God the companionship and sympathy denied it among men. Every word and act of his life was a manifestation of this love—

> My food is to do the will of him that sent me,
> And to accomplish his work.([1])

When, therefore, Jesus was asked, "What is the first commandment of the Law?" without hesitation he repeated the words, the *Shema* of the synagogue service:

Hear O Israel:
Jehovah our God is one Jehovah:
And thou shalt love Jehovah thy God with all the heart,
> And with all the soul,
> And with all the mind,
> And with all the strength!([2])

And because Jesus saw that if God were so loved, as a merciful and tender and holy Father, there could be but one result, he gave as the second commandment, again quoting familiar words of the Law:

> Thou shalt love thy neighbor as thyself.([3])

([1]) John 4:34.
([2]) Mark 12:29; Deut. 6:4, 5.
([3]) Mark 12:31; Lev. 19:18. To Matthew Arnold it seemed passing strange to find these words in Leviticus, but that was because he did not fully understand their significance there. In Leviticus the words are clan ethics—"neighbor" is another Jew; as Jesus spoke them, they are universal ethics, "neighbor" is any fellow man. Inasmuch as Jesus did thus quote from the Law to express his own profoundest teaching, all modern Jews and some modern Christians, deny his originality. He is not the one and only Teacher, they declare, but the last in a long line of Jewish prophets, and if his outlook seems a little broader and further, it is not so much that he is greater as that he is later. As somebody has said, "A dwarf can see further than a giant—if he is mounted on the shoulders of the giant." We need not pause to controvert this view.

Fatherhood and brotherhood, then, were correlative and complementary ideas and words with Jesus. Love of God necessarily implied love of fellow, and the two constituted the principle of the Kingdom of God: a human society of which God was founder and head and all men members; bound together, not by laws and institutions, but by the stronger, if less palpable, tie of human brotherhood. A Kingdom would seem logically to imply a king and subjects, but Jesus never uses either word, or anything equivalent to them. God is not King but Father; men are not subjects but children—that is his way of describing both; and this is a fact that is unimpeachable testimony to his habitual thought of God.

And it is equally fact that Jesus had little to say about man's relations and duties to God; he confined himself mainly to men's duties and relations to each other. What he did say about worship and service of God was, that it might not be suffered to take the place of justice and mercy to our fellows. Nothing so stirred Jesus to holy indignation as pretense of piety by men who robbed and maltreated those whom they should have loved and served as brothers. To the outcast sinner he was always tender, and to such of these as showed desire to forsake their sins he spoke words of peace and pardon. To the sinful woman who anointed his feet and kissed them weeping, he said, "Your sins are forgiven"—she had learned love and was "saved." To Zaccheus, eager to make restitution to any whom he had wronged, he said, "To-day has salvation come to this house"—the grafting tax-gatherer had learned social righteousness and so had become a new man. But for the proud Pharisee Jesus had only words that sting and burn. Forms and creeds were nothing to him; he looked straight through them to the reality.

Jesus summoned all men to the noble life: the life of personal purity, of sacrifice of self, of service to others, as the one cure for the world's otherwise immedicable ills.

He appealed to the heroic strain not wholly lacking in any of us. Wickedness was in his eyes nothing else than the ignoble life, the self-centered life, and this was the only "heresy" that he recognized.

> The Law came by Moses,
> But grace and truth by Jesus Christ.(¹)

If we accept the words of Jesus as the guide of life, he becomes our Saviour from the theologians, as well as our Saviour from sin. For theologians of all ages have, wittingly or unwittingly, led men back to the Pharisaic notion that right belief is the all-important thing, whereas with Jesus right conduct is all-important. And the theologian has justified himself on the ground that belief determines conduct, and therefore to have right conduct you must first have right belief. Which is true to a degree, but leaves unstated this yet more weighty truth: right belief may be necessary to right conduct, but is no guarantee of right conduct. The belief of the Pharisees was mainly right; their conduct was wholly wrong, and so Jesus condemned them. Nothing can be clearer than that Jesus never intended to make "salvation," or deliverance from moral evil, dependent upon any theory of what he was or did. He made it depend on a changed attitude towards God and man, and it was his chief mission to be the means of so changing the relations of men to God that His will should be done upon the earth and thereby His Kingdom be established.

No, we cannot get away from the fact that Jesus said very little about beliefs, that he spoke almost wholly of conduct. He made the real test of character, the real righteousness, consist in the behavior of men towards their fellows. If he does not say it in so many words, he everywhere implies, that if a man is in right relations to his fellows he cannot be in wrong relations to God. And he

(¹) John 1:17.

does say, in just so many words, that a man cannot be in right relation to God, so long as he leaves unrighted a wrong done to a fellow. The remedy for injury to a fellow man is not prayers and gifts to God—what men call piety—but restitution, redress, apology. When David had stolen Uriah's wife and murdered her husband, his repentance was wholly inadequate when he declared:

> Against Thee, Thee only, have I sinned,
> And done this evil in Thy sight.([1])

That might have answered the ethical demands of an earlier time, but Jesus taught a very different ethic:

> So, if you are bringing your gift to the altar,
> And there remember that your brother has something
>   against you,
> Leave your gift there before the altar
>   And go your way—
> First be reconciled to your brother,
>   And then come and offer your gift.([2])

It is perhaps in his parables that Jesus illustrates most clearly, certainly most strikingly, the behavior appropriate to members of his Kingdom. The Good Samaritan([3]) will instantly occur to every one. Hardly less known is the parable of the Sheep and the Goats,([4]) wherein the ultimate test of character and determination of final destiny is made to depend on mercy and kindness shown to one's fellows in distress. The necessity of cultivating a forgiving spirit towards one's brother, instead of a spirit of bitterness and revenge, is illustrated in the possibly less read parable of the Two Slaves.([5]) Even harsh judgment of a brother is forbidden; criticism of a brother's faults is

---

([1]) Ps. 51:4. Of course the ethical question is wholly unaltered if the critical view be accepted that David did not write the Psalm.

([2]) Matt. 5:23, 24.

([3]) Luke 10:30-37.

([4]) Matt. 25:31-46.

([5]) Matt. 23:18-35.

reproved with gentle irony; ([1]) and as for anger, it is declared to be equivalent to murder. ([2])   These are so hard
lessons for human nature to learn and obey, that Jesus
repeats them in various forms, again and again; and on the
duty of forgiveness, in particular, more stress is laid than
on any other element of his teaching.   He practically makes
willingness to forgive a test of membership in the Kingdom:

> If your brother wrongs you, rebuke him,
>   And if he repents, forgive him.
> And if he wrongs you seven times a day,
>   And seven times a day turns to you and says, "For-
>   give,"
>   Forgive him! ([3])

> For, if you forgive men their trespasses,
>   Your Heavenly Father will forgive you also;
> But if you do not forgive men,
>   Neither will your Father forgive your trespasses. ([4])

And that this is no arbitrary decree, any student of the
teachings of Jesus, who has really tried to walk in his
ways, well knows.   No one can receive love who is not
ready to give love.   That was why the sin of Dives was ir-
reparable—he had refused love to Lazarus, his brother
who was in poverty and want, and so was incapable of receiving God's love.   In the parable of the Workers in the
Vineyard, ([5]) Jesus teaches his followers what is for them
perhaps the hardest lesson of all: that they must treat
men, not according to seeming desert, but according to
actual want.   We must not ask, What have they done?
but, What do they need?   We must give them, not what
justice requires, but what love prompts; not the least they

[1] Matt. 7:1-5.
[2] Matt. 5:21, 22.
[3] Luke 17:4.
[4] Matt. 6:14, 15.
[5] Matt. 20:1-16.

will accept and our conscience permit, but the most we can spare, and even more than we can spare. As we often say, but seldom do, we must give until it hurts. How unbusinesslike! But how divine! For to give men what they have earned, or what they seem to us to have deserved, is justice—a good thing, but a cold. To give men what they have not earned or deserved, yet need, is that greatest thing in the world, that godlike thing we call love. And this, Jesus said, is the whole of Law and Prophets. It is also the whole of his gospel. And it is man's only adequate self-expression.

CHAPTER IV

JESUS THE HERALD OF THE KINGDOM

I

THOSE who account themselves the only "orthodox" Christians are usually quite insistent that ministers shall "preach the simple gospel." This cant phrase (for such it now is) is oftenest on the lips of those who have not the slightest idea of what the real "gospel" is. Gospel is Good News, the English equivalent of εὐαγγέλιον, the word used in the New Testament documents to denote the Message of Jesus and his apostles. The original content of that Message is very clear. According to Mark, the oldest record that we have of the ministry of Jesus, he began his work in Galilee by announcing:

> The time is completed,
> And the Kingdom of God is at hand.
> Repent and believe in the Good News.[1]

This was the gospel of Jesus: a declaration that the Kingdom of God was about to be established, and a summons to men to "repent" and "believe" as conditions of membership in the Kingdom. In other words, they were to accept the Message and relate themselves to it. It was a call to a new ideal of life, to a new purpose in life, to a new conduct of life.

And the kernel of the Good News was the immediate coming of the Kingdom of God. By this Jesus seems to have intended his hearers to understand the world as God's

[1] Mark 1:15.

spiritual empire, a realm on earth with the fundamental characteristics of Heaven, a world in which men will be godlike. The chief note of Heaven, in the mind of Jesus, clearly was that it was a divine realm of ideal perfection, because in it God was all in all, and his will was perfectly done. The Kingdom of God on earth would be realized when God became the dominating influence in the hearts and lives of men, when his will is done here as it is in Heaven.

Our word "kingdom" fails to express the idea of Jesus; for, while βασιλεία did originally mean "kingdom," to the generation of Jesus it had come to be the equivalent of the Latin *imperium,* and to mean the Roman Empire, an authority conterminous with the world itself. There could be, in the nature of the case, but one such universal *imperium,* in the sense of a visible government, with an Imperator at its head, divided into provinces, each with its administrator responsible to the Emperor; and its great army, distributed into legions, all absolutely loyal to the Imperator or commander-in-chief. But there could be alongside of this political and military *imperium,* and conflicting with it not at all, because moving in a totally different sphere, a religious or "spiritual" Empire, as vast, as perfectly organized, as loyal to its Head. But the words of Jesus nowhere afford us a hint that he had any conception of a Kingdom like that. He never describes the Kingdom of God in terms that can be stretched to cover such a conception. That was a notion of the Kingdom that came to prevail among Christians in consequence of Imperial favor, after Constantine and his successors had made the Holy Catholic Church both in form and spirit a more or less religious counterpart of the political institutions of the Roman State.

Jesus used the word that he found on the lips of all men, because it was the only word available. If a religious teacher is to make himself understood at all, he must conform to the speech of his day. He may indeed introduce a few new words, or he may try to give a deeper significance to commonplace words, and in either case he takes the risk of being misunderstood. Nothing is plainer from the Gospels than that, in this matter of the Kingdom, Jesus shot over the heads of his entire generation. True, his hearers hung upon his lips. They remembered many sayings with wonderful accuracy. In due time they wrote down his words and passed them on to others. But they misunderstood, with unanimity and perseverance that one refrains from calling perversity only because they so evidently could not help themselves. Their misunderstanding was as honest as it was tragic.

For the mind of the Jew was then full of an idea of the Kingdom of God that he derived from the Empire under which he lived. He was more than he realized under the spell of that tremendous institution, the like of which had never been known before. The "Empires" of Egypt and Babylonia, of Assyria and Persia, and even that of the great Alexander, had been limited and ephemeral things to which it was a joke to apply the name *imperium*. But here was an authority extending to the very confines of civilization, with common laws, institutions, language. There seemed every reason why it should endure forever. No forces were visible or computable by ordinary human foresight that could smash this vast military, legal and social organization. And as matter of fact, it did endure through fourteen centuries thereafter. Nothing else human and mundane has so nearly deserved the oft-applied epithets, "perpetual" and "eternal."

It is rather common to say that the Jew hated the Roman Empire. It might be more exact to say that the Jew hated the Roman, not the Empire. A universal *imperium* of which Jerusalem should be the centre, the power of which should be wielded by a Son of David, was his dearest dream—that vision summed up his ideas of

human felicity and glory. So much admiration did the
Roman Empire exact from those who unwillingly sub-
mitted to it. So completely as this did it dominate their
thought and imagination. The Jew translated the Kingdom of God into terms of this visible organization.

It was to a generation with mind preoccupied by such
an ideal that Jesus vainly tried to communicate his ideal
of a Kingdom of spirit. He said again and again, to men
as unreceptive as blocks of wood, things like these:

> The Kingdom of God is not coming so that you can
> see it,
> Nor will men say, "Here it is!" or "There it is!"
> For the Kingdom of God is within you.([1])

Jesus could not hope, so far as we can see, to get on with
his hearers save by using the accepted word, but the
moment he uttered it their minds were obsessed by the
phantasy of an empire of this world. It was the only word
available, for there were no alternatives that his hearers
could have understood better. There were then no repub-
lics, still more no democracies. The old Roman *res publica*
had perished, and the Greek "democracies" were never
democratic, for they were founded on the economic basis
of slavery. But it is notable that, though he uses the word
Kingdom, Jesus never describes his ideal as a monarchy,
but as a commonwealth, a democracy. The Kingdom is a
state of equality, of brotherhood, of mutual service. There
can be no aristocracy in it; no one can claim to be greater
than his fellows:

> You know that those considered rulers among the heathen
> lord it over them,
> And their great men exercise authority over them;
> It will not be so among you.
> So, whoever of you wishes to become first,
> Let him be slave of all!([2])

([1]) Or "among you."   Luke 17:20, 21.
([2]) Matt. 20:25-27; Luke 22:25, 26.

The Kingdom of God,([2]) in other words, is a social order dominated in all the relations of men with each other by the spirit that God shows in his dealings with us—the spirit of love, of universal good will, shown by each to each. In the Kingdom good will is to conquer hatred, trust is to take the place of fear, mutual helpfulness will be found instead of strife. Cooperation will supplant competition, service will be the standard of greatness, and the chief reward will be neither honor nor wealth, but the consciousness of having done one's best for the common welfare.

II

"Repent and believe in the Kingdom of God," was the Good News of Jesus. But theologians have read into these words meanings of which he never dreamed, as well as read out of them all the meaning that he put there, until a positive perversion of his "simple gospel" has resulted. "Repent" and "repentance" are the English words long ago chosen to render the Greek μετανοέω, μετάνοια. We must evacuate the words of theological subtleties and get back to the meaning that they had for Jesus and his generation. The words are not very common in classical

---

([1]) This is the phrase used by Mark thirteen times and by Luke thirty-three times, while Matthew uses it only five times, in all other cases (twenty-four) preferring Kingdom of Heaven (lit. of the heavens). The word βασιλεία occurs fifty-six times in Matthew, and of these cases it is attributed to Jesus forty-nine times in direct quotation, besides twice in indirect. This is characteristic of the Synoptics generally. But in John the word occurs but four times, in every instance in words credited to Jesus himself. To those who really wish to understand the teaching of Jesus regarding the Kingdom, a little book by F. Herbert Stead is worth its weight in gold. It is an inductive study of the Gospels, and as a result this definition is formulated: "The Kingdom of God is the fellowship of souls divine and human, of which the law and the life are love, wherein the Fatherhood of God and the Brotherhood of man, as both are embodied in Jesus the Christ, are recognized and realized." (Edinburgh, T & T Clark, "Bible Class Primers".)

Greek, but when used they always denote a change of opinion or purpose. A sober second thought often leads a man to change his first opinion, or to do something other than he at first intended. It is this fact of *change* that is the fundamental meaning of these words.

It is in this sense that Jesus always uses them, and throughout the New Testament there is no apparent variation from his usage. When a man perceives his past misdeeds and determines to change his conduct and lead a different life, he "repents" in the Gospel sense. The prodigal, when he "came to himself" and became convinced of his folly, resolved, "I will rise and go to my father," and that was his "repentance." So every man through "repentance" finds himself and becomes a new man in his attitude towards God and his fellows. He becomes ready to do his part in reorganizing the social order on the basis of brotherhood. He becomes a member of the Kingdom of God.

With such a change of mind and purpose often goes an abhorrence of the past life, a new sense of the meaning of moral obliquity, which theologians have called "conviction of sin." But this emotional accompaniment of the change is of no ethical value in itself; it may even exist without repentance, or change of mind and purpose, in which case we call it remorse. Repentance is nothing else than change of ethical perception, change of attitude, change of conduct, all resulting ultimately in change of character. It is a deliberate facing about and going in the opposite direction. It amounts to an ethical revolution. It is the birth of a new man. It may be preceded by experiences of greatly various kinds, by moral turpitude of different degrees; it may be accompanied by great spiritual disturbances or may be without marked emotional quality. All these are trifling considerations: the real thing, the only thing of moment, is the change.

Jesus treats this change as something within the power

of every man's will: he assumes that any man can, if he chooses, turn about and amend his life. And so every man is summoned to do just this. He has hitherto lived the life of selfhood: he must henceforth live the life of brotherhood. He has hitherto been absorbed in schemes for promoting his own advantage; he must henceforth seek first the Kingdom of God and his righteousness. His entire plan of life must be revised and new ideals must take the place of old.

But it should not be inferred, because repentance is so plain and simple a matter, that Jesus thought it an easy thing, a change requiring little or no effort. Quite the contrary. He clearly recognized that God will not, because he cannot, save a man who will not "agonize," strive as an athlete for victory, to enter the narrow gate that leads to eternal life. To be a follower of Jesus is not for the lazy, the indifferent, the cowardly, the mentally limp, the quitters; it demands an alert mind, a well-braced will; it offers opportunities for all that may be in us of the heroic, the aspiring, the intrepid, the enduring.

"Master," said another, "I will follow you, but permit me first to bid farewell to my friends at home."

"No man," replied Jesus, "who has put his hand to the plough and looks at things behind, is fit for the Kingdom of God."[1]

If any man would come after me,
Let him take up his cross and follow me.
For he that would save his life will lose it,
But he that loses his life for my sake will find it.
For what good will it do a man to gain the whole world,
But lose his own life?
Or what will a man give in exchange for his life?[2]

[1] Luke 9:61, 62.
[2] Matt. 16:24-26; Mark 8:34-37; Luke 9:23-25.

Modern evangelism, based upon the false interpretation of theologians, has made "repentance" an adjunct of what they call "conversion," the chief end of which is supposed to be to secure a sinner's deliverance from God's wrath and condemnation and the consequent danger of eternal punishment. The accepted test of a "conversion" is an emotional "experience," the stages of which are: first, "conviction of sin," second, "repentance," and third, "faith," all of which results in the joyful assurance of sins forgiven. Lack of any one of these elements used to be regarded as invalidating the "experience"; and though judgment is now more lenient, this is still regarded as the normal type.

But an emotional crisis is no proof of change of character. The fact that a man has a firm conviction that his sins have been forgiven—that he is "saved"—is not adequate proof of God's forgiveness; he may be altogether deluded about his standing with God. The real proof of forgiveness of his sins is the man's attitude towards them; for the only sins that God forgives are the sins that man has forsaken and hated. The convincing proof of conversion is not an inward experience, but an outward and visible alteration of conduct.

Christian history has shown all forms of "experience" to be only too often wholly illusory. The New Testament writings nowhere propose an emotional test of Christian character. The apostles and Jesus are at one on this point, as perhaps they are not on any other: the reality of the Christian life is to be tested, not by subjective emotion, but by objective fact—the tree is to be known by its fruits, that is, by conduct. Does an alleged conversion make a complete change in a man's life, so as to show that he is ruled by new ideals? May he be judged on the basis of what he is and does to be a man reborn? Does he show by word and deed that he has renounced self and is living the life of brotherhood? Is he plainly seeking first the Kingdom and its righteousness—the reign of justice, mercy and peace in this world—and is he doing what he may to make this ideal a reality? Never mind how he *feels;* what is he *doing?*

Nothing so clearly emerges from the present condition of our "evangelical" churches as this damning fact: these emotional "conversions" do not result in the kind of repentance that Jesus demanded. Our churches are full of people, as every candid pastor will sorrowfully admit in private, though he might not care to say it in public, who give no slightest indication of changed attitude or purpose. Some, it is true, are changed in the sense of better individualistic ethics, but that is all. The "converted" man curbs some of his former vices, perhaps, but he goes right on in his old life of selfhood, without any notion that his life calls for amendment or change. In religious meetings he talks about "love" and "brotherhood," while in his daily business he practices all the ruthlessness of the Hun. Thousands of such "conversions" bring the Kingdom no nearer. How should they? They have no relation to the Kingdom and are not in sight of its ideals. The churches will utterly fail to achieve their declared purpose until there is complete reform of methods and standards.

It is the theological perversion of "repentance" that has so disastrously promoted the exaggerated individualism of Protestant Christianity, and all but caused men to forget the social implications of the gospel. On the lips of Jesus, Kingdom of God and "eternal life" are synonymous. He did not teach men to flee from the world, but to overcome it. The main idea of his gospel was not a personal deliverance from sin and the individual's attainment of peace and happiness here and hereafter, as the immediate end to be sought. His goal was the salvation of the world, of society, as the only way to save the individual—the deliverance of all men, not merely a chosen few, from a maze of evil conditions that make individual transgression inevitable. Religion was not, in his view, a force for personal uplift merely, but a social force to be felt throughout the complex relationships of life. And it is precisely that quality of his teaching that made it so unpalatable to his hearers; and it has ever since been so unacceptable, that men have devoted themselves chiefly to devising excuses for not doing what he demanded they should do. For, as has been well remarked, men will wrangle for religion, write for it, fight for it, die for it—anything but live for it.

The popular form of Protestant religion was never more happily expressed than by John Bunyan. His Pilgrim, putting his fingers in his ears to shut out everything but the inner voice urging him to flee from the City of Destruction, reckless of the fate of wife and children, with no idea that he owed anything to his fellow-citizens, in a passion of selfish fear lest he himself should be eternally miserable and ready to sacrific every consideration of honor and duty if he might thereby secure his own eternal happiness—that is the portrait of the ideal Christian that John Bunyan gives us. Look on this picture and then on that, compare this ideal with the words of Jesus, and see how little they agree. There could not be a more total or a more fatal perversion of the ideal of Jesus.

The pilgrim's objective in Bunyan's narrative is hopelessly wrong; our business is not to get ourselves into the Celestial City as speedily as we may, regardless of what may happen to others, like a man who should rush out of a burning house without stopping to see how his wife and children were to be rescued, so intent on saving his own life as to forget that other lives were to be saved. Our business is to make our own city celestial, to bring into it and make real all that we can imagine possible of splendor and purity and blessedness in Jerusalem the Golden. The true story of a Pilgrim's Progress in the twentieth century would show him remaining in the City of Destruction and striving to make of it a City of Salvation. It would picture a man so concerned for the salvation of wife and children and neighbors as to lose all thought about his own.[1]

It would show him leading his companions to drain the Slough of Despond and batter down the castle of Despair about the giant's ears. It would show him reforming the abuses of Vanity Fair and making it a place of helpful amusement and recreation. And the man who did all this would be none the less but rather all the more capable of appreciating the view from the top of the Delectable Mountains.

And theological perversions of "believe" and "faith" have been equally disastrous. Since the Reformation and the proclamation by Luther of "justification by faith alone" as the article of a standing or falling Church, there has been a steady drift in the direction of making "faith" an intellectual process, the acceptance of a body of teaching, of ecclesiastical dogma, regarding religion. This has made orthodoxy of more value than character. Some religious bodies have explicitly defined faith as acceptance of the historic facts about Jesus and the truth of his teaching. Even in those religious circles where this definition is formally repudiated, and it is insisted that faith is something more than intellectual assent, there is a tendency too strong to be resisted to make faith mean just this and only this.

But on the lips of Jesus, and throughout the New Testament writings, "faith," "believe" denote an act of the will rather than of the intellect. It has an intellectual basis, as every act of the will has, but the essential thing in

[1] William Wilberforce, who spent his life in procuring the emancipation of slaves in all English domains, was once reproached by a good "evangelical" woman for showing so little concern for the salvation of his soul. "Madam," he replied, "I had almost forgotten that I had a soul."

"faith" is a decision and an act. To "believe in the Good News," as Jesus used the phrase, is to have such confidence in the gospel as leads to obedience. "Faith" is trust; not mere assent of the mind, but consent of the will, resulting in conduct. It is to have such an attitude towards Jesus as the pupil has towards his teacher, as the soldier has towards his commander. It is an ethical quality, that is influenced by intellectual processes, but still moves in another plane.

To have such faith in the founder of the Kingdom is necessary to entrance into it, not because such an arbitrary condition of entrance has been imposed, but because without such trust in Jesus and his teaching nobody would make the faintest effort to realize his ideal. Thousands of years of professed allegiance to him have hardly advanced us a step towards the goal that he proposed; and that is, plainly enough, because men have professed allegiance yet failed to give it. Their failure is not to be justly condemned, in the majority of cases at least, either as hypocrisy or as deliberate disobedience, but as ignorance. For the teachers and leaders of the Christian world have not themselves comprehended the ideals of Jesus, and so of course could not instruct people regarding them. We are just recovering knowledge of the real significance of the Master's teaching.

The humility that Jesus prescribed, equally with trust, as a condition of entering the Kingdom, has proved a stone of stumbling to many. It is probable that for some time to come humility will not be a popular virtue. What we are exhorted in these days to do, is to seek all means of "self-expression," by which is far too often meant a ruthless egoism that asserts an inalienable right to live one's own life and scorns regard for the lives of others as a cramping of personality. But much of the prejudice against the teaching of Jesus rests on a misconception of its nature.   Perhaps the word "modesty" would come nearer to conveying the real meaning of Jesus to the present generation. To be humble is not to cringe and sneak, to be meek is not to be abject and craven; it is to cultivate a modest estimate of self and forbear arrogance, haughtiness and bluster.   It is the domineering, flaunting, supercilious spirit that we are to eschew, for these are anti-social, they prevent mutual goodwill.   But the Kingdom has no place for the timid, the obsequious, the mean-spirited; it is a Kingdom of gentlemen and gentlewomen, and all that is urbane and companionable, highminded or honorable, breathes in this realm its native air.   It was because he taught such a Kingdom as this that the professed followers of Jesus have from the beginning followed him with greatest reluctance, and no further than they must; and that has proved to be a very little way indeed.   It is only quite recently that any considerable number of people were ready for such a Kingdom as this, saw in it anything to be desired, or believed that it was possible to establish it.   And those people are beginning very seriously to doubt whether the realization of the Kingdom is to be hoped through the agency of that Church which claims Jesus as Founder and Head, notwithstanding it professes to exist only for bringing in the Kingdom.   For, in spite of loud professions and claims of loyalty to Jesus, only in the fewest instances can the Christian churches be induced to take any serious interest in the Kingdom propaganda, or to undertake anything that has a real tendency to hasten the Kingdom's coming.   Nietzsche thought the Sermon on the Mount was "doctrine for weaklings," but the difficulty with that teaching has always been that men were not strong enough to follow it.   They have feebly evaded its obligations by declaring them impracticable.   Jesus is the one Superman.

III

When we interpret "the Good News of the Kingdom" to mean that Jesus taught a social gospel, we do not imply that Jesus was in any sense a professor of Sociology. There is no reason to suppose that he held any definite scientific theory regarding society, any more than he held a definite scientific theory regarding religion. He was entirely concerned with the practical aspects of society and religion. But he saw, as clearly as any modern professor, that society and the individual are mutually related; that each is indispensable to the other, each complements the other, each reacts on the other.

But which should stand first in our thinking, and which should we regard as of first practical importance? Or should there be no first? A perfect dualism in thought may be possible, but practical dualism is virtually impossible. In actual life, either the Kingdom or the individual will take precedence. The conviction is gaining ground that, if we would be true to the ideals of Jesus, we must give first place to the Kingdom and not to the individual— that the hope of future salvation for the race depends on our giving greatly intensified emphasis to the idea of social salvation.

The study of biology has done much in recent years to alter our views of the meaning of history and the significance of social institutions, as well as of the method of social progress. Our notion of the importance of the individual has suffered diminution, and our estimate of the value of the species has been correspondingly enlarged. Throughout nature it is seen that the individual is of comparatively slight importance; individuals are born, live and die, but the species remains. We begin to see a reality in what we had come to regard as barren metaphysical speculations—that there was truth, though perhaps not all the "truth" for which they contended, in the "ideas" of Plato and the "universals" of the schoolmen. We no longer conceive of the species as the mere classification of individuals, but as a separate entity, of which individuals are manifestations. It is true that our senses report to us only men, yet we refuse to believe that "man" is a mere figment of the mind, and deny that the only reality is that which the senses perceive. This change of mental attitude should help us to understand better the insistence of Jesus on the supremacy of the Kingdom as compared with the individual.

And just here Anthropology comes forward with its contribution. It assures us that religion was, in its earlier and cruder forms, essentially a system for securing the welfare of the social group, and all its rites and rules had as their underlying principle the sacrifice of individual interests to social needs. *The preservation of the group* was the paramount necessity, inasmuch as it was the only means by which the preservation of the individual could be secured. As Kipling puts it, in "The Law of the Jungle,"

> The strength of the Pack is the Wolf, and the strength of the Wolf is the Pack.

Everything else must bend to the one imperious necessity of promoting the highest practicable measure of security and comfort for all, or there could be no life for any. Individualism in religion is a comparatively late development, and has been fully realized only in modern Protestantism. Jesus recognized the equal claims of social and individual interests, so far as these are capable of distinction and realization; he avoided the undue sacrifice of the individual to the group, which was the chief defect of the early religions, and insisted on the dignity and rights of each human soul; he equally avoided the disintegrating effect that proclaiming the individual's complete independence of social obligations inevitably has, by requiring the voluntary subjection of the individual to the social order. He recognized both the individual's right to himself and his duties to his fellows. He established a workable equilibrium between two principles hitherto antagonistic, fully reconciled them in his thinking and teaching, and contemplated the best realization of each in his Kingdom.

IV

From this conception of the Kingdom as a brotherhood, with its implication of equal rights, privileges and opportunities for all, come all the sayings of Jesus regarding property and wealth. For the members of the Kingdom there is no such thing as property, something that is one's very own, on which nobody else has any claim. To become a member of the Kingdom, one must renounce property forever—henceforth one does not own, one administers. The property is the King's; we are his stewards. So much has been said of late about "stewardship," a good part of it having nothing but a verbal relation to the teaching of Jesus, that it is fast becoming a cant word that real men and women shun.

For the Christian ideal that a member of the Kingdom holds all that is nominally his as a trust from God, to be administered for God, a large part of the Christian world is trying hard to substitute the Jewish ideal of the tithe. We will compound with God by scrupulously giving him a tenth, and then the other nine-tenths will belong to us in fee simple. Stewards? Yes, stewards of a tenth, but absolute owners of the rest. When we have given God his tenth, he must in justice leave us to the undisturbed enjoyment of what remains—not even our conscience must give us a surreptitious twinge.

Whatever misguided advocates of tithing may intend, the practical effect of tithing must be to dry up the springs of Christian benevolence. For it substitutes the Jewish law of mathematics for the Christian law of love. Not to mention that it utterly misconstrues the significance of

the tithe in Jewish history. The later prophets, like Mal-
achi, coming from the priestly class, were pleased to
represent the tithe as a payment to God, but it was historically a payment to the tribe of Levi. That tribe did
not receive an allotment of land, what would have been
its share being allotted to the other tribes; and in lieu of
their share of land, the Levites were to receive a tenth of
all produce from the other tribes that had received more
than their just portion.([1])   Tithe was really rent, and its
payment was no gift of God but discharge of a just obligation to men. The Jew's religious giving began *after* he
had paid his tithe, and is called in the Law "offering" or
"sacrifice." The natural tendency of a priesthood to identify itself with its deity explains the later treatment of the
debt owed the Levites as an obligation to God. Jesus
says nothing about religious giving by his followers; he
was not in the least concerned with such questions. But
Paul, in strict conformity to the principles of his Master,
puts the matter on the proper basis, and makes all giving
voluntary, not legal: *as God hath prospered him.*([2])

The implications of the Kingdom teaching are far-
reaching. This universal, redeemed community was to
be co-extensive with mankind, not limited to Judea and
the Jews. Because of this ultimate solidarity of God
and men in a divine community, all men should be delivered from undue anxiety about the future. The fruit-
fulness of the earth and the toil of men have always produced enough for all, and wisely directed labor of all
might produce immeasurably more. It is not because the
bounty of God has failed, but because the greed and sel
fishness of the strong has taken from the weak, that some
men are choked with luxury while others die of starvation.
Famine is not God's curse upon the race, but man's curse
on his fellow.

([1]) Num. 18:21-24; Josh. 14:3, 4.
([2]) 1 Cor. 16:2.

And this is why Jesus said that it is impossible for the rich to enter his Kingdom. Orthodox exegesis, in its complicity with those who exploit and its fear of arousing their wrath, has found all sorts of explanations but the right one of the uncommonly plain and absolutely decisive words of Jesus. It has said that riches tend to make the heart proud, to absorb the mind in many cares, to lead men to worship Mammon rather than God, and other truisms that throw no light on the teaching, but rather obscure it with a mass of unmeaning generalities. When in fact, the teaching of Jesus is so sharp and clear and unmistakable that it can be misunderstood only by those who are determined to misunderstand. Wealth is anti-social. Wealth is therefore impossible in the Kingdom of God. Because wealth is never the honest result of a man's effort as producer, but always the result of exploitation of his brother. No man, by any amount of industry and thrift, ever accumulated a fortune from the product of his own hand and brain—it has never been done in the history of the race, and it never can be done. The rich man is rich because he has by some means, socially recognized as more or less "honest," obtained possession of what others have produced. No rich man can enter the Kingdom, not because Jesus pronounced a fiat of his exclusion, but because he has excluded himself by adopting and pursuing a mode of life incompatible with the Kingdom. Exploitation is irreconcilable with love of the brother as self; it is the antipodes of brotherhood. Love of the brother is the law of the Kingdom; it is the only law the Kingdom has. Wealth and the Kingdom cannot coexist; the rich man has worked and lived for himself, and so he cannot belong to a brotherhood of love. He must do as the rich young man of the gospels was invited to do, renounce his wealth and follow Jesus, and he can enter the Kingdom on no other terms.

Wealth is anti-social and unbrotherly, in the same way precisely that slavery was. Everybody can see now the essential iniquity of permitting some men to own others, in order that the owners might live by the labor of the owned. That form of exploitation has come to be in very bad odor. But the odor of sanctity still clings to another form of exploitation, and we are very slow to see that Jesus was right in forbidding men to own *things,* in order that they may live by the labor of others. There are, in fact, but two ways of getting a living in this world: by *doing* something or by *owning* something. The former is social and ethical: the latter is anti-social and unethical. Any system that permits one man to say to another: "You shall work and sweat to earn bread and I will eat it without work," is a more or less modified form of slavery, and is absolutely indefensible on ethical grounds. Such a system is the negation of the Kingdom that Jesus proclaimed. "A noble heart," says Bishop Barrow, "will disdain to subsist like a drone on the honey gained by others' labor; or like vermin to filch its food from the public granary; or like a shark to prey on the lesser fry; but will one way or another earn his subsistence, for he that does not earn can hardly be said to own his daily bread."

Jesus condemns wealth, but he never praises poverty. Some of his followers have been less wise and have glorified poverty in his name. Men like Francis of Assisi have believed that they found in a life of indigence great spiritual compensations. But this is to misread both the words of Jesus and the facts of life. A few exceptional men have been able to live the life of the spirit in spite of poverty, but never by means of it; and only the few, the uniquely endowed, have been able to surmount the obstacles of privation and want, and reach the heights of moral excellence. To the many, poverty interposes insurmountable barriers to the higher life. A rather advanced stage of wealth is shown by the general experience of mankind to be necessary for any community to make appreciable ethical and intellectual advance. The Renaissance, the age of Louis Quatorze, the Elizabethan period, were times of great social prosperity and rapidly increasing wealth.

It is quite true that spiritual gifts cannot be directly acquired by wealth; millions will not buy intelligence, culture, the enjoyment of music, appreciation of art, love of literature, a pure mind, a lofty soul. These are acquisitions of effort, painful, long-continued; each must win them for himself. But a certain degree of physical comfort, a certain amount of leisure, are the indispensable conditions of winning them. Without community wealth, no one could long enjoy bodily vigor, culture, recreation and social intercourse. Nothing is more deadly to spiritual interests than continual struggle with grinding poverty. Money in pocket will not ensure a well-dressed man; it only makes him possible; he may be a Russell Sage and elect to go shabby, though possessor of millions; but the man without money has no choice—he must go in rags.

It was individual wealth that Jesus condemned; he had nothing to say against community wealth. Community wealth means possibility of a worthy life for all, but does not make certain that all will live worthily. It is an instrument by use of which the higher life is realizable, a material good through which we may acquire the spiritual. Education, art, letters, are the costliest products of civilization and the most precious. To have them in the highest degree of perfection has always required great expenditure of wealth. It can never be otherwise; in any state of society the best things will be produced at heavy cost. But they are worth as much as they cost. And their value will be incalculably increased when they cease to be the perquisite of the few and become the property of all.

What Jesus accomplished for the world was the moralizing of wealth. He was not an economist, but a prophet; he did not teach science but conduct. He marked out the way to the larger production of wealth for the common good, for its juster distribution and nobler use, not by giving us a theory of social progress, but by emphasizing the sole practical method by which men may hope to advance in social relations: the way of brotherhood, the life of the spirit, the selfless life.

V

During the lifetime of Jesus his disciples again and again showed how completely they had failed to grasp his idea of the Kingdom. He took great pains to show them how wrong they were and to replace the ideas of their nation and generation with his own. He seems to have made some temporary impression, so far at least that they remembered some of his instructions and afterwards wrote them down. But he had hardly expired when they promptly reverted to type, re-embraced the ideas from which he had temporarily weaned them, and proceeded to establish a cult and form an organization differing as much from the Kingdom in spirit as in name. Peter's second fall was much worse than his first. In the Gospels he is shown us in the act of denying his Master's person; in the Acts he is shown us in the process of denying his Master's doctrine. In the first denial he was conscious of his disloyalty and promptly repented; in the second he was not disloyal but stupid, a blunderer, and so he remained to the end.

And Paul was, as he boasted, not a whit behind the very chief of the apostles in this matter. Together with Peter he made the religion of Jesus the religion of a cult. Jesus teaches that men are brothers because they are sons of a common Father: Paul teaches that Christians are members of each other, because they have become members of a mystical Body of Christ. Jesus laid the great stress on his ethical teaching; the aspostles, and Paul above all, lay the great stress, almost the whole stress, on the Person and

Office of the Christ. It is noteworthy that though Jesus fully believed himself to be the Messiah, he did not make belief in his Messiahship the condition of entrance into the Kingdom. Peter and Paul made such belief the condition of entrance into the Church.

When the enemies of Jesus crucified him, they did him a smaller injury than his disciples did him by perverting his teachings. The death of Jesus is not the real tragedy of his career, but the denial of all that he had taught. The change was so subtly made, that the very men who made it were not conscious of what they were doing. And the change was so completely made, in a single generation, that the publication of the words of Jesus in the Gospels found men's minds preoccupied with other ideas and his teachings made little impression. The Christians of A. D. 80, and afterward, supposed that they were following closely in the footsteps of their Master, when they had in reality cast aside the important part of his instructions, and adopted an ideal of life altogether foreign to his. It required nineteen centuries after that for men to catch sight once more of what Jesus intended and hoped to accomplish.

Men are saying continually, and almost with exultation, that Christianity has failed. Why should a religion succeed that has never been believed nor practiced?

CHAPTER V

JESUS THE SAVIOUR OF THE WORLD

JESUS is the Greek form of the well-known Hebrew name, *Jeho-shua,* more common in its shortened form, Joshua, which means, "Jehovah-help," or, "Jehovah is my deliverer." The name was by no means uncommon among the Jews, either before or after the day of Jesus of Nazareth; but everywhere in the New Testament it is implied, if not explicitly declared, that his name was generally believed by his followers to be not an ordinary cognomen, but prophetically descriptive of his mission and work. The Greek word of similar meaning was Σωτήρ, Saviour, Deliverer. This title was often applied to rulers or generals who were regarded by nations as having effected for them some form of deliverance. It is found, for example, in inscriptions in Asia Minor, as one of the titles of Augustus Caesar. When so used, it always implies a state of captivity, or a condition of great danger, from which a people has been rescued.

We have not only the authority of apostles, but of Jesus himself, for saying that he conceived his mission to be one of Deliverance for men. "The Son of Man is come to seek and to save that which was lost."(¹) "The Son of Man came not to destroy men's lives but to save them."(²) "For I came not to judge the world but to save the world."(³) These are instances in which Jesus is said so to have described himself and his work as to

(¹) Luke 19:10.
(²) Luke 9:56; omitted from the text in the Revised Version.
(³) John 12:47.

make his mission of Deliverance its principal feature. But this still leaves to be answered the question, What is the content of this idea of Deliverance? In what sense and to what degree is Jesus the Saviour of the world? There have been many answers to this question; some of them deserve careful consideration.

I

The popular idea of the nature of salvation is vividly set forth in "evangelistic" campaigns. Our fathers used to talk of salvation by divine grace; we have come to believe in salvation by committees and a Tabernacle and an "evangelist." These religious mass-meetings, commonly known as "revivals," are considered, by the majority of Protestant Christians at least, a sort of panacea for all the ills of the world. And the Roman Catholics have their "missions," which are essentially the same thing. To the student of religious history, modern revivals seem little more than recrudescence of primitive religious orgies, such as marked the cult of Dionysius and Cybele, and are found among the howling dervishes of today. The violence of emotion manifested by their votaries is directly proportioned to their lack of culture, and rises to climax among the unlettered negroes of the South. Religion in bondage to the emotions is always extravagant, shallow, ephemeral and even dangerous. It often illustrates in the spiritual realm the principle of mechanics: action and reaction are equal. Nothing can equal the spiritual fervor of a community during a revival—except its spiritual deadness after the revival is over. There are still a few people sane enough to question whether a condition of alternate chills and fever is any more salubrious for the soul than for the body.

It may be objected, however, that a revival should be considered rather as a means of obtaining salvation than as having any direct relation to salvation itself. If we accept that view of the case, we may next ask, What is the popular idea of salvation that makes possible the revival and the evangelist? And the answer must be, that the commonly accepted idea of salvation is, safety and happiness in another world. Salvation is identified in the minds of ordinary folk with "going to heaven when you die," just as to be lost means "to go to hell." Is that the idea that Jesus stresses in his teaching?

Not at all. Jesus offered men an immediate Deliverance, a salvation for this world, the consequences of which would be valid for any and all worlds. This Deliverance was to come to men through the Kingdom of God. And this positive content of his teaching was balanced by the negative idea, what it was to be "lost." To be lost was to stray away from the Father's home and love, and by consequence to forfeit all that makes life worth living. "What shall it profit a man to gain the whole world and lose his own soul?"([1]) was the reading of our old version; and the Christian world came with a unanimity quite remarkable to interpret this to mean "fail to obtain eternal happiness." But we have other translations now, and what is more, another idea of this saying of Jesus. "What will it profit a man to gain the whole world and lose his own life?" we read to-day. And we understand by this "life" something less speculative and distant than the old interpretation recognized, something much more immediate and certain and practical, namely, man's entire life, present and future, but especially this present life, with all its possibilities of making character for the future. It is a life of love, that transcends time and death.

How different from this word of Jesus the preaching that seems to find most favor to-day—at least, it draws the biggest crowds. "Salvation, salvation! Come and be saved!" thunder the Billy Sundays. Saved from what? "From the wrath of God," answers the evangelist. But

---

([1]) Mark 8:36; Matt. 16:26; Luke 9:25.

this is not the Gospel, it is a relic of Judaism. A divine ὀργή correlated with a divine righteousness, is taught throughout the Old Testament, and Paul and most of the apostles borrowed the thought from that source without questioning its truth. But the distinction of Jesus is that he rejected this teaching concerning God. According to him, it is love that is correlated with righteousness in the divine character. The "wrath" of God can be reconciled with his teaching only by so spiritualizing wrath as to evaporate all real significance from the word.

Yes, according to Jesus, there is no wrath of God. God is our Father; he loves us; he has never ceased to love us, all his creatures, the sinful no less than the sinless. His love is like the sunlight, like the rain and dew, bestowed with equal prodigality on all. The Jews once believed in a God who permitted his prophets to send lying oracles, and even himself lied to his own prophets on occasion;(¹) a God who commanded his chosen people to slaughter all the Canaanites;(²) a God who would bless one who dashed the babes of an enemy against the stones.(³) But we cannot believe in any great Hun in the heavens who have learned from Jesus what God is like. The man who wrote the seventh Psalm knew no better than to say, "God is angry with the wicked every day," but Jesus knew better, and the disciples of Jesus should know better. The older religion and ethics of that progressive revelation contained in the Bible must be compared with and corrected by that highest revelation that God made of himself in Jesus the Christ. Others knew God in part; Jesus only had such knowledge of the Eternal Father as makes his teaching final, the norm of all religion and ethics to his followers.

(¹) Thus Elisha, "the man of God," is said to have sent a lying oracle to Benhadad, King of Syria: 2 Kings 8:8, 10—quite legitimate in dealing with an enemy. Ezekiel tells us that Jehovah deceived his own prophets. Eze. 14:19.
(²) Deut. 20:16-18, and cf. Joshua *passim*.
(³) Ps. 137:9.

"Come and be saved!" Saved from what? "From hell," says the evangelist. But there is no hell. The popular superstition about hell, so far as it is supposed to rest on Scripture, rests on a complete misunderstanding. "Hell" is the translation in our common English version of two Greek words. One of these is ᾅδης (Hades), which means · simply (as the alternative phrase of the Prayer-Book has it) "the place of departed spirits." The other word is γέεννα (Gehenna), not a place of the future world, but a definite place in this world, namely, the Valley of Hinnon, a ravine outside the walls of Jerusalem where the refuse of the city was burned. Jesus speaks of it as the "Gehenna of fire," and further describes it as a place "where their worm dieth not and their fire is not quenched." That is, since fires were always burning in this valley, the place was a fitting symbol of prolonged suffering. For Jesus as undoubtedly taught retribution in the life to come for sins committed in this life, as he undoubtedly taught nothing about "hell" as a place of future unending torment.

The popular imagery of hell and its accompanying theological statements are mainly derived from the vision of John in the Revelation—the "lake of fire" into which he beheld the wicked cast. But it is no more rational to suppose that this "lake" has an objective existence, than to believe literally in a New Jerusalem whose streets are pure gold and its gates single pearls. These are the figures of an Oriental writer, of a naturally poetic temperament, by aid of which he sought to convey the truth that character, good or bad, is the most permanent thing we know; that we shall carry with us into the next world the character that we form here; that moral evil involves consequences imperfectly represented by physical suffering, since they are incomparably worse: loss of spiritual blessedness, alienation from God and good, that must remain as long as moral evil remains.

But why should a disciple of Jesus believe, or how can he believe if he would, that God's love for his creatures ends with the grave? How can we say, as Jonathan Edwards and his generation said, that the blessed will look down from Heaven on the torments of the damned, not with a pity and sympathy that would mar their enjoyment of eternal felicity, but with a holy joy, seeing in these sufferings the crowning glory of God, the vindication of his holiness before the universe? That generation could not understand that one who could be content with his own salvation has no idea of what real salvation consists. Nor could it comprehend that one who could rejoice over the sufferings of the lost would be himself a fitting subject of that damnation dealt out so freely by his theology to others. But our generation can understand that it is vain to exhort men in the name of God to forgive their enemies, if that same God so hates his enemies as to cast them into everlasting fire. We have been shuddering much the last few years over the atrocities of war. What are the atrocities of war, compared with the atrocities of theology?

He who maintains that, but for fear of a future hell, men would rush into unbridled license, unconsciously betrays his own ethical limitations. He shows himself to be convinced that the only successful appeal to men is through their selfish fears, possibly because he is secretly conscious that he is himself swayed by selfish impulses, and does not believe in his heart of hearts that there are in the world any interests worth considering but his own. In addition, he indicates that he probably has a low and gross idea of pleasures, and in his secret thinking identifies pleasure with vice. The man of nobler impulses, of unselfish aims, who delights in refined pleasures, will not be so afraid to trust men as a whole to behave themselves decently, if the whip of hell is no longer flourished in their faces.

A better exegesis of Scripture, a better understanding of the nature of God, a better ethic, have together almost deprived even the most orthodox of their last hope of eternal damnation.

II

An idea of salvation differing from this popular notion has been held by the ascetics and mystics of all ages. Salvation has seemed to them the attainment of "holiness," or the moral perfection of the individual. The ascetics proposed to reach this goal by withdrawal from the world and "mortification of the flesh"—scourgings, fastings, vigils, and the like. The method of the mystics was withdrawal from the world and a life of contemplation. No argument is required to show that this is a worthier ideal of salvation than that proposed by the evangelist. The philosopher and the saint have turned their faces towards the light and are moving upward. They have done much as ethical teachers of the race. Men as widely separated in time and ways of thinking as Epictetus, Marcus Aurelius and Bernard of Clairvaux have urged this ideal upon men, with no small success. But both methods come from the pagan Orient; both are egoistic; both are anti-social; both are, therefore, unchristian.

Since this notion of salvation is only a baptized paganism—Aristotle's hedonism somewhat spiritualized—we cannot expect to find the theory and practice of it among Christians much exceeding the best pagan ideals and attainments. Greek sages found a point of contact between this theory of salvation and their racial love of beauty. They thought of beauty as perfection: they conceived it as symmetry, balance, proportion, enough of everything, too much of nothing. Their first effort to realize this ideal of beauty was through form and color; but they discovered at length in character and conduct a still higher ideal of perfection. There is an inseparable connection, therefore, between Greek art and Greek ethics, the aim of both being the embodiment of an ideal perfection, of which symmetry is the fundamental principle, and the result τὸ καλὸν, the beautiful. Art makes its appeal to the soul through the senses of sight and hearing; character and conduct appeal directly to the spiritual intuition, the inner sense of fitness, proportion, beauty. This is why the feeling for beauty has in all ages been clearly perceived to be a powerful ally of the forces that make for righteousness; and when art and morals become divorced, art becomes lawless and life unlovely—as Puritanism once demonstrated.

The intellectual clarity of the Greeks led them to recognize danger in egoistic emphasis of moral perfection. The Stoics, in particular, strove against this error, with a good measure of success. They did much to weaken the barriers of class and race feeling, and prepare the way for universal brotherhood of men. The Stoics were, in truth, not far from the Kingdom of God. The mediæval ascetics and mystics never reached this wideness of vision; they went to school rather to the Cynics, whose chief distinction was to cherish a proud scorn of pride and to find their highest pleasure in contempt of pleasures.

The mystical element in modern Christianity gives to it much of its spiritual fervor and elevation: yet is at the same time one of the chief sources of weakness, since it encourages an egoistic, exclusive, Pharisaic type of religion. Even granting its point of view as partially true, experience convinces most people that perfect keeping of the Law is possible only to such as cherish a narrow and inadequate conception of the scope of moral Law. To one who regards his ethical obligations in the spirit of the Sermon on the Mount, a Pharisaic self-satisfaction becomes permanently impossible,

The mystics, however, approached the truth so nearly that their missing it becomes a wonder. They held part of the truth. They were right in exalting spirit above flesh. If the outer life becomes too rich, the inner life will not be rich enough. Life does not consist in what we possess, but in how we possess it. The mystics were right in considering moral perfection as the goal of salvation. Jesus regarded the Deliverance of the individual that he came to effect as nothing less than his restoration to wholeness, to ethical normality. Salvation is to have all our functions and activities brought into harmony with each other, and with the Power that controls and directs all things. Not merely freedom from sin, but capacity to work righteousness, is the promised Deliverance. But a man cannot be thus set in harmony with himself, without being set right with all his fellows. Internal harmony cannot exist while external disharmony prevails. Social salvation and individual salvation must proceed together, and neither can be perfected apart from the other.

Hence, though individual perfection is the ultimate goal, it is not the immediate aim. As St. Ambrose said, "We heal our own wounds in binding those of others." The highest welfare of each man is one tissue with the highest welfare of his social group; and, equally, the highest welfare of mankind includes the happiness and perfection of the individual. But happiness and perfection are subject to a law that governs all the highest values: they cannot be attained as direct objects of quest, but are by-products of the quest for other things. This is the meaning of the saying, "He who seeks his life loses it, but he who loses his life finds it." Altruism is the only way to social progress, but also the only way to individual perfection. This is the Great Paradox of Jesus and his profoundest truth.

For always he taught that salvation is not the quest of the individual after his own spiritual good, but strenuous endeavor to secure the good of others. In scientific phrase, if he had been acquainted with it, he might have said that salvation is not individual but biological, not personal but racial, not the rescue of men singly but the rescue of society. Organized religion, the Church and its agencies, have up to this time directed effort to the salvation of men after the fashion of a fire department, summoned to a great conflagration threatening destruction to a whole city, that should busy itself with the rescue of a few from this house and one or two from that building, but make no attempt to put out the fire. Social salvation is putting out the fire, in the first place, and then investigating its causes with a view to preventing other fires. All experience and analogy show the utter futility of the method religion has pursued for ages, with the result of bettering the world so little that men sincerely wonder if it is not growing worse.

No man can solve the problem of sin for himself alone or solve it by himself, nor can he escape by himself from sin, because sin is social as well as individual. To make possible escape for one, there must be escape for all; we are all members of one another, in a profounder sense than the apostle realized when he wrote those words. Instead of seeking personal salvation, one must seek the salvation of his neighbors, and in this social salvation he will find his own. To reverse the process, and make his own salvation the quest, is to cut oneself off from social salvation and make his own impossible. This is to save life and yet lose it. The true saint is not the man withdrawn from the world, and seeking a purification of self from all evil, but the man living in the world who is seeking to make the evil good, trying with all his powers to increase the intelligence, beauty and happiness of the entire social order.

III

Jesus seemed always more concerned with what happens to a man after he is "saved" than with the process.

As compared with the average Christian preacher, and certainly as compared with the "evangelist," he might be described as saying nothing about the process. It is Life that is the great thing in the teaching of Jesus. He does not always use the word, but ten-tenths of his words have to do with life—that is to say, with living. Usually he speaks of *the* Life, with the emphatic definite article. Sometimes he calls it "eternal" (aeonian, agelong) life. The word "life" occurs often enough in the Synoptics to mark it as a characteristic of the thought of Jesus, and only a little careful reading is needed to convince us that where the word does not occur the idea is everywhere present. The fourth Gospel was written, according to its author, expressly to persuade men to believe (trust) in Jesus and so "have Life in his Name." Further than this, Jesus is represented as declaring this to be his great mission on earth:

> I came that they may have Life,
> And may have it abundantly.[1]

It is this new Life in him, as the result of accepting his teaching as the guide of life, the product of personal trust in him, that Jesus has in mind continually, as he makes plain in all his discourses about the Kingdom. Salvation is commonly conceived nowadays as deliverance from divine condemnation on account of sin. Ever since Melanchthon, the accepted definition of the "gospel" has been "the assurance of forgiveness of sins through faith in Jesus Christ." But what Jesus lays stress upon is deliverance from self and resulting devotion of life to others.

> If any man would come after me,
> Let him renounce self,
> And take up his cross daily,
> And follow me.[2]

---

[1] John 10:10.
[2] Luke 9:23; cf. 12:27; Matt. 10:38; 16:24; Mark 8:34.

Whosoever would become great among you
Will be your servant;
And whosoever would be first among you
Will be slave of all.([1])

Christian moralists have ever found this doctrine of renunciation a doctrine too hard for them, and have sought by all means in their power to soften the words of Jesus and turn them aside from their plain intent. For this renunciation of self, they have substituted self-renunciation; in place of his unselfishness they exhort us to an enlightened selfishness—the sacrifice of a lower good to gain a higher. In their desire to make religion easy for men, preachers have been tempted to be discreetly silent about the yoke and the cross, but Jesus never concealed the fact that to be his disciple is the acid test of manhood. His idea of the cross, as Ruskin says, "has been exactly reversed by modern Protestantism, which sees in the cross, not a *furca* to which it is to be nailed, but a raft on which it, and all its valuable properties, are to be floated into Paradise."

The law of renunciation is not popular, but it is imperative. We must deny self or deny God. The result of putting this truth into the background is a saltless Church, that has lost its antiseptic power—a Church that has forgotten the high ideals of its (nominal) Head, and has learned to speak the world's language and live the world's life; a Church that puts men's consciences to sleep instead of wakening them, that offers men a soft couch in place of a cross, that finds it easier to camouflage the world's pits of iniquity and misery than to find a remedy for them.

It would have been fortunate, perhaps, if Christian people had accustomed themselves to use of another equally Scriptural word in place of "salvation," namely, redemption. Salvation seems to imply chiefly, if not wholly,

([1]) Matt. 20:26, 27; cf. 23:11; Mark 9:35; 10:44; Luke 22:26.

rescue from impending danger, while redemption implies
restoration to a former status.   We are saved *from* some
thing; we are redeemed *to* something.   Mr. H. G. Wells
struggles to express a thought like this, when he says.
"Religion is the development and synthesis of the conflicting and divergent motives of the unconverted, and the
identification of the individual life with the immortal
purpose of God."([1])   The thought of Mr. Wells suffers
from his too sophisticated vocabulary.   Jesus says the
same thing and says it much better, because more simply:

> My food is to do the will of Him who sent me,
> And to finish his work.([2])

And just there we reach the *crux* of the whole matter:
what is the will of God?   Christians have always recognized that doing the divine will is the essence of religion,
but have given all sorts of answers as to what this will is.
While always talking about it, they have had for the most
part only very hazy ideas of what constitutes the purpose
of God in redemption and have often interpreted the divine will in terms of their own desires.

So it has come about that most people who call themselves Christians have scarcely the faintest notion of what
Jesus taught and required as the fulfilment of God's will.
They talk vaguely about "leading the Christian life," by
which they show how deep-rooted is the Pharisaic conception of religion as the avoidance of gross sins and the
performance of conventional duties.   In those inclined to
be Puritanical, the Christian life appears to be mostly
avoidance of certain amusements long by common consent
tabooed.   Those who have progressed a little further tell
us that a Christian must "be a good citizen," by which
they mean that he must obey the laws, pay his taxes without dodging and vote regularly.   O yes! if he would be
perfect, he must not evade jury duty.   That to be a good

([1]) "God the Invisible King," p. 94.   New York, 1917.
([2]) John 4:34.

Christian or a good citizen means anything more than these things, Christians in general have no more comprehension than if Jesus had never lived or the Gospels never been written. And it is impossible, or virtually so, to induce "good" Christian people to go beneath these superficial matters and see that Jesus taught a social gospel, not an individualistic—that he was more concerned with the salvation of men in society than with men as separate entities. This is so far from being understood by the majority of Christians that they stare and gasp when such an idea is suggested, and at once break forth into indignant denial.

Our difficulty in urging forward the Kingdom is almost exactly the opposite to that which Jesus experienced. The thinking of his generation was less foreign to his ideas than the thinking of ours. The coming of the Kingdom of God was what the Jew understood to be salvation, the Deliverance of his race and nation. "Saviour" and "Messiah" were one to him. The deliverance that he looked for was so entirely social and political, especially the latter, that Jesus was compelled to stress rather heavily at times the idea of individual redemption and insist that it was included in any scheme of social redemption. Nicodemus found it impossible to comprehend this. He could easily understand why great social changes were necessary and possible, but why any individual change? Was not he a son of Abraham? What more could be asked to make any man an heir of the Kingdom? In our day it is the other aspect of truth that demands stress. Men must be taught with iteration that not seldom becomes tiresome, that a disciple of Jesus is he, and he only, who accepts the Kingdom ideal of Jesus and who tries to convert to this ideal the society of which he is a part. Only such a man has fully experienced the "salvation" that Jesus came to bring to men. When we all learn to practice social righteousness, moral perfection of individuals will come almost of itself.

IV

Very important in this necessary process of orientation is a redefining of terms. Our entire religious vocabulary requires to be recast, reinterpreted, recharged with meaning, to make it fit the idea of salvation taught by Jesus. A few specific instances will make plain the necessity and the method.

There is no commoner word on our lips than "fellowship," and none from which the true significance has more completely evaporated. "Fellowship with God" we have come to think of as some mystical union of our spirits with the Divine, accompanied or followed by some remarkable emotional and ethical experiences. But fellowship with God is not peace of mind or unity with the divine will or any other subjective state; it is wholly an objective thing, most practical. Fellowship is partnership. To have fellowship with God is to become his partner in the great enterprise of rescuing the world from the grip of evil. In like manner, to have "fellowship with Christ's sufferings," of which Paul writes so eloquently, is not to feel sympathetic pangs as we read of his poverty, his loneliness, his scornful rejection, his agonizing death. It is rather to share actively whatever may be necessary of like experiences, in order to be his partners in the glorious enterprise of saving humanity. And "Christian fellowship" is not merely to cultivate pleasant relations with our fellow-Christians and enjoy their society, but to be partners with them in carrying on the work of redeeming men for which Jesus gave his life.

A right view of "salvation" will give new meaning to another much abused phrase in common use, "Christian unity." Jesus prayed for a unity of believers; we are straining every nerve to bring about a unity of beliefs; and we can see no difference between the two ideals. Our objective is the wrong one, and we shall never get anywhere by our present method; or, if we do, we shall get somewhere not worth reaching. An irreducible minimum of creed, "a general union of total dissent," as Lowell sarcastically calls it, if it were possible, would not be worth striving after. But we shall have unity of beliefs in religion when we have unity of beliefs in politics and science and business, or unity of taste in music and painting and literature.

Conventions to discuss unity are futile, because they always concentrate on questions of creed, when the real issue is a question of deed. The only unity possible or desirable is a unity of believers, the willingness of all Christians to be one in the prosecution of a common task. Such unity must be based, as all social and political unity is based, on the principle of inclusion, not of exclusion. If a man does not agree with us on the merits of a poem or a painting, we do not say that he is no gentleman and refuse to dine with him. If a man differs from us about the tariff or government ownership of railways we do not advocate his expulsion from the United States as an undesirable citizen. We maintain social and political relations and coöperation in spite of all such differences. Christian unity, like salvation, is social, not intellectual. The vague and timid efforts at coöperation in Christian enterprises in past years, and the larger coöperation in a measure forced upon us by the recent war, point out the only possible way of advance. The war did not last long enough to form in us a habit of coöperation. Sectarian feeling, almost forcibly repressed for a time, showed a tendency to react with fresh violence as soon as the war pressure was removed.

"Holiness" marks another idea that demands readjustment to the true conception of salvation. Anything was "holy" to the Jew, not because of its ethical character, but because it had been set apart to the service of Jehovah. We have so emphasized the element of aloofness as to let the element of service escape altogether from our idea of holiness. Yet service was the principal thing, the very relation that constituted the holiness. We have made for ourselves an ideal of holiness that is essentially ascetic and egoistic. Our favorite texts with which we have defined and defended our ideal have been such as: "Come out from among them and be ye separate,"(¹) and "Pure religion and undefiled is . . . to keep oneself unspotted from the world,"(²) or perhaps, "A glorious church, not having spot or wrinkle or any such thing."(³) It is evident that we must again emphasize service as the chief element of holiness, and get back to the original altruistic ideal of the world. Holiness should not mean to us a selfish withdrawal beyond the influence of evil, but a strenuous conflict with evil. It is not a life of self-exaltation, but a life of self-immolation, or self-surrender—a life devoted to realizing the purpose of God in uplifting men out of the slough of sin. We must care much more about cleaning up the foul places of the world than for keeping our own garments immaculate, if we would be really holy.

"Christian work"—is there a more abused phrase in all our religious vocabulary? It has come to mean little more than getting up bazaars and suppers and other Mrs. Jellyby activities, and serving on the numerous committees of our much organized churches. Most of the so-called "Christian work" of our day is about as valuable as the buzzing of flies on a window-pane: there is no end of bustle and hustle, but nothing of real value is accomplished. Viewed in the light of delivering men from sin, of rescuing society from its manifold evils, of making this a better world for men to live in, as a means of making better men to live in this world, what could be more pathetically childish or more tragically futile than most of our "Christian work"?

(¹) 2 Cor. 6:17, quoted from Isa. 52:11.
(²) Jam. 1:27.
(³) Eph. 5:27.

CHAPTER VI

SAUL THE URBAN PHARISEE
I

Two facts stand out above all others in the formative period of Saul's life: he was city-bred, and he was rabbi-bred. He tells us that he was a native of Tarsus, in the province of Cilicia; "no mean city," as he justifiably boasts, for it ranked with Athens and Alexandria as a centre of education and culture, since it rejoiced in a university of the first rank and was the home of poets and sages. It retained this eminence for several centuries, and celebrated Fathers of the Church, like Theodore of Mopsuestia and Chrysostom, studied there. It is not likely that Saul attended the heathen schools of his native town; Jewish prejudice would be too strong for that;[1] but he could hardly fail to absorb some of the culture of the place, and he shows acquaintance with at least one of its poets, Aratus, from whom he quoted in his address at Athens the line,

For of him also we are offspring.

Of Saul's parentage we know positively only one fact, that his father, though a Hebrew, was a Roman citizen; but inferences drawn from this fact are extremely uncertain, since we do not know how this citizenship was secured. Of his extraction, Paul tells us further that he was "of the tribe of Benjamin, a Hebrew of Hebrews."[2] This indicates a pride of race in himself and family, from

---

[1] The Palestinian Talmud says: "Cursed be he who breeds swine, and who teaches his son the wisdom of the Greeks."

[2] Phil. 3:5; Rom. 11:1.

which we may fairly infer that his training would be of strict Jewish type, beginning in the home and continued in the synagogue school. Almost literally from infancy he would be taught the Law, both in word and in scrupulous observance. This theoretic and practical reverence for the Law continued to be characteristic of him, so that in later years he could say with perfect honesty, no man challenging, "as to the righteousness that is in the Law, blameless."

In his speech to the multitude at Jerusalem, Paul said, "I am a Jew, born in Tarsus of Cilicia, but brought up in this city, taught at the feet of Gamaliel according to the strictness of the Law of the fathers, being a zealot for God, even as you all are to-day."[1] This implies that at an age not later than twelve or thirteen he was sent to Jerusalem, the centre of Jewish culture, to complete his education. From this fact it seems a tolerably certain inference that his family was one of wealth, or at least well-to-do; no mere peasant or artisan could have sent his son to Jerusalem in this way. Luke tells us incidentally[2] that Paul had a nephew in Jerusalem towards the end of his life, and some have inferred that the apostle may have had a married sister in the city and lived with her while studying the Law. But we do not know that his sister was in Jerusalem at any time, as absolutely nothing is said about that.

Like all Jewish boys, Saul was taught a trade, no doubt before he left Tarsus, since his trade was tent-making and that was a prominent Cilician industry. It included weaving the cloth of which tents were made, a heavy canvas made from the long hair of goats, with which the hills of that region then abounded. Nothing can be inferred from this as to the wealth or social status of his family, for the Jews had a proverb to the effect that "he who

[1] Acts 22:3.
[2] Acts 23:16.

brings up a son without a trade, brings him up to be a thief." His trade was more an anchor to windward than a real dependence, though at Thessalonica and Corinth Paul found it very serviceable to him, since he was thus enabled to support himself while he preached the gospel to the people, and so convinced them of his utter disinterestedness—as he put it, he sought not theirs but them.(¹)

This, however, was but a little eddy in the main current of the apostle's life. Nothing that we know about him warrants us in supposing that he ever had the discipline of want and struggle; he never enjoyed close contact with the soil and the toilers of his world. Easy circumstances and a habit more studious than active may be assumed during the pre-christian years of his life. His associations were with those who think rather than with those that do, and in spite of his trade he was scholar and not artisan. A youth in which the bitter pinch of poverty was unknown, association during his growing years with the best people of his day and nation, the unconscious effect on his character of experiences in the life of two great cities, may be traced in all Paul's writings. His trade counted for so little in his life that he barely refers to it by way of illustration. The most conspicuous instance is, "For if the earthly house of our tabernacle (tent) be dissolved, we have a dwelling from God, a house not made with hands, eternal, in the heavens."(²) It is superfluous to dwell further on the contrast between him and Jesus in their youth and breeding.

The ambition of Saul and his family was evidently that he might himself become a famous rabbi, and so he would give himself to study with all zeal. We can get a tolerably clear idea of the instruction in the school of Gamaliel. The curriculum, as we should say, consisted almost wholly of the Law, by which was then meant, first of all, the com-

(¹) 2 Cor. 12:14.
(²) 2 Cor. 5:1.

mitting to memory of the text of the Pentateuch, and following that a like memorizing of the comments handed down from rabbi to rabbi, that were eventually reduced to writing in the Talmud. Such education does not deserve the name of culture, hardly that of intellectual discipline. It was almost purely an exercise of memory, with little to develop the judgment or reasoning powers. Anything like imagination, coordination, initiative, was repressed rather than encouraged.

This is most apparent when we consider the rabbinic method of interpreting the Law that was so zealously studied. A curious combination of slavish literalism and free allegorizing was the Jewish exegesis, which resulted on the one hand in those glosses so characteristic of the Pharisees, and on the other in a kind of "spiritualizing" of the most prosaic texts which made them mean whatever the interpreter desired them to mean. Paul tells us that he was not only a Pharisee but a son of Pharisees,[1] so it is nowise surprising that he acquired in the school of Gamaliel, and never lost, a full faith in the rabbinic ideals and methods, and continued to practice as a Christian what he had learned as a Jew.

Not only was the early life of Saul such, but his conversion made little change in his external conditions. As preacher of the gospel he was distinctly urban. So far as we know, he never went into the little towns and villages, as Jesus did in Galilee, but sought out the large cities of the Roman Empire. This was undoubtedly good missionary strategy; he could thus find a quicker hearing of his message by a larger number of people, than by any other method. Good generalship always aims to capture the enemy's key positions, and this Paul did when he planted strong churches in the principal Roman cities. Jesus was an intensive Teacher; Paul was a world evangelist.

[1] Acts 23:6.

It is no impeachment of the apostle's judgment, or belittling of his mission, to recognize the fact that the necessary result of his labors was to keep him all his life in a single groove, and in an environment altogether different from that of Jesus. To suppose their personalities to be unaffected by surroundings so different would be to defy all experience and observation. To expect lives so diverse to produce a common type of teaching would be silly—a sort of silliness of which only some students of the Bible appear to be capable, and they merely because they will not think about the Bible and its characters as they think of other books and men.

II

Because Saul was such as we have seen him to be, by heredity, environment and training, the writings of Paul are what they are: exactly what we should expect from one sprung from commercial conditions rather than agricultural, from the well-to-do middle class and not from peasantry or proletariat, bred in cities and given chiefly to books and study. If the words of Jesus are redolent of the country, those of Paul smell of the city street and the student's lamp. The apostle has neither eye nor ear for the beauties of nature, he can only hear it groaning and travailing together because of man's sin.([1]) He can, to be sure, appreciate the splendor of the heavens,([2]), since sun and star shine equally for town and country. But could there be greater contrast, in their whole attitude towards the world about them, than is afforded by Paul's, "Does God then care for oxen?",([3]) and the saying of Jesus about the sparrows, "Not one of them falls to the ground without your Father"?([4])

([1]) Rom. 8:23.
([2]) 1 Cor. 15:40, 41.
([3]) 1 Cor. 9:9.
([4]) Matt. 10:29.

It is seldom from the country and from nature, therefore, that Paul draws illustrations—that inexhaustible fount of Jesus. But even a city-bred man knows a few primary facts about agriculture, and so Paul does several times allude to sowing and reaping as analogies of spiritual processes.([1]) He describes character as "fruit of the Spirit."([2]) We find also single references to a few other like matters, as plowing, ([3]) the grafting of fruit trees,([4]) planting and watering,([5]) and the shepherd's work.([6]) This about exhausts the apostle's illustrations from nature. Unless, indeed, we include in "nature" the human body, which would not ordinarily be suggested to the mind when we speak of nature.

The body, its members and functions, suggests to Paul many illustrations of spiritual truth. On one occasion he draws an elaborate parallel between the members that together constitute the body and the various gifts and endowments of the individuals who compose the church. The body is not one member, but many, he says, and each is indispensable in its place and function. From this he concludes that we are all one body in Christ, and so "if any member suffers all the members suffer with it; or one member is honored, all the members rejoice with it."([7]) He uses the same figure in addressing the Romans, but with a slightly different application. To the Corinthians he had occasion to insist on the unity of the body, because the spirit of disunion was rife among them; to the Romans he emphasizes the importance of each member fulfilling its function. As the body has members differing in use, so the church has members of varying gifts; as the efficiency of the body depends on the proper functioning of each

([1]) 1 Cor. 3:6-8; 9:7; 2 Cor. 9:6; Gal. 6:8.
([2]) Gal. 5:22.
([3]) 1 Cor. 9:10.
([4]) Rom. 11:17 sq.
([5]) 1 Cor. 3:6-9.
([6]) 1 Cor. 9:7.
([7]) 1 Cor. 12:26.

member, each doing well the thing for which it is fitted,
so also in the church.([1])

Writing some years later to the Ephesians, Paul recurs
to the same figure, but this time to lay emphasis on the
union of believers with Christ, as the body is united to the
head, so that through that union and resulting union of
all parts, the body grows in strength and usefulness.([2])
To the Corinthians again, in another connection he argues
that this union with Christ as head is the great incentive
to avoidance of all moral evil, especially of those sexual
lapses that were so common in heathen society as to affect
even the Christian brotherhood.([3])   That disease should
suggest analogy with sin would be natural, and the apostle
represents ungodly teaching and conduct as a "gangrene,"
that eats away the flesh.([4])

How completely Paul's thought was conditioned by his
urban life, we appreciate more fully when we extend our
study of his illustrations.   They almost uniformly indicate the city-bred man.   Architecture furnished him with
numerous and striking analogies, as we might expect from
one whose daily wont it had been to gaze on stately temples
and palaces.   He compares his preaching the gospel where
others had preceded him to "building on another man's
foundation."([5])   The making of character he many times
likens to the erection of a building—"edify" is one of his
favorite words.   As a skilled master-builder, by his preaching he laid the foundation, Jesus Christ, and on that
foundation men built: some gold, silver, precious stones;
others wood, hay stubble; but a day would come when fire
would test the quality of the superstructure.([6])   To the
same intent, but with a slight change of the metaphor, the

([1]) Rom. 12:4 sq.
([2]) Eph. 4:12, 15, 16.
([3]) 1 Cor. 6:15-20.
([4]) 2 Tim. 2:17.
([5]) Rom. 15:20.
([6]) 1 Cor. 3:10-12.

apostle likens the entire body of Christians to a Temple,
built on Christ as corner-stone.(1)   More briefly, he says
to the Corinthians, "We are a Temple of the living
God,"(2) where the thought may be that each believer is
a Temple in whom God dwells.

Next to architecture, the amphitheatre is most fruitful
of suggestion, if indeed it should not be put first.   The
Greek games, as they would be celebrated in a city like
Tarsus, and still more at Corinth, seem to have made a
deep impression on Saul's mind.   One cannot resist the
inference that he had often looked on them, and was human enough to enjoy those contests of strength and skill.
He most frequently refers to the foot-races, and to the
rigorous training(3) necessary for winning them, as well as
to the leafy crown that was the victor's reward and held in
such high esteem.   "Every man that contends in the games
exercises self-control in all things.   Now they (do this)
to receive a perishable wrath, but we an imperishable."(4)
The Christian life he compares to a race, and declares, "I
press on toward the goal of the prize of the high calling of
God in Christ Jesus."(5)   "You were running well, who
fouled you," he asks of the fickle Galatians.(6)   And he
reminds his converts that a principle of the games is ap-
plicable to their new life, one who contends "is not crowned
unless he contends according to the rules."(7)   Contests
with the cestus also afford the apostle a striking and effective illustration: "So do I box, not as one beating the
air, but I hit my body under the eye and bring it under
control."(8)   Not asceticism, but mastery of self is the
apostle's idea.   In his first letter to his younger disciple,

(1) Eph. 2:20.
(2) 1 Cor. 3:16, 17; 2 Cor. 6:16.
(3) 2 Tim. 4:7, 8.
(4) 1 Cor. 9:25.
(5) Gal. 2:2; Phil. 3:14; 2 Thess. 3:1.
(6) Gal. 5:7.
(7) 2 Tim. 2:5.
(8) 1 Cor. 9:26, 27.

Timothy, he exhorts to contend well as an athlete.([1]) And when his own life was fast drawing to a close, he summed it all up in the words, "I have contended in the noble contest"—which is quite spoiled and meaningless in our ordinary English version of "I have fought the good fight."([2])

Of those deadlier contests in the arena, in which Christians were pitted against wild beasts, Paul was doubtless never an eye-witness, at least never a willing witness. But though he knew of them only by hearsay, he nevertheless makes two references to them. The first is of a general character, when he speaks of all the apostles, including of course himself, as "men doomed to death . . . made a spectacle to the world, both to angels and men."([3]) In the other case the reference is usually thought to be merely figurative, expressive of the writer's vivid sense of the mortal combat he had waged with heathenism in one of its strongholds: "What would it profit me if, humanly speaking, I fought with wild beasts at Ephesus?"([4])

But the favorite source of illustration for Paul is the law, both Jewish and Roman. In the former he might be called an expert, and with the latter he had much more than a casual acquaintance. Many of his allusions have to do with general principles of equity, that find recognition and enforcement in all codes, ancient and modern. Among these may be placed his frequent references to the law of inheritance. In his letter to the Galatians he compares the state of the Jews under the Law to a minor who is under guardians until he comes of age, when he enters into possession of his inheritance.([5]) Again, he reminds them that a son of a slave cannot be an heir when there is a son of a freewoman, and Christians are sons of the freewoman. Often he informs his readers that they are

([1]) 1 Tim. 6:12.
([2]) 2 Tim. 4:7.
([3]) 1 Cor. 4:9.
([4]) 1 Cor. 15:32.
([5]) Gal. 4:1, 2.

children of God, and as such are his heirs, co-heirs with Christ,([1]) and gentiles are co-heirs with Jews.([2]) The kindred law of adoption suggests to the apostle another illustration of our new relation to God as believers in his Son: we become sons of God by adoption.([3]) The law of marriage, as distinguished from the status, affords several illustrations. Both Jewish and Roman law gave complete control of the wife to the husband; so Paul says, "a husband is head of the wife as also Christ is of the Church."([4]) By most legal codes a wife is freed from the bond of matrimony by the death of her husband and is permitted to marry again if she chooses. The apostle finds in this an analogy to our being made free from the Law by the death of Christ.([5])

Paul was student and preacher, but enough man of affairs to draw some of his illustrations from business and social transactions. Death he describes as "the wages of sin";([6]) he exhorts Christians to keep out of debt, "Owe no man anything, save to love one another";([7]) and to "buy up the opportunity",([8]) as a shrewd merchant buys goods when they are cheap. Many times the apostle compares himself and his fellows to stewards—"We are stewards of the mysteries of God"—and at the same time points out, as the explanation and defence of his zeal, that the first duty of a steward is the faithful discharge of his trust.([9]) The privileges of Roman citizenship suggest a passing allusion to the much greater joys and privileges of the believer, "Our citizenship is in the Heavens."([10])

([1]) Rom. 8:17; Gal. 4:7.
([2]) Eph. 3:6.
([3]) Rom. 8:3, 23; 9:4.
([4]) Eph. 5:23.
([5]) Rom. 7:1-3.
([6]) Rom. 6:23.
([7]) Rom. 13:8.
([8]) Eph. 5:16; Col. 4:5.
([9]) 1 Cor. 4:1, 2; Eph. 3:9; Col. 1:25.
([10]) Phil. 3:20.

Though he was by no means deficient in manly spirit, perhaps nobody would think of calling Paul a warlike man. Yet circumstances had made him very familiar with Roman soldiers and their discipline and arms, and these often furnish him an apposite illustration. "War the good warfare" he exhorts Timothy.(¹) One of the best known passages in his letters is his elaborate series of analogies between the "panoply" or complete armor of the soldier and the Christian virtues. "Stand," he says to the Ephesians, "having belted your loins with truth, and having put on the breastplate of righteousness, and having shod your feet with the preparation of the gospel of peace; in addition to all having taken on the shield of faith . . . and receive the helmet of salvation, and the sword of the Spirit."(²) Less elaborately, but to the same general effect, he writes to the Thessalonians.(³) He speaks to the Corinthians of "armor of righteousness on the right hand and on the left,"(⁴) i.e. sword and shield; but reminds his readers that the weapons of Christian warfare are spiritual, not material.(⁵) He argues that as a soldier does not serve at his own charges, so apostles and other Christian workers are entitled to support;(⁶) and again, as a soldier does not engage in business outside of his warfare, so as to give an undivided heart and service, so must the Christian do.(⁷) In quick flash of metaphor he alludes to the trumpet that sounds the onset,(⁸) the triumph that follows victory,(⁹) and the garrisons in time of peace.(¹⁰)

(¹) 1 Tim. 1:18.
(²) Eph. 6:11.
(³) 1 Thess. 5:8.
(⁴) 2 Cor. 6:7.
(⁵) 2 Cor. 10:4.
(⁶) 1 Cor. 9:7.
(⁷) 2 Tim. 2:4.
(⁸) 1 Cor. 14:8.
(⁹) 2 Cor. 2:14-16; Col. 2:15.
(¹⁰) Phil. 4:7.

Family life and occupations, which figure so largely in the words of Jesus, find but small place in the writings of Paul. He speaks of various household utensils in a single passage,([1]) and of musical instruments in another.([2]) The relationships of husband and wife, parents and children, freemen and slaves, suggest spiritual analogies, but these are of the most conventional type and without much straining cannot be regarded as distinctive features in the Pauline writings. The apostle writes almost as one who had never known a home and home life. His exile for so many years in Jerusalem, apart from kindred, may in some measure account for this strange lack in his letters.

III

Wit and humor are as conspicuous for their absence from the writings of Paul as for their presence in the sayings of Jesus. The apostle was what is commonly called "a serious minded man," a phrase that usually stamps those that use it as unable to distinguish between the seriousness of the genuine humorist and the frivolity of the habitual joker. The one thing that might pass for wit is the occasional pointed antithesis of clauses or sentences. A good example is, "For the good that I wish, I do not; but the evil that I wish not, that I practice."([3]) This is certainly wit of a very mild type. Occasionally antithesis amounts to paradox, "But the foolishness of God is wiser than men, and the weakness of God is stronger than men."([4]) And is not this a case of rather rare hyperbole? "Howbeit, in the church I had rather speak five words with my understanding, that I might instruct others also, than ten thousand words in a foreign language."([5])

---

[1] 2 Tim. 2:20, 21.
[2] 1 Cor. 14:7.
[3] Rom. 7:20.
[4] 1 Cor. 1:25.
[5] 1 Cor. 14:19.

On the infrequent occasions when Paul does permit himself the use of humor, it takes the form of grave irony or biting sarcasm. Humor is for him a weapon to be employed in emergencies, rather than a habitual way of looking at men and things. He never plays with an idea or a person; his earnestness is too deadly for that. Such earnestness is well called "deadly," for it is often fatal, or nearly so, to him who possesses it—or is possessed by it. A good instance of what is meant by his grave irony is this from his second letter to the Corinthians: "What is there in which you were inferior to the rest of the churches, except that I was myself not a burden to you? Forgive me this wrong!"([1]) And again, "For you bear with the foolish gladly, being wise."([2]) The most extended sample of irony in Paul's letters is perhaps that allegory of the body and its members, already cited for another purpose. The apostle is gently rebuking those Corinthians who were puffed up with pride, because they believed themselves possessed of exalted spiritual gifts, and so looked down on those less favored than themselves:

The body is not one member but many. If the foot say, 'Because I am not a hand, I am not of the body,' it is not therefore not of the body. And if the ear say, 'Because I am not an eye, I am not of the body,' it is not therefore not of the body. If the whole body were an eye, where were the hearing? If the whole were hearing, where were the smelling? But as it is, God has set the members in the body, even as he wished. And if they were all one member, where were the body? But now there are many members, but one body. And the eye cannot say to the hand, 'I have no need of you'; nor again the head to the feet, 'I have no need of you.'([3])

Of the sarcasm that the apostle occasionally uses, this is perhaps as good a specimen as any: "Man, do you reason thus: that judging those who practice such things

([1]) 2 Cor. 12:13.
([2]) 2 Cor. 11:19.
([3]) 1 Cor. 12:12 sq.

and doing the same, *you* will escape God's judgment?"([1])
Or this: "Was Paul crucified for you? Or were you
baptized into the name of Paul?"([2])   Less severe, but
still quite unmistakable, is his reply to the brother who
makes his "faith" justification for eating things offered to
idols, irrespective of the effect of his conduct on others:
"Have you faith? Have it to yourself before God.
Happy is he that does not condemn himself in what he ap-
proves."([3])   Sometimes the apostle begins ironically, but
warms as he proceeds, and ends with a strong sarcastic
thrust.   Thus to the Corinthians: "We are fools for
Christ's sake, but you are wise in Christ; we are weak,
but you are strong; you are glorious, but we are without
honor."

IV

As to the literary form of Paul's writings, it is for the
most part the plain sober prose appropriate to correspondence.   His letters, though intended to be read publicly,
bear no marks of purpose or expectation on his part that
they would be preserved as contributions to a new collection of sacred writings.   It was a sound instinct, nevertheless, that led to their preservation, since the qualities
of the letters that made them valuable for instruction in
the writer's age have proved to be of equal worth in all
ages.   The saying in the second letter of Peter, whether
that is the work of the apostle or another, is most judicious: that there are some things in the letters of "our
beloved brother Paul" that are "hard to understand," so
that the ignorant and unstable use them to their own dam-
age.([4])   And, could the writer have foreseen the course

([1]) Rom. 2:3.
([2]) 1 Cor. 1:13.
([3]) Rom. 14:22.
([4]) 2 Pet. 3;15, 16,

of Christian thought, he might have added that the learned and wise would make even worse use of them. It is still true, however, that to understand the more important parts of them the only requisites are an honest intent and a fair degree of good sense.

Every Hebrew writer seems to have had in him the makings of a poet; and a few times, in moments of special exaltation, Paul breaks into the rhythmical utterance of psalmists and prophets. One notable instance is his panegyric on love in the first letter to the Corinthians. Inasmuch as, in every one of our current versions, the poetic character of this passage is disguised, in some by being split up into unequal numbered "verses," and in all by being printed as plain prose, it may be pardonable to give it a literary form that indicates its real character:

Though I speak with the tongues of men and angels,
   But have not Love,
I am become a brazen trumpet or clanging cymbal.

And though I have [the gift of] prophecy,
   And know all mysteries and all knowledge,
And though I have all faith, so as to remove mountains,
   But have not Love,
I am nothing.

And though I spend all my property to feed the poor,
   Yea, if I give my body to be burned,
     But have not Love,
It profits me nothing.
   Love suffers long, is kind;

Love envies not, Love boasts not herself, is not arrogant,
   Does nothing shameful, seeks not her own,
    Takes no offence, imputes no evil,
     Is not joyful over wrong,
      But is joyful with the truth,
     Overlooks all, trusts all,
      Hopes all, endures all.
    Love never fails.

But if [there be] prophecies, they will be made vain;
　Or tongues, they will cease,
　Or knowledge, it will be made vain.
For we know in part and prophecy in part,
　But when the perfect shall come, the partial will be made
　　vain.

When I was a child, I talked like a child,
　I understood like a child,
　I reasoned like a child;
Now that I have become a man I have renounced the [con-
　duct] of a child.

For now we behold through a mirror, in shadow,
　But then face to face.
Now I know in part,
　But then I shall know as I have been known.

So now there remain with us Faith, Hope, Love—these three;
　But the greatest of these is Love.

There is one other passage in Paul's writings com-
parable with this in length and poetic exaltation, at the
close of the discussion of the resurrection.　Here the
apostle's passion again demands rhythmical expression:

All flesh is not the same flesh;

　But there is one flesh of men and another of beasts,
　One of birds and another of fish.
There are both heavenly bodies and earthly bodies,
　But the glory of the heavenly is one, and of the earthly
　　another.

　　There is one glory of sun,
　　And another glory of moon,
　　And another glory of stars;
　　For star differs from star in glory.(¹)

____

(¹) The poetry of this fine passage is completely spoiled in all English versions by insistence of translators on "supplying" (which
in this case means needlessly inserting) definite articles and other
words not in the forceful and poetic original, whereby they have
given us, not Paul, but Paul-and-water.

And so is the resurrection of the dead:
  It is sown in corruption,
    It is raised in incorruption;
  It is sown in dishonor,
    It is raised in glory;
  It is sown in weakness,
    It is raised in power;
  It is sown a natural body,
    It is raised a spiritual body.

        *   *   *

So also it is written:
  The first Adam became a living soul,
  The last Adam a life-giving Spirit.
But not first is the natural, but the spiritual,
  Then the natural.
The first man is from the earth, earthly,
    The second man is from Heaven.

        *   *   *

  But this I say, brothers:
Flesh and blood will not inherit God's Kingdom,
  Nor will corruption inherit incorruption.
Lo, I tell you a secret!
  We shall not all sleep, but all will be changed,
  In a moment, in the wink of an eye, at the last trump.
  For the trumpet will blow,
  And the dead will be raised incorruptible,
  And we shall be changed.

For this corruptible must put on incorruption
  And this mortal must put on immortality.
And when this corruptible shall put on incorruption,
  And this mortal shall put on immortality,
Then will come to pass the word that is written:
  Death has been swallowed up in victory.
    Where is *thy* sting, O Death?
      Where is *thy* victory, O Death?
    The sting of death is sin,
      And the power of sin is the Law.
    But to God be thanks, who gives *us* the victory
      Through our Lord Jesus Christ!

V

The ethics of Paul are such as we should infer from our knowledge of his experience. On the surface they do not differ materially from those of Jesus; so far as they have to do with individual character and conduct they may be pronounced practically identical with those of Jesus. But the ethics of Jesus are mainly social; his point of view is the conduct of those who are members of the Kingdom of God. The ethics of Paul are individualistic. There is no social teaching in Paul's writings, because he never got the social point of view.[1] He virtually tells us nothing about the Kingdom of God, because, although he sometimes uses the phrase, he almost never uses it in the sense of Jesus. He either leaves the words quite undefined, or else uses in the context words that appear to indicate a conception of the Kingdom as future and heavenly, not present and earthly. If we accept 2 Timothy as genuine, we can hardly avoid the conclusion that at the close of his life "Kingdom" and "heaven" had become synonymous: "The Lord will deliver me from every evil work, and will bring me safe to his heavenly Kingdom."[2]

Jesus was therefore an original ethical teacher, Paul a derivative. The maxims of Jesus have been incessantly cited through the Christian ages as guides of life, to be approved or opposed; with few exceptions, Paul's maxims are seldom mentioned, and those most often cited are mere echoes of the words of Jesus. It is not the ethics of Paul but the theology, that has been recognized as distinctive. No Christian can discuss a theme like sin, or atonement,

---

[1] One of the best books in English on the practical teachings of Paul is Archibald Alexander's "The Ethics of St. Paul," Glasgow, 1910. It is instructive to note that while many pages are devoted to the apostle's ideas of individual virtue, a single brief paragraph quite suffices for an account of his social and economic ideas (p. 321).

[2] 2 Tim. **4:18.**

justification, sanctification, without constant reference to Paul. He may agree with the apostle or he may repudiate him; the one impossible thing is to ignore him. But Paul may be entirely ignored in a discussion of Christian ethics, for he made no contribution to the subject.

Even when Paul repeats the ethical teaching of Jesus, he sometimes narrows the scope of his Master's words. Thus, while he apparently insists as strenuously as Jesus on the primacy of love, the effect of love, in his view, is the transformation of the individual rather than of the world. Still, at his best, he gives us applications of the principles of Jesus worthy of the Great Teacher himself. Such instances are his cluster of "fruits of the Spirit,"(¹) and his word to the Ephesians, "Become kind to one another, tender-hearted, forgiving one another, as also God in Christ forgave you."(²) An entire paragraph in his letter to the Romans is of this character:

"Let your love be sincere. Hate the wrong; cling to the right. In brotherly love, be affectionate to one another; never flagging in zeal; fervent in spirit; serving the Master; rejoicing in your hope; steadfast in persecution; persevering in prayer; relieving the wants of Christ's people; devoted to hospitality. Bless your persecutors—bless and never curse. Rejoice with those who are rejoicing, and weep with those who are weeping. Let the same spirit of sympathy animate you all, not a spirit of pride. Be glad to associate with the lowly; do not think too highly of yourselves. Never return injury for injury. Aim at doing what all men will recognize as honorable. If it is possible, as far as it rests with you, live peaceably with every one. . . . Never be conquered by evil, but conquer evil with good."(³)

Of like character are many single maxims, such as: "Love works no ill to one's neighbor; therefore love is

---

(¹) Gal. 5:22, 23.
(²) Eph. 4:32; cf. Col. 3:12.
(³) Rom. 12:9-21. From the Nineteenth Century New Testament.

the fulfilment of the Law."([1]) "Now we, the strong, ought to bear the infirmities of the weak."([2])

What we are entitled, therefore, to say of the ethics of Paul is not that, on the whole, they are so different from those of Jesus in quality, as that they are other in the place they take in his thinking. That place is distinctly second. What our fathers called "the plan of salvation" was always first in his mind. And precisely because ethics stood in second place in Paul's thinking, they have always been second in his influence upon succeeding generations. Paul's is the greatest name in the history of Christianity, next to that of Jesus, because of his theology and without regard to his ethics.

For, as has already been implied, his ethics are not uniformly good. Nobody, for example, can reconcile with his own favorite principle of love, still less with the spirit of Jesus, that injunction of his to the Corinthians regarding the sinful brother. After admitting that his advice or command "to have no social relations" with fornicators and idolators could not be too literally followed, "for in that case you must needs go out of the world," he repeats the command, in the case of a "brother," a fellow-Christian, who is guilty of any great sin, "with such a one, no, not to eat."([3]) This does not seem to mean, as some have interpreted it, that he is to be excluded from formal fellowship—not to eat with him ceremonially in the Lord's Supper—but that he is to be cast out of the community and utterly boycotted. The Christian conscience of our age can by no means approve that as good ethics. Nor would enlightened Christians of the twentieth century hesitate a single moment to condemn as essentially unchristian such advice, if they found it outside of what they call Holy Writ. Why not

([1]) Rom. 13:10.
([2]) Rom. 15:1.
([3]) 1 Cor. 5:11.

have the courage, then, to say that such words may be writ, but are not holy, wherever they occur?

Nor can Paul's instructions about the veiling of women and the silence of women in the churches be longer regarded as good ethics, at least for our day. The good sense of modern Christians has practically blotted those words out of our Bibles. Even men whose boast is that they "believe every word of the Bible, from the first verse of Genesis to the last of Revelation" openly approve of women addressing large assemblies on religious topics. They act precisely as if Paul had never written those words—which is, of course, the only sensible thing to do, though it accords ill with their professions of belief in Paul's inspiration and infallibility. For the reasoning by which he supports his commands, if it gave them any authority when he issued them, gives them permanent validity to those who accept the historicity of Genesis. For Paul distinctly bases his words on the principle that woman is man's natural inferior and subordinate,([1]) created after him and for him, and that her spiritual inferiority is manifest in the fact that she was first in the great transgression of Eden.([2]) Milton caught Paul's spirit exactly when he wrote of Adam and Eve,

He for God only, she for God in him.

We repudiate both Milton and Paul. We no longer believe that woman is in any sense man's inferior, or that man is in any sense woman's "head." We do not believe that the family is a little despotism, of which man is ruler by divine right, and wife and children are his obedient subjects. The divine right of husbands has gone into the limbo whither the divine right of priests and the divine right of kings preceded it. There are no "divine rights" among men. Christianity is the religion of democracy, of equal rights for all.

([1]) 1 Cor. 11:1-16; 14:34-36; Tit. 2:5.
([2]) 1 Tim. 2:11-15.

And it is to be further noted that even when Paul's ethics are apparently identical with those of Jesus, closer scrutiny discloses a fundamental difference. He exhorts the Romans not to seek revenge against those who have injured them; but the ground on which he bases his exhortation is that God will avenge them; since he quotes (not quite accurately) as his authority from the "Song of Moses" in Deuteronomy,

> Vengeance is mine, and recompense.[1]

The ground on which Jesus urges men to forego vengeance is precisely the reverse of this—not because God will avenge, but because God forgives and we must forgive to be like God.

Of Paul's exegesis of the Old Testament in general it must be said that its authority, and often its correctness, is quite repudiated by the scholarship of our day. It is based on the Septuagint, not on the original Hebrew, and is such as he learned from Hebrew rabbis, whose interpretations were often logically as well as grammatically unsound, and absurdly allegorical. A crucial case is the apostle's argument to the Galatians that the promise to Abraham, "to him and to his seed," meant Christ, because God said "seed" and not "seeds."[2] But the word in the Hebrew, though singular in form is a collective noun, like our word "sheep," and may mean one or a multitude. The context shows clearly that the promise related to all the descendants of Abraham, "and I will make thy seed as the dust of the earth."[3] Paul's exegesis is not even doubtful; it is quite impossible. On the other hand, his allegorizing of the story of Hagar and the two children of Abraham[4] is not impossible—it is merely absurd.

---

[1] Deut. 32:35.
[2] Gal. 3:16.
[3] Gen. 13:16.
[4] Gal. 4:22-31.

CHAPTER VII

THE MAKING OF PAUL THE APOSTLE

I

PAUL and Jesus were as unlike in spirit as in heredity and environment. No two human personalities could well be more dissimilar; hardly a single quality, bodily or mental, is common to the two.

The notable thing in the personality of Jesus is the exquisite balance of his faculties and qualities. His spirit was at once strong and restful; he was masculine without brutality, gentle without weakness. Normally equable and tranquil, without a trace of irritability or impatience, he was yet capable of fiery indignation. Yet at the summit of his passion he never loses his poise, his sense of proportion. His speech is calm and measured for the most part, yet when occasion demands it can be vitriolic and burn into the conscience as no other human speech can. He was an idealist, but not a dreamer; an enthusiast but no fanatic.

The bodily powers of Jesus were as remarkable as the spiritual. His vitality is wonderful; he surpassed in endurance his disciples, men inured to labor, of exceptional toughness of physique, and though often wearied he was never ill. This vitality, no less than his faith in God, kept him from discouragement. His clarity of vision is surpassed only by his steadfastness of hope. He began each day with fresh and exultant spirit. He was the great Optimist, an optimist without an illusion, who desired all men to share his present joy and coming triumph. He was the one man who wanted nothing for himself, everything for others. In every respect he seems the normal man, a human being raised to the nth power.

In contrast we need not take too literally Paul's ironical self-depreciation, "his bodily presence is weak and his speech despicable";[1] but the fact that the people of Lystra, supposing them to be gods, called Barnabas Jupiter and Paul Mercury,[2] is sufficient warrant for the conclusion that Paul was by no means of imposing physique. And while few have surpassed him in keenness of intellect, he lacked the temperamental balance of Jesus. Where the one was conspicuous for poise and power, a placid and unruffled spirit, the other stands forth a fiery, tempestuous, impulsive, vehement, volcanic nature.

Jesus was a Seer of God, not a philosophizer about God. From an early age he became conscious of a peculiar relation to his Father, and his spiritual experiences were an uninterrupted process of development, conditioned by this consciousness. There was no moral crisis, no "conversion" in his life. He studied the Scriptures, to be sure, but as a revelation of his Father's mind and heart, not as a guide to salvation. He did not need the Law whose food it was to do his Father's will.

Paul had no such relation to God, whom he feared more than he loved, because he believed (and never ceased to believe) that God's wrath is kindled against the evildoer, and he knew himself to be an evil-doer. To him, therefore, the Law was an inflexible code, an infallible rule of conduct, a means of salvation if its requirements could be met. And so he became "of the strictest sect of the Pharisees," differing from those against whom Jesus hurled his fiercest invectives only in possessing greater sincerity than they. But he was sincerely wrong, as he came at last to see, and perhaps dimly suspected all along.

---

[1] 2 Cor. 10:10.
[2] Acts 14:12.

It was entirely in harmony with such a spiritual experience and such a theory of life that Saul became a fierce persecutor of the Christians. The more doubt he had concerning the foundations of his legalism, the more urgently he may have sought the punishment of those who offered a way of salvation apart from the Law. He was probably not the first, and certainly not the last, to seek an anodyne for intellectual difficulties in some form of activity. There are to-day Christians not a few who will tell you that the one best cure for all doubts is to engage strenuously in "Christian work." That may stifle doubt, it will never solve it, as Saul found.

It is not difficult to comprehend the hatred of Saul and his Pharisaic fellows for Jesus and his teachings. To the good, pious Jews of his day, Jesus gave apparently quite sufficient reason for them to suspect him of hostility to their religion. It is true that he sometimes said that he had come not to destroy the Law, but to fulfil it, that is, both to render full obedience to it and to expound it in fulness of meaning. Yet how could his contemporaries reconcile this declaration with his conduct at other times? Did he not violate their Sabbath rules and justify his conduct? Did he not criticise their feasts and sacrifices and set aside their taboos? Did he not show disregard for practical piety by eating with unwashed hands, and was he not the unashamed associate of those accounted irreligious and even immoral? If his example should be followed, if his teaching and conduct should be accepted as the norm, what would become of Judaism and its traditions?

Jesus had outraged the orthodoxy, he had opposed and denounced the plutocracy, of his time. He was undermining both, threatening both with destruction. Under guise of completing the old, he was in reality establishing a new religion and a new social order. Pharisee and Sadducee saw this with equal clearness, and for a time forgot their ancient enmity in their common interest to crush this innovator. Instead of wondering, as we sometimes do, that so much opposition was quickly developed against the teaching and person of Jesus, we should rather wonder that he was permitted to continue his work so long.

And the disciples of Jesus, after their Master's death, had been even more revolutionary in conduct and teaching. They taught salvation through this crucified Jesus, and not through the Law. The course of Paul the apostle was the justification of Saul the Pharisee—but for one thing: Saul was wrong in denying to Jesus the character of the Anointed of God, while Paul accepted Jesus as such.

Paul's conversion opened to him a new world of love and victorious energy. Up to the very moment of his conversion he had believed that Jesus had been justly crucified as an impostor. The crucifixion proved to any normal Jew that Jesus was not the Messiah—could not be, for God's Anointed was to be a conquering King. No Messiah could be a suffering malefactor, because God would never permit his Anointed, his Vicegerent, to undergo a death of ignominy. But when Jesus appeared to Saul on the way to Damascus, in an instant it became clear to the persecuting Pharisee that he had been absolutely wrong. Jesus, crucified as a malefactor, was alive; he was in glory with God; and this Jesus had spoken to him. His whole life lay in ruins at his feet. He had been fighting against God, even while he supposed himself to be an exceptionally faithful and zealous servant of God! There was not so much a change of character and purpose wrought in his soul during that fateful hour, as a tremendous revulsion of mind and heart against all that he had taught and done. As soon as he could orient himself, he amazed his fellow Jews by proclaiming the very views he had hitherto tried to suppress. Naturally, they could not understand such tergiversation; to them it seemed treason, betrayal of the religion of their fathers.

Paul now sought seclusion and the opportunity for meditation and study of the Scriptures of his people from his new point of view. This was necessary, in order to adjust himself to his new life and somehow to reconcile his new experience with his old knowledge, so that he might have a definite message to proclaim. Neither at this time nor at any other did he seek information or advice from other Christians, and he seems to have taken particular pains to keep himself aloof from the Twelve. He understood himself to have received a special and independent mission from the lips of Jesus, and he was always very sensitive about his apostolic authority. He was not only outside of the original Twelve, but he was not even of the Jerusalem circle, like Barnabas and Mark; and for this reason his apostleship was often challenged and he felt obliged to assert it with the greater emphasis. "Am I not an apostle?" he asks the Corinthians; "have I not seen Jesus our Lord?"([1]) And he reminds the Galatians that his apostleship had been recognized by the Twelve—"James and Cephas and John, they who were reputed to be pillars, gave to me and Barnabas the right hands of fellowship."([2])

Something Paul learned later about the life and work of Jesus, but so far as the record shows he made no special attempt to do this and was quite satisfied with such knowledge as incidentally fell in his way. He was rather inclined to depreciate knowledge of Jesus "after the flesh."([3]) Of all the New Testament writers, he is least affected by the personality of Jesus, for the obvious reason that he never came into contact with his Master. It is a heavenly Christ, not the historic Jesus, that pro-

([1]) 1 Cor. 9:1.
([2]) Gal. 2:9.
([3]) See, for example, 2 Cor. 5:16.

foundly influences Paul; and if the only Christian literature of the first century now remaining to us were his
letters, we should know only a few cardinal facts about
the life and teaching of Jesus—indeed, practically nothing about the teaching.   These letters direct almost exclusive attention to the death and resurrection of Jesus.
It is the *work* of Jesus, not his *words,* that is significant
to Paul.

The reason is obvious, though it may have been partly
unconscious: Paul knew as much as any other about
these themes and could reason about them better than
most; while, if he should dwell upon the life and teachings of Jesus, he would necessarily expose himself to
unfavorable comparison with those who had been daily
companions of their Master, and knew his words at first
hand.   Possibly the exact truth is, that Paul was not so
much ignorant of the teaching of Jesus as determined
to ignore it.   The very nature of his apostolate ("as one
born out of due time") virtually compelled this course.
If he were to vindicate his apostolate as specially bestowed, he must have a special message and be something
other than a mere echo of the Twelve.   And so, in all
his writings, we seldom or never find him confirming or
illustrating his own teaching by quoting the words of
Jesus.   His message is indeed "*my* gospel." ([1])

II

It should not surprise us, therefore, to discover that
Paul claims for his teaching a special quality.   He says
that he received it "by revelation," that he "received
from the Lord," and the like.   These assertions have been
interpreted to mean that, through Paul, Jesus has given
us teaching that supplements and even overrides his words
in the Gospels; so that the letters of Paul are primary

([1]) So in Rom. 2:16; 16:25; 2 Tim. 2:8; besides three times
"our" gospel; "the gospel preached by me" (Gal. 1:11), etc.

authority for Christians. The practical result of this
interpretation, if not the intended, is to make the words
of Jesus secondary in importance. In this view of the
case, Paul is not a religious teacher to be studied as a
separate personality, but is to be regarded as the organ of
the glorified Christ, through whom Jesus has given us
his final message to his Church and the world. We have,
in reality, two gospels of Jesus: one which he gave the
world in the days of his flesh, the other spoken through
the lips of Paul, after he ascended into glory.

This astounding theory of the relation of Paul to
Jesus is furthermore declared to be the article of a standing or falling Church.[1] Failure to accept it is denounced as "infidelity" and "treason." Concerning
charges like these, one need only say that a theological
cause must be in a desperate way, when its advocates
resort to the tactics of children, who, unable to argue
and afraid to fight, sometimes fancy that they are in-
juring their adversaries by "calling names." Let us
who have become men put away these acts of the child,
as Paul himself teaches us. Personal abuse is the last
shift of the weak.

To the writings of the apostle, then, be our chief appeal.
To any candid reader of these letters, will they present
themselves as a second edition, revised and improved,
of the gospel of Jesus, or as a new and original work?
The first thing that will strike such a reader, and the
last thing that will linger in his memory, is the vast
difference in tone and content between a Gospel and a
Pauline letter. Paul is silent, or virtually so, about the
things on which Jesus lays most stress, while on the other
hand, Jesus does not hint at, or at most only hints at,
the things that are the burden of Paul's teaching. They

---

[1] William C. Wilkinson, "Paul and the Revolt Against Him,"
Philadelphia, 1914, pp. 45, 48, 69, 241. The lamented death of the
author, since the above words were written, does not make the criticism of his views less proper or less necessary; his book still lives.

move in different planes of thought. They cannot be said to contradict each other, they so seldom meet.

It may also be pointed out that to assert Paul's importance, as the unique organ of a new revelation by Jesus, is to make for him a claim not only in itself incredible, but never made by himself. He makes a different claim, not that Jesus always spoke through him, but that the Holy Spirit sometimes spoke through him. Sometimes, not always. The Holy Spirit, not Jesus. This is not mere verbal quibble, sheer pettifogging of the question, as every "orthodox" reader is bound to admit, unless he is prepared to evacuate the doctrine of the Trinity of all real meaning, in which case he ceases to be "orthodox." We cannot ignore this real, this vital distinction of the Persons in the Godhead, in discussing the teaching of Paul. If it is right to say that Jesus spoke through Paul, it is right to say that the Father died on the cross. Orthodoxy long ago decided that such confusions of the persons are inadmissible. According to the whole tenor of the New Testament, the glorified Jesus does not speak, never did speak, through anybody. He spoke *to* Paul on the way to Damascus, but never *through* him.

A careful scrutiny of Paul's statements about this "revelation" justifies the conclusion that he makes no claim to supernatural or abnormal impartation of knowledge to him. When he speaks of "revelation" he seems oftenest to refer to the "appearance" or "manifestation" of Jesus to him near Damascus. In other cases, the term seems to describe that solid conviction to which he came, by aid of the Spirit of God, through meditation and study of the Old Testament, that salvation was not to be found through works of Law, but by trust in Jesus the Christ. That was his "gospel" of which he speaks so frequently, the fundamental thesis of his two most theological letters, those addressed to the Galatians and Romans. "Man is not justified by works of Law, but only

through trust in Jesus Christ,"(¹) is the keynote of the
Galatian letter; and of the Roman, "For we reckon that
a man is justified by trust, apart from works of Law."(²)
That is what Paul calls "my gospel," and it is of this that
he insists, "For I also did not receive it from man, nor
was I taught it, but I received it through an appearance
(revelation) of Jesus Christ."(³)

It is his originality, not any supernatural revelation,
that Paul stresses. "But when God, who set me apart
from birth, was pleased to make his Son manifest in me,
that I should make known his gospel among the
nations, straightway I did not confer with flesh and
blood . . . but I went away into Arabia."(⁴) The appearance of Jesus to him was his "revelation," and Paul
was convinced that then and there he received his commission of apostleship, and the conviction that Jesus was the
Messiah and Saviour, especially his own personal Saviour.
A new man was born in that hour, and out of that experience and much subsequent study and thought developed
those ideas of "faith" and "Law," of "works" and "righteousness," that became fundamental in his thinking and
teaching.

To stretch Paul's "gospel" so as to make it cover all
of his later writings, and to assert in his name that whatever he taught is to be regarded as part of his "revelation,"
and therefore to be clothed with a character of supernatural authority; in a word, to strive to invest all the
teachings of Paul with the authority of Jesus himself—
this is an interpretation of Paul's words that Christian
scholarship has never authorized, nor Christian good sense
approved. Nothing that the apostle says about his experiences requires us to believe that they are different in
kind from those of his fellow Christians, though they

(¹) Gal. 2:16.
(²) Rom. 3:28.
(³) Gal. 1:12.
(⁴) Gal. 1:15.

may well have differed in degree. They were, in quality, for all that appears to the contrary, just such experiences as all disciples in all ages have had.

There are just two exceptions to this statement: the appearance of Jesus was admittedly unique; and Paul speaks once of special revelations in which he heard "unspeakable words, which it is not lawful for a man to utter."[1] Since he never uttered them it is the same to us as if they never occurred. Normally he seems to have been led into the truth by the Spirit of God, according to the promise of Jesus.[2] To assume the supernatural to explain the natural is gratuitous and irrational.

This is particularly true of the "revelation" regarding the Lord's supper.[3] Paul says: "For I received from the Lord, what I also delivered to you, that the Lord Jesus, in the night in which he was betrayed, took a loaf; and having given thanks he broke it and said, 'This is my body, which is for you; this do in remembrance of me.' In like manner also the cup, after they had supped, saying, 'This cup is the new covenant in my blood; this do, as oft as you drink it, in remembrance of me.'" The great majority of commentators on this passage insist on interpreting the words "I received from the Lord" as meaning "I received this by direct revelation."

Did Jesus appear to Paul again and relate this story to him, giving him the exact words in which the holy supper was instituted? Is it credible that Paul would have passed over in silence an event of so enormous significance as such a second appearance of Jesus to him? And if that is the meaning of Paul's words, it follows that the narratives in the Gospels are quite incorrect, and that we have here the only trustworthy account of the Last Supper—for, of peculiar authority as if Jesus spoke through him, must be

[1] 2 Cor. 12:1-4.
[2] John 16:13.
[3] 1 Cor. 11:23-25.

accurate to the last detail. But is not the other alternative far preferable, is it not virtually the only sane opinion, that Paul received this account from his Lord mediately, through some disciple who was present, or through current tradition?

Such, then, must be regarded as the true content of the apostle's idea of "revelation."

III

It would be most unfair to Paul to hold him in any way responsible for the exaggerated claims in his behalf of those who have admired him not wisely but too well. To do him mere justice, he never thought of making such claims. If he had ever put forward pretensions so enormous, no one of his generation would have listened to him. And Jesus excluded the very possibility of such claims by anybody coming after him and professing to speak in his name, when he enjoined his followers not to be called Rabbi (which of course included a prohibition to call any other man Rabbi) but to regard him as their sole Teacher and themselves equally his disciples. He thus signified in words unmistakable that his teaching was final for them and for all who should trust in him. Any who should come later, claiming special authority from him as religious teachers, were to be reckoned impostors.

When Jesus knew himself about to leave his followers, did he modify this injunction in any way? Did he, even by subtlest hint, give warning of his intention to appoint some one outside of the Twelve to a higher authority than theirs, one who was to be his chief accredited organ, through whom he was to continue to be the Teacher of his Church? He did not. On the contrary, he assured the Twelve that he would send in his stead the Paraclete, the Spirit of Truth, to teach them in all things and guide them into all the truth. And this was his last word to them, as it is his last word to us.

We have the explicit warrant, therefore, of our Master himself for asserting that anybody who puts himself forward, or is put forward by others, in the character of organ or mouthpiece or viceregent of Christ, or in any other way unique representative of Jesus, and so to speak with peculiar authority as if Jesus spoke through him, must be rejected as at the very least the victim of megalomania or delusion or unwise hero-worship. Yet there are those who think they honor both Jesus and Paul when they contradict the words of Jesus and cast Paul for the role of impostor. The utmost that can be said truthfully for Paul, as it is the utmost that he claimed for himself, is that the promise of Jesus was fulfilled to him, and that he, like the Twelve, like all sincere disciples of Jesus, was taught by the Spirit of Truth.

The Roman claim, that in the Pope the Church has an infallible organ, through whom Christ still speaks to his faithful ones, is little more incredible or unhistorical than the claim that Paul was made the chief accredited organ of Jesus. For Jesus has no "organ," has never had one, though he has millions of organs, since every Christian believer is the mouthpiece of the Christ, in just so far as he permits the Holy Spirit to dwell in him and speak through him. This is the teaching of all the New Testament documents, including the writings of Paul himself.

That Jesus of Nazareth spent his public life in giving to the Twelve a teaching that he declared to be the Way of Life; and that he had no sooner left the world than from his state in glory he straightway deputed another man to be his chief accredited organ; and that through this new mouthpiece he proceeded to set aside the chief part of what he had taught during his lifetime, substituting for his simple ethics a complicated group of theological speculations, so as to make a system of theology the gospel, instead of a proclamation of the Kingdom of God—this is a hypothesis so fantastic, so lacking in all elements of

credibility, that one marvels how it could find a sane advocate anywhere. Who can credit that the Heavenly Christ
taught through Paul something so different from what
the earthly Jesus taught the Twelve? There is the *crux*
of the whole matter. Can we, if we would, regard the
Gospels and the Pauline epistles as literary products or
thought products of the same personality?

It is a historical fact, of course, that the entire Church
of the following centuries proceeded to substitute Paul
for Jesus, as the authoritative teacher of Christianity.
For "the truth as it is in Jesus" the Fathers taught the
truth as it is in Paul. But they did this without consciousness of what they were doing, never attempting dogmatic
justification for their conduct. Had they stated a reason
in the bald terms employed above, it would no doubt have
seemed incredible, even in those times when almost anything was credible and credited but the truth. The
most gullible and careless of the "Fathers" would never
have admitted in so many words, that the glorified Jesus
speaking through Paul could stultify the earthly Jesus
speaking through his own lips. Such a proposition must
be carefully sugar-coated to be swallowed by any. But
though this reason was never explicitly given, the Church
acted as if it believed this to be true. Paul's teaching
was quietly put in place of the teaching of Jesus. Not
one of the great theologians of the Church—Athanasius,
Augustine, Anselm, Aquinas, Melanchthon, Calvin—drew
any considerable part of his doctrine from the words of
Jesus. All without exception, Catholic or Protestant, are
expounders of Paul.

Paul insisted vehemently, almost passionately, on the
genuineness of his apostolic call, and rested it on the same
ground that validated the apostolate of the Twelve—the
risen Jesus had appeared to him also with a command
to be his witness. It would not be fair to urge against
him his deprecatory words to the Corinthians, "For I am

the least of the apostles, that am not fit to be called an apostle;" for the words following show this humility to be due to a sense of personal unworthiness, not of official inferiority: "because I persecuted the church of God."([1]) When his official authority was challenged, this humility dropped from him like a garment, and he could say to the same Corinthians, "For I reckon that I am not a whit behind the very chiefest apostles."([2])   But though he thus claimed with emphasis entire official equality with the Twelve, and did not hesitate to reprove Peter publicly when Peter was clearly in the wrong, he never claimed more than equality. He never asserted for himself such a relation to Jesus as would make the Twelve by comparison mere ciphers. Such conceit in Paul is as unthinkable as tolerance of it by the Twelve.

From the time of Constantine it was held that the promise of Jesus to send to his disciples the Spirit of Truth, had been fulfilled in such wise that the voice of the Church was the voice of Christ. A vast spiritual despotism was gradually built on the basis of that falsehood, and it required the great convulsion of the sixteenth century to win once more for Christian men a measure of that liberty wherewith Christ made us free. Now some would build a new spiritual despotism on the claim that the voice of Paul is the voice of Christ. In our day pure religion must do battle for the principle that the voice of Christ was heard once for all in the words of Jesus, and that all other pretended voices of Christ are delusion or sham.

IV

We have touched rather lightly on that event in Paul's life which marked the crisis in his thinking and doing: the appearance of Jesus to him as he was journeying

([1]) Cor. 15:9.
([2]) 2 Cor. 11:5.

toward Damascus. We have noted the significance of the event without inquiring exactly what took place. We have three accounts, all in the Acts of the Apostles, one in the words of the author of that book, the other two purporting to be the apostle's own narrative of what happened. There are some remarkable differences in these accounts, which will be made plainer if brief summaries are placed in parallel columns:

Acts 9:3-7	Acts 22:6-10	Acts 26:18-19
There flashed a light out of heaven.	There flashed around me a great light out of heaven.	I saw a light from heaven above the sun.
Saul fell to the ground.	I fell to to ground.	All fell to the ground.
Voice: Saul, Saul, why do you persecute me?	Voice: Saul, Saul, why do you persecute me?	Voice: Saul, why do you persecute me? It is hard for you to kick against the goads.
Saul: Who are you, sir?	Saul: Who are you, sir	Saul: Who are you, sir?
Voice: I am Jesus, whom you persecute; but rise and enter into the city and it will be told you what you must do.	Voice: I am Jesus of Nazareth, whom you persecute.	Voice: I am Jesus, whom you persecute (quite a long speech follows, nearly a hundred words, corresponding to nothing in the other accounts).
	Saul: What shall I do, sir?	
	Voice: Arise and go into Damascus, and there it will be told you of all things that are appointed you to do.	
Companions heard voice, but saw no one.	Companions beheld light, but did *not* hear voice.	Nothing said about companions either seeing or hearing.

From careful comparison of these three accounts, assuming that the first, in the words of Luke, was probably derived directly from Paul, certain conclusions inevitably follow:

1. *This appearance of Jesus was to Paul alone.* The first account says that his companions saw no one, and the second that they saw only the light. The first account says that they heard the voice, to which the second gives an apparently flat contradiction, that they did not hear

the voice. But the contradition may be only apparent. The Greek word used means both "sound" and "voice," and the real fact probably was that the companions of Saul heard a sound, but no words. Not one of the three accounts says or fairly implies that the companions either saw Jesus or heard him speak; the contrary conclusion is clearly implied in the second and third accounts, and is quite consistent with the first. No interpretation of the three is possible, without straining words or phrases unduly, than this: Paul alone saw Jesus and heard him speak intelligible words. The others, at most, saw a light and heard a sound.

2. *This appearance of Jesus to Paul was not objective.* By "objective" is meant an event cognizable by the senses in the ordinary way. If Jesus had appeared in visible, material form, would not the others have seen him as clearly as Paul? If Jesus had spoken audible words, would not the others have heard him as distinctly as Paul? This is no attempt to evacuate Paul's testimony of its legitimate meaning; it is an attempt to evaluate the testimony in its fair significance, accepting just what Paul tells us, but declining to read into it a meaning that the words do not fairly bear. An objective material appearance of Jesus, that could be detected by the ordinary exercise of the senses of sight and hearing, seems to be carefully excluded from the narrative by the words chosen to describe the event.[1]

3. *The appearance of Jesus was therefore made to Paul's spirit, not to his body.* It was a "heavenly vision"[2] but not a physical sight of Jesus that he had; words addressed to his soul, not to his ear, that he heard.

---

[1] The latest biography of Paul, by an "orthodox" Presbyterian, the Rev. David Smith, D.D., Professor of Theology in the M'Crea Magee College, Londonderry, a scholarly work, quite abreast of recent investigations, takes precisely the above view of the vision of Paul. "The Life and Letters of St. Paul," New York, 1921, p. 53.

[2] Acts 26:19.

This, we repeat, is his own account of the matter, in the only sense that his words will fairly bear.

4. Thus accurately to define the appearance of Jesus to Paul, according to the apostle's own testimony, *is not to deny its reality,* but only its materiality. Matter is not the only reality in the universe; it is merely the only reality that addresses eye and ear. Things visible to the eye are not the only things we see, nor are words audible to the ear the only words we hear. Seeing and hearing are spiritual processes, usually induced by impressions on the sensorium, but not always. That Jesus appeared to Paul he at least believed to be the most real thing in his life, and why need we doubt the reality of this vision of his merely because others did not see and hear? The change in his character, the total transformation of his life, are things inexplicable on any theory other than his own: the inexpungable conviction of his soul that Jesus met him in the way to Damascus and commissioned him to preach the gospel to the nations. Others have pronounced this Delusion; to Paul it was Fact, less open to doubt than any other fact, as certain to him as his own existence.

Nor is there any answer, except mere refusal to accept it, to the view that this appearance may have had a material basis of an extraordinary kind. In saying above that it was immaterial and subjective we have only used words in their ordinary sense, as describing ordinary experiences of ordinary folk. At both ends of the spectrum there are rays invisible to our eyes, because our nerves are not sensitive enough to react to these vibrations of the ether. Above and below the musical sounds that we hear are tones inaudible to us, or audible only as noise. Were our ears sufficiently acute, it is possible that every sound would be musical. Science assures us that these are dependable facts, and we cannot therefore say that things do not exist because we cannot perceive them. A Superman is conceivable, with senses of sight and hearing so far developed, that his range of knowledge would be immeasurably greater than ours. In the realm of spirit, Jesus was a Superman. And there have been other choice spirits, so much more exquisitely attuned to the Infinite, that they have apprehended things beyond the ken of most. Such was Paul, such was Francis of Assisi. We lesser breeds can do no better than receive gratefully from such men what we cannot perceive for ourselves. The only obstacle to our doing this is our reluctance to admit that others surpass us in spiritual insight.

The one thing that cannot be questioned is the permanent effect of this vision upon Paul. It transformed the whole man. Once for all he was convinced that Jesus was still living, Son of God, revelation of God's love, enthroned with power. He "was laid hold on by Christ Jesus,"(¹) who had now appeared to him "as to the child untimely born."(²) Henceforth Christ was to him the centre of all things and he could say "for me to live is Christ."(³) And with this new hope of salvation through love, not through Law, came another conviction into his soul, from which he never wavered, that he was specially commissioned to preach the Christ among the gentiles.(⁴)

V

Men's religious experiences are determined by the forms under which they conceive religious truth—though it is equally true that religious concepts are modified by experience. Paul early learned to think of God as Sovereign, and of men as subject to a system of divine Law, and he never learned to think otherwise. To the statutes of God he believed that penalties were attached, penalties both demanded and inflicted by the justice of God, who would

(¹) Phil. 3:12.
(²) 1 Cor. 15:8.
(³) Phil. 1:21; Gal. 2:20.
(⁴) Gal. 1:16; Acts 22:21.

bring every man to judgment.([1]) The divine Law differed from the human, in that to violate a single statute
was to be "guilty of all"—that is, a single offence as irre-
vocably established the status of a sinner as if he had
transgressed all. In this view, one sin was fatal. All
men, Jew and Gentile alike, were subject to God's wrath,
because all had sinned.([2])

This was Paul's idea of Law. Saul had a quite different notion. He believed that for the Jew, God had provided a way of deliverance from sin through the Law
given to Moses. He diligently sought salvation by this
means, as "a Pharisee of Pharisees," and he has given us
a vivid account of the result of this effort in the seventh
of Romans. His diligence to obey the Law only increased
his sense of guilt, and brought him to the brink of despair.
He continued in increasing agony of soul, until the vision
of Jesus prompted surrender to him as Lord and trust in
him as Saviour, and this brought peace to his troubled
spirit. Martin Luther and John Bunyan have left us
records of a similar experience, minus the personal appearance of Jesus to them. Either of them could have
written the seventh of Romans out of his experience before
conversion, and the eighth afterwards.

Paul was thoroughly loyal to the Master who had appeared to him and appointed him an apostle. Loyalty is
an attitude of soul, a product chiefly of the affections and
will, only partially of the intellect. The most loyal souls
sometimes misunderstand their leader. And all experience shows that out of an intensely loyal multitude only
a few will have real comprehension of the person or institution that is the object of their utter trust. It need
not surprise us, still less dismay, if we find from the
letters of Paul evidence that he was loyal, not to the
Jesus of fact, the real Jesus disclosed to us in the Gospels,
but to an ideal Jesus whom he had created out of the

([1]) 2 Cor. 5:19; 2 Thess. 1:7, 8.
([2]) Rom. ch. 1.

Messianic hopes of his race, the sacrificial system of Judaism and the philosophic ideas that were "in the air" in his day.

Paul did not claim to be the disciple and expounder of Jesus of Nazareth. He never appeals to the teaching of Jesus for confirmation of his own doctrine. It cannot justly be said that this was due to his vivid consciousness of the indwelling Spirit of Jesus, so that he felt no need of confirmation of anything that he taught. He often sought confirmation, but nearly always went for it to "the Scriptures," that is the Old Testament, or else appealed to the facts of his own experience. He by no means expected, as Jesus so uniformly did, that his teaching would be accepted for its own inherent, self-demonstrating truth. It was the Heavenly Christ whose disciple Paul professed himself to be, and he all but boasted of his ignorance of the Jesus whose words we have in the Gospels. The Jesus of history, the Jesus of real life, has little to do with the teachings of Paul, and certainly the words of Jesus were not the chief formative influence in his life.

Being what he was, a theologian by instinct and training, and deeply versed in the Jewish Scriptures and their rabbinic interpretations, Paul was impelled to find an adequate theory of the change that had taken place in him and for the new gospel that he felt himself commanded to proclaim. His type cannot exist with a religion alone; it must have also a theology, a philosophy of religion. The heart of the apostle was fully satisfied with the love of the Christ who had redeemed him from the bondage of sin and death, but his mind craved an intellectual basis for his new religion, a theory that would reconcile his experience with his changed conception of the Messiah, and at the same time save out of the wreck as much as possible of his old Jewish ideas. His conversion, his trust in the Jesus whom he had once fought, must be justified to his intellect as well as be testified by his consciousness.

It was this imperious necessity that produced Paul's theology, and the conditions under which it was wrought out help us to understand both its value and its limitations.

The organizing thought of Paul's theology is the character and work of the Christ, but above all the work. As before his conversion the cross had been his chief reason for rejecting Jesus as Messiah, so now he became convinced that the cross was the chief feature of Messianic work. He now saw that the Messiah could die, because Jesus had died yet still lived. He did not die for himself—that were unthinkable—then necessarily for others. The cross from which Paul had formerly revolted now became his glory; from a badge of shame it was transformed into an emblem of unspeakable honor. His gospel became the gospel of the cross. The death of Jesus was of so much greater significance than his life that Paul felt he could afford to know little about the life. So too he could truly protest that his gospel was not of men, not based on what he had been told of the deeds and words of Jesus, but on his personal vision of Jesus and his personal apprehension of the significance of the cross.

In the light of this conviction, the Jewish sacrifices took on a new meaning, and Paul worked out a theory of the sacrificial character of the death of Jesus. He did not understand the significance of that system in the history of his own people. He was quite ignorant of the fact that the Jewish sacrifices were part and parcel of that system of exploitation, grafting and priestcraft against which the prophets inveighed so bitterly and so vainly.[1]

---

[1] Isa. 1:11 sq; 5:23; Micah, Chs. 3; 6: Hos. 4:1, 2; 6:6; Amos 5:21 sq. In his so-called "temple sermon" (7:22, 23) the prophet Jeremiah is most explicit. "Thus says Jehovah of hosts, the God of Irsael: 'Add your burnt offerings to your sacrifices and eat the meat. For on the day I brought your fathers out of Egypt I said naught to them, nor did I give them any command, concerning burnt-offerings or sacrifices. But only this did I command them, "Hearken unto my voice and I will be your God and you will be my people; and walk in the way that I ever enjoin upon you, so that it may be well with you."'"

He accepted the system as it existed in his own day, as undoubtedly of divine origin, and saw in it a forecast of the cross. The Christ had died in man's stead, bearing the penalty of man's sin, and God accepted that death as a satisfaction of the demands of divine justice.

Through "faith," or trust in Jesus and his work, a sinner obtains the benefit of this sacrifice; so that, by a legal fiction, the righteousness of Christ, the perfect fulfilment of the divine Law, is transferred to him who thus trusts, so that he is "justified" or acquitted of guilt.([1]) This idea of justification by the transference of Christ's righteousness (or God's righteousness, as Paul also calls it) to the sinner through "faith," is illustrated at length in the letters to the Galatians and Romans by the case of Abraham, whose confidence in the promise of God was accounted to him as righteousness. Faith and its resulting justification constitute "salvation" in Paul's mind, that is, deliverance from the wrath of God and the power of sin and entrance into the eternal life of Christ. Jesus as the Messiah has become a second Adam, a new head of the race. As a result of accepting salvation through him, we have peace with God,([2]) real freedom([3]) and a new character.([4])

This makes no pretense to being a complete outline of the Pauline theology, but purports to be no more than a tracing of the process by which its cardinal doctrines seem to have developed in his thinking. Many things are omitted, notably the doctrine that has made the greatest noise in the world, that of "election." The point at present to note is, that this conception of Jesus and his work is the result of Paul's training in the school of Gamaliel, plus some knowledge of Roman law, such as would be

([1]) Rom. 3:21-24.
([2]) Rom. 5:1.
([3]) Rom. 6:4.
([4]) Rom. 6:22.

acquired easily by one who possessed and valued the privileges of Roman citizenship.

The notion of Adam's sin as the sin of all men, and physical death as well as spiritual the result of sin, is rabbinic theology.([1])   The conception of vicarious sin-bearing is Jewish—and pagan also, for it is found in nearly all religions, especially in such as make much of animal sacrifices.   Jewish are also other elements of Paul's teaching, of less fundamental importance, such as his incidental remarks about angels and demons.   The Law, he says, was given by angels,([2]) thus following rabbinic tradition in preference to the Old Testament record.   His doctrine of the divine predestination, hinted by the prophets, developed by the rabbis, is another case of his indebtedness to Gamaliel.

Of probably Gnostic origin is his idea of two contrasted aeons, the earthly present and the heavenly future, which took so strong hold of his imagination.   He differs from such later Gnostics as Valentinian or Basilides chiefly in ethical passion; intellectually he is their blood brother. His doctrine of the Son([3]) is hardly distinguishable from pure Gnosticism—an emanation of the divine essence, begotten before all worlds and made the agent of God in creation.   The difference is that Paul puts into his doctrine an ethical content not found in the cold speculations of later Gnosticism.   It is these Judaeo-pagan notions in Paul's writings that for ages, with unconscious irony, men have been proclaiming as the real gospel of Jesus, the only pure and undefiled "Christianity."

Paul has another doctrine of the cross, to be sure, which is essentially that of Jesus, when he says, "I have been crucified with Christ."   But this, the really Christian

---

([1]) Rom. ch. 5.
([2]) Gal. 3:19.
([3]) It has often been pointed out that the classical passage, Phil. 2:6-9, is more easily reconcilable with the later heretical *homoiousion* than with the orthodox *homoousion*.

doctrine of the cross, Paul's admirers have always practically ignored. If challenged, no doubt they would give it a perfunctory assent; but it cuts no figure in their theology or in their preaching.

CHAPTER VIII

PAUL THE CHRISTIAN RABBI

I

His contemporaries scarcely thought of Paul as a theologian. It was left to his successors to appreciate his greatness as a Christian thinker, but to the men of his own age he was preëminent as missionary and organizer. It was to John, the "beloved disciple," and not to Paul, that the title "Theologian" was given by the early Church. The last three centuries have been as much inclined to underrate John, as the first three underrated Paul. Nevertheless, it was the underrated Paul whom the Church actually followed.

We have already seen that the fundamental idea of Paul, as of all who have followed him as a theological leader, was the Sovereignty of God. He was probably not conscious that this was a doctrine of the Jewish priesthood, deeply embedded in the Law, which was mainly of priestly origin, and little sympathized with by the prophets, to whom God's Fatherhood made a stronger appeal. The apostle's idea, derived primarily from the Law, was also much shaped by the social and political institutions of his age. It was natural that the Roman Empire should become the type of divine government among its subjects, even its unwilling and rebellious subjects, like the Jews. And so Paul generally illustrates God's character and acts from the thrones of emperors and kings and from their courts. His own function appears to him that of am-

bassador,(¹) and the life of Jesus on earth and his exaltation at the right hand of God are described in terms of
sovereignty.(²) To him God is King, Ruler of the world,
absolute despot, and therefore supreme Lawgiver and
Judge. The mere good pleasure of God is the cause of
all existence and events, and no other explanation is necessary or even possible. In God's relation to us, justice
therefore becomes the chief element. He is merciful, to
be sure, but he must exercise his power of pardon so as
not to impair the validity of his Law. And, like the des-
pots of this world, he is capricious in his mercy—"He
will have mercy on whom he will have mercy,"(³) and
there is nothing more to be said. To violate his Law,
which is holy and good, is to deserve a penalty inconceiv-
ably great; and the wrath of God is kindled against all
evil-doers. As all men have sinned, all are alike help-
less and hopeless before this wrath—nothing remains to
them but misery in this world and in the world to come.

But we have also seen that Jesus in the Gospels presents
to us a wholly different ideal of God, which John caught
and set forth better than Paul. Jesus illustrates the character of God, not from the State, but from the family.
God is "Our Father who is in Heaven." His chief characteristic is love of all the world, an impartial love that
sends rain alike on just and unjust. If Paul conceives
the mercy of God as arbitrary and bestowed on a few
chosen ones, Jesus conceives God's mercy as freely given
to all who will receive it. The "wrath" of the Father-
God is directed, not against the sinner, but against sin—
it is the revolt of purity from impurity, of goodness from
everything evil. Even an earthly father, just so far as
he is good, "hates" evil, but does not hate his sinning
child; the moment his wrath is kindled against his child,

(¹) 2 Cor. 5:20.
(²) Phil. 2:1-11.
(³) Rom. 9:15; cf. Ex. 33:19.

he ceases to measure up to our ideal of a truly good father.

These decided differences in ideas of God necessitate corresponding differences regarding "law" and "penalty." Paul conceives the Law of a Sovereign in the heavens as like human law in principle: it is a definite statute, whose validity rests on the will and authority of the maker, and has a definite penalty affixed, proportioned to the gravity of the offense. This penalty must be regarded as just punishment of a lawbreaker by an offended ruler, and is imposed, not for the offender's sake, but for the ruler's, to uphold his dignity and authority. On the other hand, a Heavenly Father's law is an ethical principle, an expression of his goodness and love, a demand for that perfection in his people which is found in himself. Jesus says little about penalty, and leaves us to infer its nature from what he does say about the Father's love. The inference that seems best to accord with his teaching is: since God's Law is the expression of his love, what we call the penalty of sin is but the discipline by which he seeks to turn the erring back to himself. As in nature, so in grace, penalty is the inevitable consequence of transgressing Law; it is not suffering inflicted in retaliation for transgression.

Let us pursue this parallel a little further, for it is full of instruction. God has ordained such a connection between things in nature that when we transgress a "law" we suffer certain consequences. What we call a "law of nature" is simply a uniform method in which God operates through things. If we act by another method, we experience results more or less disagreeable, and by repeated results of this kind we are taught to respect the "law" and conform our conduct to it. When, in our baby days, we put our hand on a hot stove, in spite of maternal warnings, the smart taught us to respect God's method of operation that we call heat, and so to adjust our relations to it as to make it minister to our comfort, not discomfort.

The burn was not punishment, not an act of God's vengeance because we have disobeyed one of his "laws," but a means of salutary discipline. But for such lessons in our tender years, we might at a later time do ourselves a far worse mischief.

Ethical penalty is just like that: a necessary consequence of wrong-doing, a discipline into right-doing, not an act of vengeance on the part of an angry God. There is no such thing in nature as retribution or punishment, and we have no ground to assume such a principle in God's moral order. Men have transferred their imperfect laws and institutions to the heavens, and imputed to God the shortcomings and inconsistencies and brutalities of their "justice." A loving father cannot inflict bruises and wounds on his child as retaliation for wrong-doing; but he may permit a large liberty, in the exercise of which his child may bruise and wound himself into a better knowledge of safe and right conduct. The father will do this for the child's own good, because no other knowledge than that gained through personal experience is of real or permanent value. So the Father of our spirits, we may be very sure, will condemn no child of his to misery, temporary or everlasting; but, in order to form in us an ethical character, and to discipline us into righteousness, he will permit us to incur the misery that certainly follows wrong-doing, and to remain in misery until we turn to him and seek forgiveness and righteousness.

The principles of right conduct are founded in human nature and express its highest possibilities and joys. To act contrary to these principles is to fail to realize our best, to establish a state of disharmony and suffering within; it is not to be conceived as losing eternal blessedness, except as such loss is the necessary accompaniment of losing present blessedness. The consequences of ethical transgression are sometimes spiritual, sometimes physical, generally both; and both are as certain as gravitation.

There is no rational justification for "punishment" under human law, but the welfare of society and the welfare of the individual. God needs no protection from what man can do; consequently, the only rational justification for penalty inflicted by him is that it promotes human welfare, disciplines men into higher character, brings the wandering child of God back to his Father.

It appears from comparison of these ideas of God, sin, penalty, that Paul's teachings are not so much wrong as inadequate. His ideas are too exclusively legalistic and not sufficiently ethical. "Where there is no law, neither is there transgression"([1]) is a saying that clearly marks his limitations. In this he does not stand alone among the apostles, for even the spiritual John defines sin as "transgression of law."([2]) Both Paul and Jesus attempted to make known the character of God and his relations to man through human analogies, and human analogies are imperfect illustrations of the divine. That God is both Sovereign and Father may well be our conclusion. Both methods of illustrating his character are valid and helpful. But in our conception of God, one function or the other is almost certain to predominate. Shall it be paternal love or kingly authority? In the teaching of Jesus, paternal love certainly predominates. In the teaching of Paul kingly authority takes first place. Which shall we follow in our thinking, Jesus or Paul?

In our idea of law we must likewise choose as its basal principle either the will of the lawmaker or his character. Is the moral law binding on us because God wills it so, or because this is his only possible self-expression? From Jesus we get one idea of God's law, from Paul another. To which shall we attribute greater authority? The answer cannot be refused by any genuine disciple of Jesus: He is the fullest, the clearest, the highest revelation of God, and his word is for us final authority.

([1]) Rom. 4:15.
([2]) 1 John 3:4.

II

From these fundamental postulates of Jesus and Paul follow divergent ideas of sin and salvation. Paul's favorite word for sin is ἁμαρτία, a missing of the mark, failure to reach a standard; but he occasionally uses other words, like ἀδικία, unrighteousness, and παράπτωμα. transgression, a turning aside from the way of right and truth. It is not so much the use of these words, which are also found in the Gospels, as their constant recurrence in connection with the Law ὁ νόμος, that marks the apostle's conception of sin as essentially legalistic.([1])

It is not so easy to deduce from what Jesus says about sin what his fundamental idea is; he specifies and illustrates rather than defines. But one can gather from his teaching as a whole that his conception of sin is the assertion of self against God and our brothers, since he makes the prime condition of discipleship that a man should utterly renounce self. In the mind of Jesus, therefore, sin would appear to be the choice of individual good in place of the common good. It is the opposite of righteousness, which means every method by which man shows love to God and his fellows. Jesus never indicated that he regarded sin as primarily the violation of law, but he virtually defined it when he gave as his summary of the Law, "Thou shalt love." Sin is failure to love, refusal to love, and love is essentially selfless.

"Salvation," as regards the individual, has a twofold meaning in the New Testament, and in all Christian literature. It denotes first of all that inward harmony and peace, assurance of safety here and hereafter, which results from trust in Jesus and conformity to the will of God. The attainment of this peace is usually called "con-

---

([1]) The word ἁμαρτία occurs 47 times in Romans alone, more than one-fourth of the number of times (171) in the entire N. T. νόμος is found in Romans 71 times out of 192; but ἀδικία (7) and παράπτωμα (9) are much less frequent.

version," and is normally a sudden and joyful experience. But salvation also denotes the process of fashioning life and character into likeness of the new ideals that this experience brings us—a process that begins at once and continues to the end of life, called by theologians "sanctification." It is an experience of deep and growing blessedness, rather than of great joy. The goal of salvation is attainment of perfect character.

Jesus conceived and described his own mission as that of a Deliverer. What sort of deliverance he brought to men he himself explained in the synagogue at Nazareth: it is deliverance from captivity. Men are slaves of sin: Jesus offers freedom. It is also described as rescue of the lost, those who have wandered from Father and home. To effect his purpose he said that he gave his life as a ransom(¹)—his life, not merely his death, as theologians have narrowly interpreted him. He also came to reveal God to man, because to know God is Eternal Life;(²) and so his mission may be described as the giving of abundant Life to all who trust in him.(³)

The works of Jesus illustrate his words, especially the works of healing that fill so large a place in the Gospels. The blind, deaf, palsied, leprous, demoniacs, have bodily infirmities that correspond to spiritual defects and deformities, from which Jesus is men's Deliverer or Saviour. He came to seek and deliver such, as he makes plain in his parables of the Lost Sheep, the Lost Coin, the Lost Son. Nowhere perhaps is this idea of salvation more sharply defined than in the story of Zaccheus. When this unjust and oppressive tax-collector was convinced of the error of his ways and declared his purpose to live a new life, Jesus said, "To-day is salvation come to this house." The salvation of Zaccheus consisted in his adop-

---

(¹) Mark 10:45.
(²) John 17:3.
(³) John 3:15; 6:53; 10:10, 28.

tion of a wholly new attitude toward God and men, which was expressed in his offer of restitution. He had acquired a new social conscience; he had experienced the sense of brotherhood; he had promptly accepted and conformed to the new standard of conduct that brotherly love required of him.

Jesus represents such an ethical *volte face* also in the case of the Prodigal. The key-word of that story is, "But when he came to himself." For the first time the young man saw himself and his conduct in the true light, and the consequence was immediate revulsion of feeling, determination to forsake the past and change his relation to his father. But Paul represents a like change in our relations to God, we are told, as not of our will but wholly of divine grace, "Faith is the gift of God."(1) No doubt there is a sense in which this is true; everything we have and are is God's gracious gift. Sight is the gift of God, but God does not see for us; food is the gift of God, but we must procure food for ourselves and eat it for ourselves. Capacity of trust is God's gift, but exercise of trust in a particular case is our act. God does not save us by any miracle. He does not snatch us as brands from the burning, or rescue us from the slough of evil, and at once place us on the pinnacle of righteousness. With his aid, to be sure, but by our own effort, we must painfully climb from the depths to the heights. Salvation must be won, not given, and no other salvation would be worth having, even if it were possible.

That is common sense and sound psychology and Christian experience. Paul's teaching is not irreconcilable with it, if fairly interpreted; but it has been given an interpretation for many generations that makes it totally contradictory of our consciousness. If God produces or compels or gives faith, it is his faith, not ours.

Paul's first premise in working out his doctrine of sal-

(1) Eph. 2:8.

vation was: The wrath of God impends over a sinful world, which he will soon bring to judgment. The way of deliverance from this wrath has been provided by the mercy of God, through the death of His Son, which constitutes a propitiation for the world's sin, because of its sacrificial efficacy. The method of deliverance is "faith," or glad and thankful acceptance of this sacrifice that divine love in the Father conceived and divine love in the Son consummated. On the ground of this faith, God holds the sinner to be "justified"([1]) or acquitted at the bar of justice, the righteousness of Christ being by a legal fiction attributed or "imputed" to him. The result is a new man, who brings forth the "fruits of the Spirit," conduct and character such as a man delivered from sin should exhibit.

Dante endeavors to improve on the theologians in his statement of this forensic view of salvation, in his *De Monarchia*. In the conclusion of the second book he elaborately argues that Jesus, by suffering under the sentence of Pilate, delegate and servant of the Emperor, and so the agent of a worldwide *imperium,* made salvation certain. For all mankind were sinners through the fall of Adam, and so a penalty inflicted by one who had jurisdiction over less than the entire human race, would have been insufficient to atone for the sins of all men. In attempting to strengthen Paul's argument, Dante has very effectively reduced it to absurdity. No such frigid and rigid calculations can be admitted into modern theology, however germane they may have seemed to the mediæval.

Another part of the theological notion of sin cannot fairly be charged to Paul, namely, the doctrine known as "total depravity." Total depravity is a doctrine equally slanderous to Paul and to human nature. It is violently

---

([1]) In the Jewish and Roman law of Paul's time, "justification" was the acquittal of the accused by the judge. It was not pardon of an offence, but a declaration that he was not guilty of offence. Paul uses this procedure to describe and illustrate the Christian's experience in the forgiveness of sins.

opposed to facts of consciousness and experience, even in its milder interpretation, not that every man is as bad as he can be, but that in every part of his nature he is corrupted by sin, so that he can do nothing good. Consciousness testifies clearly that we can do good, that we do achieve good, that good and bad are intermingled in every character and in every man's conduct. If it is true that we inherit a bias toward evil from our parents, it is equally true that we inherit a bias toward good; our parents transmit to us characters, as well as estates—capitalized virtue, no less than capitalized wealth.

On the whole, it must be concluded, even after making all possible allowance for misunderstanding and distortion by interpreters, that the difference between Jesus and Paul regarding sin and salvation is a very real one, beginning in their fundamental ideas and extending through all details. Paul's salvation is a scheme for the deliverance of individuals, not of society. It does not aim at the establishment of a Kingdom of God on earth, but definitely postpones the realization of that Kingdom to the world to come, in the saying that "flesh and blood cannot inherit the Kingdom of God."[1]   A social religion was wholly outside the ideas of the great apostle to the Gentiles; but it was the chief message of Jesus to the world.

III

From his idea of God's Fatherhood and universal love, Jesus proceeded to his teaching concerning God's providence, or care for all his children. That poetic and eloquent passage in the Sermon on the Mount, beginning, "Be not anxious for your life,"[2] is perhaps his fullest exposition of his thought, but it finds frequent briefer expression in his other discourses:

[1] 1 Cor. 15:50.
[2] Matt. 6:25; cf. Luke 12:22.

> Are not two sparrows sold for a farthing,
>> And not one of them will fall on the ground without
>> your Father.
> But the very hairs of your head are all numbered:
>> So do not fear—you are worth more than many spar-
>> rows.([1])

So when he sent out his disciples two by two to proclaim the Kingdom of God through the towns of Galilee,
he bade them trust in God's providence. In this case,
God's care for them was to be shown through the love and
hospitality of their brothers:

> Heal sick, raise dead, cleanse lepers, cast out demons:
>> You received without pay, give without pay.
> Take no gold or silver or copper in your girdles,
>> No handbag for the journey, nor change of clothing,
>> Neither sandals nor staff,
> For the worker is worthy of his food.([2])

Paul also strongly emphasizes the providence of God
in the case of believers: "For we know that all things
work together for good to them that love God"—but, as
the words following show, this is a corollary, not from
the love of God for all his creatures, but from God's election of a few to a special grace; for the apostle adds, "to
them that are called according to his purpose."([3]) This
doctrine of the divine election is, according to many interpreters of Paul, his distinctive teaching, and it lies at
the basis of that system of theology known as Calvinism.

Election, according to these interpreters, is the appoint-
ment of some men to eternal life, which logically implies
that others are not elect and so cannot attain to eternal
life. Election depends upon the divine sovereignty; it
is the unconditioned exercise of the divine will, which it
is impious to question. Luther even maintained that this
act of will must be conceived as purely arbitrary and with-

([1]) Matt. 10:29-31.
([2]) Matt. 10:5-10.
([3]) Rom. 8:28.

out reason, on the ground that to make God's will depend on reason would be to suppose something higher than God. To maintain God's sovereignty, therefore, we must firmly hold that he acts irrationally! Not all interpreters have drawn so extreme a conclusion from the illustration that Paul borrowed from Jeremiah([1]) about the potter and his clay. The apostle repeats the prophet's question, "Has not the potter a right over the clay?" May he not make of it whatever seems good to him? A vessel for honor or a vessel for dishonor, a vessel for use or a vessel for destruction?([2]) And the answer is not Yes, but No, for men are not clay, not inanimate things with which man or God may do whatever pleases, but creatures made in God's image, whom, since has has made them such, God is bound by his own character of goodness and justice to treat ethically.

If the ninth of Romans were, as so many have interpreted it, an unqualified assertion of God's right to deal with men as he pleases, we could not receive from Paul or any other such a doctrine of God without serious modification. God's "rights" are the right to be God and the right to act like God. It is not in accord with God's character, as Jesus has revealed him to us, to refuse mercy to any. We must seek a better exegesis of Paul. If we study this chapter without theological prepossessions, we shall see clearly that it is of the nature of an *argumentum ad hominem,* a rebuke to Jewish racial prejudice and religious conceit. Then we shall not try to draw from it consequences that Paul has himself repudiated elsewhere.

For Paul is nearly as emphatic as Jesus himself in proclaiming the universal love and mercy of God. Nothing could be more explicit than his word to Timothy about "God our Saviour, who would have all men to be saved and come to the knowledge of the truth."([3]) And if any

([1]) Jer. 18:2.
([2]) Rom. 9:21.
([3]) 1 Tim. 2:4; cf. 2 Pet. 3:9.

doubt whether these are genuine words of Paul, they surely cannot question his assertion to the Corinthians that "God was in Christ reconciling the world to himself,"([1]) which he repeats to the Colossians in nearly the same words, that it was God's pleasure that in Christ should all the fulness dwell "and through him to reconcile all things unto himself . . . whether things on the earth or things in the heavens."([2]) Nor can any sane interpretation, other than the desire of God for all men's salvation, be placed on the argument in the fifth of Romans, especially in verses 12-21, where an elaborate parallel is drawn between the effect of Adam's sin on the race and the effect of Christ's righteousness—the one as universal as the other. This represents an ideal of salvation, no doubt, not the fact, but an ideal that cannot possibly be reconciled with God's having willed that any man shall lose eternal life. Calvin would not only set Paul at variance with Jesus, but makes Paul quarrel with Paul.

This notion of an election of the few to salvation and the many to damnation is not a Christian idea, but a Jewish. Both Jesus and Paul had to contend with it and did contend with it. The Jews were absolutely certain that they were an elect people, the special favorites of God, marked out from all others as peculiar recipients of Jehovah's mercy. They quoted with unction the saying of their great Lawgiver: "For thou art a holy people to Jehovah thy God; Jehovah thy God has chosen thee to be a special people to himself from all the peoples that are on the face of the earth."([3]) The whole world was

---

([1]) 2 Cor. 5:19.

([2]) Col. 1:20.

([3]) Deut. 7:6 and repeated in 14:2. But this was the voice of the Law, of priestly origin. Had they read their prophets better, the Jews would have had less of this conceit: "Verily you are not better to me, men of Israel, than the Kushites, saith Jehovah. I did indeed lead forth the Israelites from Egypt, but I also led forth the Philistines from Kaphtor, and the Arameans from Kir." Amos, 9:7.

ultimately to be theirs and Messiah's kingdom was to be an everlasting kingdom. In the sure word of prophecy they beheld the coming world dominion of the Jewish race, as the Roman then dominated the world. Salvation was for the Jew; the Gentile had no part or lot in it. That they were made a special people by God in order to be custodians and stewards of his grace, that they were a nation elect to be a blessing to the Gentiles whom they despised, was clearly said in their sacred writings, but never understood by them; and whatever glimmerings of truth the prophets had led some to see had faded out of mind long ago. Nothing but religious conceit and arrogance was left in the mind of a Jew of Paul's generation.

It was these ideas that Jesus found to be insuperable obstacles to success in his mission, and he vigorously combatted them on every appropriate occasion. In his discourse at Nazareth he antagonized this national conceit with great boldness and energy:

But I tell you truly, there were many widows in Israel in Elijah's days, when the heaven was shut up three years and six months, when a great famine came over all the land; and to no one of them was Elijah sent, but only to Zarephath, in the land of Sidon, to a woman that was a widow. And there were many lepers in Israel in the time of the prophet Elisha; and no one of them was cleansed, but only Naaman the Syrian.

This rebuke of their pride produced a quick and violent reaction among his hearers: those who at first had wondered at the gracious words of Jesus were turned by this discourse into an angry and murderous mob.

On the other hand, theologians have professed to draw from the writings of Paul a doctrine of election in violent contrast to that of Jesus, not to say contradiction—an election of some men to eternal life and others to eternal death, a choice having no ethical basis but only the arbitrary good pleasure of the Almighty; a decree that has condemned the majority of every generation to eternal misery, and that will continue so to condemn them to the end of time. This is the most frightful doctrine that the intellect of man has ever conceived—even Calvin had the grace to declare it "horrible," while he maintained it to be true. And the real, Simon-pure Calvinism insists that, in the eternal counsels of God, this decree to elect preceded the decree to create; so that God deliberately brought the human race into existence with the express purpose of damning the greater part of it. This doctrine imputes to God a cruelty more fiendish than even a Kaiser and his minions were able to devise; yet as a climax its advocates have the impudence to say that this is all for the "glory" of God! The blasphemy of such a doctrine is even greater than its horror. Where is the loving Father of Jesus, who does not will that one of his little ones shall perish? Ah, says the Calvinist, the "little ones" of Jesus are the "elect" of Paul. But, dear sir, who told you so? Neither Jesus nor Paul, of a certainty.

Election of some to life and of some to death is a doctrine utterly incompatible with the conception of God as Father, and not easy to reconcile even with the idea of God as King. A father must have no favorites among his children; a king should treat all his subjects with impartial justice. True, fathers do have favorite children and kings are often unjust; but that is because men are fallible and peccable. We recognize and condemn such things as shortcomings, failures to realize our highest ideals of even earthly relations; how then do we dare attribute them to God? According to Jesus, man is by nature the child of God and never loses this status, though he may ignore or deny it. However far the country into which he may wander, it is always open to him to return to his Father and be reinstated in home and love. Theology sees in man one who is by nature a child of wrath, the object of God's abhorrence and vengeance. A few become adopted sons, by the Father's choice, just as, in Roman law, one not a son by blood became one in law by act of the paterfamilias.

If such could be shown to be the teaching of Paul, he could no longer be accepted as a religious teacher of the Christian world. The God of orthodoxy can no more be ours than the German God. The day is long past when such a theology can be believed. We know today that Jesus understood God better than John Calvin did. But it is by no means certain that such theology is contained in Paul's writings, fairly interpreted; he has had fathered upon him many things that he never taught, for which he should not be held responsible. Paul does teach a doctrine of election, not an election to eternal life or death, but an election to service. God has chosen all men to salvation, but he has chosen a certain few to be the special means of making salvation known and available to the rest. In one sense all Israel was so chosen, "because to them were committed the oracles of God." The divine election was not for the salvation of the elect, but for the salvation of men generally. In Abraham, not merely his descendants, but all the nations were to be blessed.

Theology has hitherto been a deductive science like geometry, a system logically perfect, a chain of inferences from a few definitions and axioms. Theology should be an inductive science, like physics or chemistry. Human experience of what God and man are should furnish its fundamental material, from which its first principles should be obtained by induction. Deduction should be limited to inferences properly drawn from these materials. So, for example, a doctrine of divine decrees cannot be deduced from assumed facts about God and his plans, or metaphysical speculations about his mental processes, or from assumptions regarding a divine "nature" of which we know less than nothing; what God has "decreed" must be learned by patient induction from the facts of nature and history, in which he has given us the only trustworthy revelation of himself. The Bible is of course a most important part of this historical revelation, but it is not the whole.

CHAPTER IX

PAUL THE SPECULATIVE THEOLOGIAN

I

It is in regard to the forgiveness of sins that Jesus and Paul differ most. So little was Jesus a theologian, that in regard to all the "great doctrines"—esteemed so essential by theologians, ancient and modern, that to deny them is to deprive one of right to call himself a Christian—the nominal founder of Christianity either said nothing at all, or so little and so vaguely as to make it impossible to say just what he did mean. Impossible, of course, for any but a theologian. And the theologians by no means agree among themselves as to what he did mean, while agreeing that he meant something. It is sheer fact, with no whit of exaggeration, that if we had for the documents of our religion only the Gospels, nobody could formulate a Scriptural doctrine of the Trinity, Predestination, Original Sin, Atonement or Justification by faith. What most people call "the gospel" is not in the Gospels.

It is to Paul that we must turn for material out of which to formulate these doctrines. He teaches a doctrine of Atonement, in distinction from Jesus,([1]) who teaches only the fact that the Atonement is supposed to explain and justify—the fact, namely, that God forgives sins. Jesus teaches nothing formally and systematically, but his ideas

([1]) It is no doubt true that theologians, having drawn from extraneous sources a doctrine of vicarious sacrifice and expiation of sin, have read this back into some of the words of Jesus. It is incontrovertible, however, that, had we the words of Jesus only, no doctrine of vicarious atonement would ever have been invented.

are unmistakable. Forgiveness of sins, as he looks at it, is the restoration of the relation of Father and sons which has been interrupted, but not destroyed, by wrong-doing. The Old Testament correctly represents this transaction under several different figures:

Yea, thou wilt cast into the depths of the sea all our sins.—Mi. 7:19.

For thou hast cast all my sins behind thy back.—Isa. 38:17.

Thou didst take away the iniquity of thy people,
Didst cover all their sins.—Ps. 85:2.

I have blotted out, as a thick cloud, thy transgressions,
And, as a cloud, thy sins.—Isa. 44:22.

In that day a fountain will be opened for the house of David and for the inhabitants of Jerusalem, for sin and for uncleanness.—Zech. 13:1.

For I will forgive their guilt and their sin will I remember no more.—Jer. 31:34.

As a consequence of the divine forgiveness, we are received into the same intimate and loving relations with our Father as if we had never sinned. Jesus says nothing that implies any power in forgiveness to restore lost innocence, or undo the effects of sin, or annul penalty. The father of the parable could and did restore the wanderer to his place as son in the household, but not all his love could restore the innocence of youth or give back those wasted years or make good the squandered inheritance.

Forgiveness is a personal act; it restores status; it does not directly affect character; it cannot alter the past. Theologians have confused personal relationship, always subject to change, with accomplished facts that are unchangeable. They have not discriminated the unrighteousness of sin from its penalty, and popular theology shows, as might be expected, more confusion of ideas than systematic. Jesus sharply makes these discriminations. He shows us that God is willing to forgive just as soon as the erring child will let himself be forgiven; and his forgiveness is free and unconditional, restoring the child completely to his former status. More than this God cannot do; the sinner must bear the penalty of his misdeeds; and he must painfully work out for himself a new character. Here God can help; he cannot give.

Jesus shows that the forgiveness of God is exactly like man's in quality, when he commands his disciples to forgive one another. We are to forgive our erring brother "until seventy times seven," that is, without limit. And the reason assigned is, because God's mercy to us is limitless. The principle is stated in many forms, of which this is one:

> But love your enemies and do them good,
>> And lend never despairing;
>> And your reward will be great,
>> And you will be sons of the Most High!
> For he is kind toward the unthankful and evil.([1])

Even the one word of Jesus that seems to indicate an implacable attitude on God's part toward any,

> The blasphemy against the Holy Spirit will never be forgiven,

is misunderstood when it is taken in that sense. This sin is unforgivable, not because the sin is so heinous that the mercy of God here reaches its impassable limit, but because the nature of the sin is proof of a fixed state of wickedness and hatred of God that makes reception of forgiveness impossible. One who blasphemes the Holy Spirit desires no forgiveness, will not let himself be forgiven. Here is also the key to the parable of the Pharisee and Publican. God was no less willing to forgive one than the other; but the Publican sought forgiveness and obtained it, while the proud Pharisee would not be for-

([1]) Luke 6:36.

given since he had no consciousness that he needed forgiveness.([1])

When we forgive a man who has wronged us, we do not require him to pay any penalty, either in person or by proxy. We just forgive him, take him back into our confidence and love as if nothing had happened, and strive so to forget what he has done that in time it fades out of memory altogether. But along comes the theologian and tells us that analogies drawn from human forgiveness are misleading when applied to God's. God, the theologian assures us, is a Being of infinite holiness, and sin against him is an infinite wrong, deserving therefore an infinite penalty. And God cannot forgive as man does, for, because his holiness is infinite, somebody *must* pay this infinite penalty. But why? What do we really *know* of these "infinites" about which the theologian talks so glibly? Theology juggles with words as children play with "jackstones." A good part of theology is no more than an intellectual game, and among its big words, with their vague, shadowy, indefinite meanings, one searches in vain for something like reality and certain knowledge.

If a mere sinful man is under ethical obligation to forgive his brother seventy times seven, is a holy Being entirely freed from that obligation merely because he is "infinite," whatever that may mean? The holier a Being is, and the more "infinite" he is, the more ethically obligated he should seem to be to forgive, and if his holiness is perfect his forgiveness should be boundless. That is the only sound reasoning from what we know of the finite to the unknown and unknowable "infinite." And when we speak of God's "obligation" we mean, of course, an obligation from within himself, that he can be nothing else than what he is, perfectly good, hence perfectly merciful. Why is there an ethical obligation on man to for-

([1]) Luke 18:10 sq.

give? Jesus says, because God forgives. As our great poet has it, mercy

> is an attribute to God himself,
> And earthly power doth then show likest God's
> When mercy tempers justice.

Jesus even declares God's forgiveness to be exactly like man's, for he bade his disciples pray, "Forgive us our debts, *as* we have forgiven our debtors"; and in addition assured them:

> For if you forgive men their trespasses,
> Your Heavenly Father will *also* forgive you.([1])

And in these cases the words "as" and "also" mean "in the same manner."

II

One of the chief functions of Jesus, the greatest in the mind of Paul, was to assure men of the love of God and his willingness to forgive sin. But Jesus did not change the nature of God; he only revealed God more fully to the world. He did not devise any new machinery for the forgiveness of sins; he only taught men to rely more confidently on their Heavenly Father's love. God always forgave sins; he forgives sins now; he always will forgive sins. He forgives because he is God, our Father in Heaven. And Jesus is as explicit in what he teaches about the ground of forgiveness, as he is about the fact: God does not forgive because sins have been expiated, but because he loves us. He does not hate men; he never hated men; he never needed to be placated; because he loves all men and has always loved them.

Not only Jesus, but apostles and prophets, speak with one voice in this matter. "Herein is love: not that we loved God, but that he loved us and sent his Son to be the

([1]) Matt. 6:14.

propitiation for our sins."(¹)   "As I live, says the Lord
Jehovah, I have no pleasure in the death of the wicked;
but that the wicked turn from his way and live."(²)   Of
course there are texts that can be given a different sense,
but the prevailing testimony of Old Testament and New
is to the abounding love and mercy of God.   The heresy
of all heresies is the doctrine that God was once in a state
of vengeful wrath against man, that demanded somehow to
be appeased.   There was never any excuse for such a
heresy, when the Scriptures explicitly declared that God
was never so estranged from man that He needed to be
reconciled.   The orthodox theology since the time of Augustine, and perhaps before also, has been a criminal libel
on the nature of God—criminal because the theologians
deliberately closed eyes and ears to the declaration, "God
is love."   For their crime there is no excuse, though there
must be forgiveness.

Paul has been made the scapegoat for this theological
crime; theologians have professed to draw most of their
material from him.   But Paul is not guilty; at least, he
is only partially guilty; much that is found in historic
Paulinism is not Pauline.   The core of Paul's "gospel,"
as we have seen, was a message of forgiveness and redemption through trust in Christ, not through deeds of law.
"The word of reconciliation" was an inseparable element
of the Pauline gospel from the first, but it was only gradually that the simple gospel became a theological system.
For their perversion of the apostle's teaching, the theologians of a later age were able to make plausible appeal
to his fundamental idea of God, as Sovereign, Lawgiver,
Judge.   He was so conscious of his own failure to attain
salvation by works of Law that at times he thought God
was angry with him, and with all other men as like sinners.   An angry God must be placated; the sacredness

_____

(¹) 1 John 4:10.
(²) Eze. 33:11.

of Law demanded payment of penalty by somebody, if not by the sinner himself, then by somebody else in his behalf. So God set Christ forth "as a propitiation through faith in his blood, for the exhibition of his righteousness."[1] God, in the apprehension of Paul, could forgive sins only in view of the fact that Christ through his vicarious death had paid the penalty of sin. Through an act of trust in Jesus, the merit of this sacrifice is transferred to the sinner and his sins are forgiven. This is historic Paulinism.

But Jesus says nothing about his agency in procuring the forgiveness of sins. He does not so much as hint that God is ready to forgive only because of something that he has done or is about to do. In all the teaching of Jesus, man's soul stands face-to-face with God. Immediate communion with God, unmediated forgiveness by a Father who loves, was the great Message of Jesus to the world:

I say not to you that I will pray the Father for you,
For the Father himself loves you.[2]

A doctrine of the atonement must be, therefore, largely extra-scriptural and entirely outside of the teachings of Jesus. Consequently attempts to state such a doctrine have been many and contradictory. Only a single saying of Jesus can be fairly quoted in favor of any theory, and that is the remark that he had come "to give his life a ransom for many." Even if we say "give his life" is the same thing as "give his death," which is more than doubtful exegesis, is it credible that Jesus meant to teach that crude military theory of the atonement held by some of the early Fathers: that the devil had acquired possession of mankind through sin, so that men were his lawful captives, and Jesus could purchase their release only by dying as a ransom for them? Or that hardly less crude mercantile theory, like the balancing of accounts in a heavenly ledger—so much blood of Christ over against so much sin

[1] Rom. 3:25.
[2] John 16:26.

of man? If not these things, then what did Jesus mean? We do not know.([1]) It is an isolated saying of his, a metaphor on which no light is thrown by other words. But how slender basis for a doctrine of atonement, this single metaphor of doubtful significance!

This is the only saying of Jesus that may be fairly quoted as bearing on a doctrine of atonement; but there is another saying that has been unfairly pressed into service. In the account of the institution of the eucharist, Mark quotes Jesus as saying of the cup, "This is the blood of the covenant, which is poured out for many." The other Synoptics, with slight variations of no particular significance (Luke's "new" covenant is the most striking) give the same words; but Matthew alone adds, "unto remission of sins." As to this apparent connecting of the forgiveness of sins with the death of Jesus, two things are to be said: first, that these words, occurring only in the latest Synoptic, are almost certainly the accretion of tradition to what Jesus actually said; and, secondly, even if Jesus actually did speak these words, it is possible, even probable, that he meant nothing more than that the shedding of his blood, the offering of his life, would result in bringing to men deliverance from sin—which all Christians admit to be the fact.

For no means can be conceived so potent as his own voluntary and guiltless death, by which Jesus could create in his followers then and for all time that lofty type of character which gladly renounces self and welcomes death for others as the highest privilege, the crown of Christian service. It is the spectacle of that death that

([1]) There can be little doubt that this saying of Jesus is an echo of Isaiah, whose depiction of the suffering Servant of Jehovah made a deep impression on his mind. As to the fact of the life and death of Jesus constituting a "ransom" for men, that is to say, actual deliverance from sin, no follower of his would dispute it. Jesus has delivered men from sin; he has reconciled men to God; being lifted up, he has drawn all men to himself. But how? That is where men differ.

has ever since led men to repentance, change of mind and will toward God and man, a definite break with the old life and the entering on a new life, marked by unselfish love. And this new life, which Jesus came to impart to men abundantly, is salvation, deliverance from sin. For unselfish love is deliverance of man from all evil and the rock foundation of all good.

But while Jesus cannot fairly be made to support any theory of atonement, Paul's teaching may quite plausibly be made to support the Grotian or governmental theory, whether the apostle so intended or not. His argument in Rom. 3:21-26 is very like the Grotian demonstration that the death of Christ made it "safe" for the Ruler of the world to forgive sin without impairing the majesty of his law. But nothing is clearer to any student of theological thought than that it would be wasted time to advance critical objections against any theory of the atonement, for the various doctrines confute each other in turn. Grotius undermines Anselm, and Abelard and Socinus undermine both. Efforts have been made in recent years to construct some sort of "ethical" theory, that will combine the merits of all and avoid the defects of each, but with no very gratifying results.

The difficulty with all theories regarding atonement is with the very idea of atonement, if that means (as it nearly always does) anything like expiation of sin, transference of penalty, and other like notions, which are neither Christian nor Jewish, but pure pagan. Nothing but ignorance of the real nature of "moral laws" could have led men to suppose that ethical penalty could be either escaped or transferred. Nothing but such ignorance could have made men suppose that extra-ethical sanctions of a future order (the pains of hell) were necessary to ensure a penalty for sin, but for which the ways of evil might be trodden with impunity. Orthodoxy appreciates neither sin nor virtue. Theories of the atonement fail because they are pitched in too low an ethical key. There was doubtless a time when men were inclined to take a too easy view of moral evil and to regard their transgressions as mere peccadillos. It then did them good to be told of a God whose anger burned against sinners, and of a forgiveness of sins that was possible only because some one had borne the sinner's penalty for him. But Jesus gave us higher teaching regarding God, lifted the race permanently to a loftier ethical level, and made these crude views henceforth untenable. It has taken many centuries fully to realize this, and a large part of the followers of Jesus have not yet realized it, but are still obsessed by the ideas of a darker time.

III

Paul's doctrine of the atonement, in its simplest form, was, "He died for our sins according to the Scriptures." But what did Jesus say of his death and its significance? In most instances he speaks of his coming death merely as a fact. Only in one case, already considered, do his words point to any significance in his death. His plainest words about the meaning and effect of his death are:

And just as Moses lifted up the serpent in the wilderness,
    So must the Son of Man be lifted up,
That everyone who trusts in him may not perish,
    But have eternal Life.[1]

When you shall lift up the Son of Man
    Then you will know that I am he.[2]

And I, if I be lifted up from the earth, will win to myself
    all men.[3]

But the utmost that Jesus says in such cases is that his

---

[1] John 3:14, 15.
[2] 8:28.
[3] 12:32.

death will convince men that he is indeed the Messiah, the Saviour of men, and that the effect of his death will therefore be to draw all men to him. So far as this bears on the atonement, it is distinctly favorable to the "moral influence" theory, which Abelard was the first to propound and Horace Bushnell has been foremost to advocate in our day. It is not his death which Jesus says will have power to save men, but his words:

I say these things to you that you may be saved.([1])
The words I have spoken to you are spirit and life.([2])

His own view of the significance of his death, Jesus probably gave most definitely in his parable of the vine-yard.([3])   As Son of God, climax of a long line of proph-ets, he was killed because men's selfish interests were op-posed to his mission.   Death was the inevitable end of his work.   To be sure, a single parable should not be assumed to give an exhaustive exposition of truth, but at any rate, there is no hint of expiation or ransom here.

It is maintained by some that Jesus does hint at the Pauline doctrine of atonement, if he does not explicitly teach it, in what he says of the cross.   Jesus has two say-ings, and only two, about the cross, which he repeats in varied forms at different times.   The first has already been cited: it is about his own cross, and it has, as we have just seen, no sacrificial or propitiatory significance. The other saying has to do with the cross of his disciples: "Whosoever does not bear his own cross and come after me, cannot be my disciple."   *Man crucified with Christ, not Christ crucified for man, is the doctrine of the cross in the teaching of Jesus*.   The true doctrine of the cross therefore is the supreme beauty of a life of self-devotion to others—self-surrender so complete that it does not shrink from "the last full measure of devotion"; and that

([1]) John 5:34.
([2]) John 6:63.
([3]) Matt. 21:33-44.

all who would have fellowship with the joys and glories of the Kingdom must follow Jesus in the hard and thorny path of utter renunciation of self.

The same idea fills a large place in Paul's writings. "I am crucified with Christ," he tells the Galatians;([1]) and to the Corinthians he speaks of "always carrying about in the body the dying of Jesus."([2]) He elaborates the thought in many of his letters: he is to die with Christ in order to rise with him;([3]) he follows after, so that he may know the sufferings of Christ and be conformed to his death;([4]) through Christ the world is crucified to him and he to the world;([5]) and he insists that our hope of sharing the glory of Christ is based on the fact that we have first shared the passion of Christ's self-sacrificing love.([6]) But this doctrine of the cross has no relation to atonement. Christian people have, in fact, nearly evacuated this saying of all significance by their silly custom of calling every disagreeable duty "taking up the cross." The metaphor cannot be misunderstood save by wilfulness; it is what Jesus called on other occasions "renouncing life" or self. The cross was the instrument of death, and the condemned criminal bore his own cross to the place of execution, as Jesus did.

This doctrine of the cross is fundamental in the teaching of Jesus, but though it may properly enough be described as a doctrine of sacrifice, it is not a doctrine of expiation. It may even be called vicarious sacrifice, for though Jesus does not say a word about expiation, he does say much about the redemptive love that always involves the suffering of the righteous for the wicked, the innocent for and with the guilty. And this is because he con-

([1]) Gal. 2:20.
([2]) 2 Cor. 4:10.
([3]) Rom. 6:4, 8.
([4]) Phil. 3:10.
([5]) Gal. 6:14.
([6]) 2 Cor. 1:7; Rom. 8:17.

ceives salvation in social terms, not in individual. Vicarious suffering runs all through life, and finds its supreme expression upon the cross of Calvary.

But in Paul's view of Christ's death some find expiatory significance. His doctrine of atonement was worked out to solve his own personal problem, which he assumed to be the problem of all other men, because all other men are like himself, sinners. And that problem was, How could God's Anointed die a shameful death? How could God condemn his Son to the cross? It seemed to Paul that no other explanation was possible, or at least that no other was adequate, except that Christ's death was for the sins of men. The Jewish sacrifices suggested a ready explanation, one that was indubitable in the mind of one trained under that system: Jesus was the one great Offering by which the sins of mankind were expiated. "He bore our sins in his own body on the tree," as prophets had foretold, as Temple sacrifices had prefigured.

But Paul's personal problem does not concern us in the least. To us it appears natural, not abhorrent, that Jesus should die. Even if it were no more than the death of any martyr, the death of Jesus rewrote in red all that he had ever taught. And so the reasoning of Paul does not fit our case, and therefore it fails to convince. Especially do we revolt from his idea of sacrificial expiation. The whole notion of appeasing God by the sacrifice of animals, the entire machinery of altars and priests and rivers of blood, has not a point of contact with the present day thinking and feeling. The moment we make an effort of imagination to realize what it really was, our gorge rises. Paul appeals to a state of mind that has forever passed away—at least, among civilized peoples, though his theology may still be helpful to African savages.

Sacrifices are a fine mixture of popular superstition and priestly imposture. Only superstition could have made so many nations for so many ages imagine that the slaughtering of animals might propitiate a divine Being, or remove guilt from a man. And only priestly imposture could have been equal to persuading men of all races and colors for so many generations that God or the gods had ever commanded men to offer sacrifices.([1]) Whenever and wherever men have achieved a stage of civilization that enabled them to think rationally, sacrificial systems have inevitably withered and died. Beginning in the twilight of the race, they could not bear the light of noonday. They were too physically repulsive and too intellectually crude to live in the light. The whole round of Temple services in the days of Jesus and Paul would be unspeakably shocking to the twentieth century. Reader, did you ever visit a slaughter-house? Have you ever smelled burning meat? A God would be a strange Being whose eyes were pleased with such sickening sights, or who found in that horrid, nauseating stench a "sweet savor." The whole thing is so stupidly absurd as to be unworthy of serious refutation. No God that we could possibly love and worship ever devised such a method of approach to him and winning his good graces.([2])

Paul's idea of law, of penalty, of expiation, offends the modern sense of justice and contradicts our ethical values at every point of contact. Without caricature, it may be compared to ideas that prevail in certain police circles to-day. A sensational crime is committed; the public is greatly roused and demands detection and punishment of

---

([1]) Judaism was better than the pagan faiths, in that it never countenanced the offering of human beings in sacrifice. Readers of Montaigne will recall an instance that he mentions: "Amurath at the taking of Isthmus, sacrificed six hundred young Grecians to his father's soul: to the end their blood might serve as a propitiation to exculpate the sins of the deceased." Essays, bk. I, ch. xxix.

([2]) The judicious reader will observe that nothing is said above that is not fully implied by the writer of the Epistle to the Hebrews: "For it is impossible that the blood of bulls and of goats should take away sins" (10:4). The injudicious reader will, of course, perceive nothing of the sort, not even after it has been pointed out to him.

the criminal.   This the police are unable to accomplish, but obviously something must be done to silence public clamor; so they "frame up" a case against some one who can most plausibly be made the scapegoat.   He is convicted by perjury, the public cry is silenced, the majesty of the law has been vindicated, justice is satisfied!

But we are no longer content with that brand of "justice."   We insist that the guilt of the guilty cannot be expiated, justice cannot be satisfied, by the punishment of the innocent.   Yet our theology continues to teach that the Almighty could find no better expedient to save men than to "frame up" a case against his own Son and put to death the innocent for the guilty.   And that which fills us with horror when done by man to man, we praise and glorify when done by God to God.   Does the orthodox Christian *ever* think?

We have come of late to understand that there are many survivals of primitive ideas and customs in Christian doctrine and institutions.   The Pauline teaching regarding atonement is an excellent example.   He inherited his thought from Judaism, where it is a palpable survival of the clan stage of Israel's development, when the clan and the family were the social units, and any member of family or clan, or the whole of either, might be held responsible for an individual's wrong act and could pay the penalty. Transference of penalty, so unthinkable to us, was then normal and usual.   Every group must bear the sins of its members, and conversely the individuals must suffer with and for the group.   Ideas persist longer than institutions; and while, in modern society, group responsibility has given way in law to individual responsibility, ideas derived from group responsibility are still potent in theology. We find it difficult to persuade ourselves that such savage punishment could be inflicted on an entire family for the sin of one member, as the story of Achan describes, and we refuse to believe that God had anything more to do with the matter than he had with the slaughter of the citizens of Louvain because a few of them were accused of "sniping" at the German invaders. The notion of transferred or substituted penalty cannot be adjusted to our present social status, in which individual rights and individual responsibilities are so overemphasized that social responsibilities and duties are little felt and social sins not at all. Transference of penalty cannot happen to-day; not only so, it is quite inconceivable.

Only a believer in universal salvation can with logical consistency, hold the doctrine of penal substitution. If Christ actually has borne our penalty, then God cannot justly hold us to further penalties for our sins. Therefore all men must be saved. There is no escape from the conclusion if the premise be maintained; universalism is the rigorously logical deduction from the substitutionary theory of Christ's death.

And the modern ethical sense declares that sin can no more be expiated than transferred. Expiation of sin is impossible, was always impossible, unimaginable even. Nobody has ever been able to show, nobody will ever be able to explain, how a given quantity of suffering can equal a given quantity of sin. Neither sin nor suffering can be measured quantitatively, and if each could be exactly weighed or measured or computed nobody can show how one can be the equivalent of the other. The mediæval attempt to establish a money value for crime (*Wehrgelt*), was not more irrational, nor was the sliding scale for indulgences proclaimed by Tetzel a greater scandal. Sin cannot be escaped by expiation; it can be escaped only by being repented, forsaken, hated. The consequences of sin are indelible; the effect of an evil act cannot be undone, even by divine omnipotence. Suffering is the inescapable consequence of sin, penalty, but not punishment. Society only evades the problem of moral evil when it hangs or imprisons a wrong-doer; the only solution of the problem is to remake him into a doer of right. God cannot dispose of sin by sending the sinner to hell; God must make the sinner righteous.

Any theory of atonement is impossible that does not take into account these ethical ideas of our own day. So far as sin is conceived as a personal offense against God, his forgiveness may also be conceived as removing the barrier that sin has made between man and God. But we can no longer receive the teaching that any sort of atonement or forgiveness makes it possible for God to relieve man of the other effects of his sin. These the sinner must bear, and others must bear with him; for, as no man lives to himself, so no man sins to himself. The worst thing about moral evil, indeed, is not its effect on the individual who sins, but its social consequences. Its effect on his innocent fellows quite outweighs its effect on himself. The sooner we awake to the fact that the past is unalterable by the forgiveness of God, the better for our religious life and the better for the prospect of greater reality in our preaching. Untold mischief has been done by the proclamation from ten thousand pulpits that repentance and the forgiveness of sins wipes out all the consequences of sin. Hymns like Cowper's "There is a fountain filled with blood," have led thousands into a religious fool's paradise. Far truer are the words of Omar:

> The Moving Finger writes; and having writ
> Moves on: nor all thy Piety and Wit
> Shall lure it back to cancel half a Line,
> Nor all thy Tears wash out a Word of it.

The present is ours, to make a new record; the past is past. Whoever teaches men otherwise, teaches lies.

It is often made a reproach to "liberal" Christians that, in denying the efficacy of blood-atonement they take a light and inadequate view of sin. But what is often called an inadequate sense of sin will turn out on examination to be merely a sense of different sin—an appreciation of the utter inadequacy of an idea of sin that confines it entirely to wrong relations to a God whom one has not seen, with a bland unconsciousness of sin that consists in wrong relations to the brother whom one has seen. And as for "light" views of sin, which is the lighter, that which insists the sinner must forever bear the burden of consequences that accrue from his evil, or that which says he may escape the consequences utterly by a bath in the "fountain filled with blood"? No, it is your orthodox theologian or preacher with his theory of blood-atonement who takes sin too lightly. It is your evangelist who exhorts sinners to come and be washed white in the blood of the Lamb, who takes an inadequate view of sin. God has never promised to whitewash moral evil and call it good, whatever presumptuous and silly men may have rashly promised in his name. Poetic phrases of prophets that expressed religious emotion have been made into scientific theological definitions, with consequences disastrous to theology and religion.

But, after all, the great untruth of the vicarious sacrifice is that by representing the crucifixion of the Son of God as "substitutionary," theology has excused the sons of God from that daily dying on the cross which Jesus declared to be the essence of discipleship.

IV

The difference between Jesus and Paul regarding forgiveness of sins stands out clearly when we consider their terminology. The word continually on the lips of Jesus in connection with sin is "forgive"—in the Greek ἀφίημι, which means to send away, let go, disregard, and was used in classical Greek as a legal term to denote release from contract, debt, or indictment. Paul uses the same terminology a few times,([1]) thus showing that the idea of remission of sins was not unfamiliar to him. But if not unfamiliar, it seems to have been unwelcome; he preferred something quite different. The verb δικαιόω which Paul uses to denote man's deliverance from sin and guilt, occurs in his writings 27 times, not to mention its cognates, δικαίωσις (3) and δικαίωμα (5). Law knows no forgiveness; law either convicts of sin or acquits of guilt. Jesus uses δικαιόω only once or twice in speaking of man's relations to God, and then apparently not in a forensic sense.([2]) Forgiveness, utter and final, not acquittal by legal fiction, is his idea of God's way of dealing with the sinner. A Father may forgive the guilty; a judge must either convict or find some expedient to acquit. The prayer of Jesus on the cross, "Father, forgive them, *for* they know not what they do," can find no place in the Pauline theory of justification. Law can never admit ignorance to be an excuse for guilt or a reason for acquittal.

The same distinction follows in the ideas of "righteousness" δικαιοσύνη the status of being "just" in the sight of God. Jesus everywhere, but especially in the Sermon on the Mount, speaks of a righteousness that is personal and essential, a real righteousness that consists of right character and conduct. His idea of righteousness is a relation of reverence, trust and love to a Father in Heaven, which cannot but express itself in obedience. "Be perfect, as your Father in Heaven is perfect," is an ideal rather than a law, a standard but not a statute. Paul's "righteousness" is not primarily personal and essential, but legal, and therefore unreal; it is a fictitious righteousness that is "reckoned" to us, or with which we are "clothed"—not ours, but Christ's, bestowed on us by a legal fiction. "Christ *has been made unto us* wisdom

---

([1]) For example, Eph. 1:7; Col. 1:14.
([2]) Matt. 12:37.

from God, and righteousness and sanctification and redemption." (¹)

Jesus teaches the insufficiency of mere formal obedience
to law, such as the Pharisees rendered, and gives a new
and spiritual interpretation of the Decalogue—"I am come
not to destroy, but to fulfil," fill full, complete.   He holds
up to men a higher ethical standard than they had known,
and then holds them up to the standard.   But Paul insists that the Law was not intended to be kept, that man
is unable to obey it—the Law was given to awaken men's
sense of sin, to teach them their inability to obey, and so,
like a tutor, to bring them to Christ. (²)   So, while Jesus
insists that his disciples must obey the Law, in a righteousness exceeding that of Scribes and Pharisees, (³) Paul
sweeps the Law altogether away—Christ has abolished it,
nailed it to the cross, and made a sport of it. (⁴)   There
may be a way of "reconciling" these differing views of
the Law, but their likeness is not striking.

Paul represents the process of salvation as wholly of
the grace of God, with which the sinner has nothing to
do but either to accept or reject it.   Jesus represents salvation as the result of man's effort together with God:
"By your endurance you will win your lives," *i. e.,* your
true lives, eternal Life.   Life comes from God, but attainment of Life is man's work.   Eternal Life is God's
gift, as is all that we possess, but it is also a self-creation
through self-conquest.

> I am the master of my fate,
> I am the captain of my soul,

is not a pagan sentiment, as has sometimes been said, but
profoundly Christian, though its author never understood
that fact.   Posing as pure pagan, he was Christian in spite
of himself.

(¹) 1 Cor. 1:30.
(²) Gal. 3:24; Rom. 7:7.
(³) Matt. 5:20.
(⁴) Col. 2:14, 15.

In a word, Jesus came, not to satisfy divine justice and confer a fictitious righteousness, but to save sinners by making them truly righteous. The atonement is not a legal, but a vital process. God's forgiveness makes the forgiven heart the home of the love that forgives; it brings with it the promise and potency of a new life; it regenerates. Its result is not the imputation of a righteousness that does not really exist, but the impartation of a righteousness that comes really to exist. The teaching of Paul is not false, but inadequate; it does not represent the ideas of God, sin, penalty, forgiveness, righteousness, at their highest, as Jesus has helped us to apprehend them; instead, he gives us older and less perfect ideas.

Yet, if we see in Paul's doctrine of justification by faith and imputed righteousness, not a dogma to be accepted in the precise form of words in which he sets it forth, but an illustration from legal principles of his day of an eternal principle, we shall get from justification by faith and its imputation of righteousness all that it was designed to convey. To do this, we must lay the emphasis on the faith, rather than on the justification. It is justification by faith, and not by works of law, as Paul so vehemently insists, because works are a product of spiritual condition, not its cause. Faith, trust in Jesus as Deliverer, the soul committing itself to him as Teacher and Master, marks the beginning of a new life of God in the man. Henceforth he is a new creation, reborn from above, to grow in the grace and knowledge of God through the power of his indwelling Spirit. Every man who has had a genuine Christian experience knows exactly what this means, but to one who lacks that experience such words will ever appear foolishness.

The real difficulty in Paul's doctrine of a forensic justification, that depended on an "imputed" righteousness, was not felt in his day or for long afterward, but is very serious to us. We have come to see that it is an unworthy idea of God to suppose that he employs a mere "dodge" to save men. Our idea of God does not admit of his dealing in fictions. God is not merely truthful, he is Truth. No artificial, forensic expedient is conceivable in the domain of ethical and spiritual relations. If God declares a man just, if he acquits him of sin, it must be because the man is just, is no longer guilty. And that is exactly what forgiveness means. When man turns from sin and God forgives, he is no longer guilty, and therefore he must be acquitted. God judges him according to what he has become and is henceforth to be, not according to what he was. It is not legal fiction; it is ethical fact. But when we have thus evaluated Paul's forensic illustration, in the light of our highest ethical knowledge, the essential thing in justification by faith remains: There is such a thing as trust in Jesus the Christ, so vital and compelling that it grips a man's very soul and makes him completely over, reconstitutes his ideals and aims, determines anew the whole course of life, and puts him in new relation with God.

V

Next to the teaching of the unquestioned Pauline writings, and in certain respects of greater weight in the estimation of some, is the contribution to the doctrine of atonement made by the Epistle to the Hebrews, long attributed to Paul. The majority of scholars now believe that this is certainly not Paul's composition, though he in large part furnished its ideas. The letter is avowedly the work, not of an apostle, or even an original disciple of Jesus, but of a convert who has received his knowledge of Jesus and his words from apostolic sources.(1) That would quite accurately describe Apollos, whom Luther first guessed to have been the actual writer. Whoever he was, he makes no claim to inspiration or apostolic authority.

(1) Heb. 1:3.

The so-called "epistle" is not a letter at all, but a homily, a religious essay or exhortation, belonging to the same class of early Christian writings as 2 Clement.

The chief characteristic of the homily is the author's attempt to establish analogies between the Jewish system, the details of which he seems to have imperfectly understood, and the new religion of the Christ. No more than Paul did he comprehend the origin and nature of the Jewish sacrificial system. It was not his fault that the science of comparative religion did not then exist, and that he was ignorant of the correspondence between Judaism and Oriental paganism. But, waiving this fundamental defect in the homily, a careful examination of it shows that there has been widespread misinterpretation of it.

The idea of sacrifice so prominent in this writing, is not expiation or propitiation, but purification or cleansing. This is made clear at the very outset, where it is said of the Son that, "when he had made a purification for sins, he sat down on the right hand of the Majesty on high." This is the controlling thought of the homily. The argument is twofold:

First, that Jesus performs for his people essentially the same office that the High Priest performed for the Jews, only much more effectually; and that he performed it once for all, so that it does not need to be repeated. That office was to put away sin, which was accomplished in symbol by the High Priest going on the day of Atonement into the Holy of Holies and sprinkling the mercy-seat with blood. Jesus, by the shedding of his blood, has once for all effected the purification, sanctification, cleansing, perfecting (all of these terms are employed in turn) of all that trust in him. Throughout the first eight chapters, Jesus is likened to the High Priest, not the victim; he is represented as making the sacrifice of purification, not as being the sacrifice.

Second, in the ninth and tenth chapters, Jesus is also spoken of as the victim, as "being offered," but the end of the offering is still to purify his people from their sins. There is no doctrine of expiation or vicarious sacrifice anywhere in the "epistle."([1])

Hebrews is therefore wholly in accord with the view that the real significance of the death of Jesus is that it completed and perfected that revelation of God's character as the loving Father of all men, which it was the chief object of the entire life and teaching of Jesus to make to the world. It is most untrue to say that if the death of Christ was not expiatory, it was no more than the death of any martyr. His death was in any case as much greater than any martyr's, as his life and personality were greater than any martyr's. The significance of any death is not the act of dying, for we all die, but in the character of him who dies. The most orthodox theologian is compelled to stress that, and to regard the expiatory value of Christ's death as resting on his Person, not on the mere fact of his death. If we deny expiatory value to the death of Christ, the significance of his Person remains, unaffected by any theory of atonement.

Some sort of death was an inseparable part of the human life of the Son of God. Without experiencing death, he could not have been a full man. Without death, the Captain of our salvation could not have been "made perfect through suffering." The particular death of Jesus on the cross was the natural effect and culmination of his prophetic labors, Judaea being what it was in his day. He could not be faithful to his mission and fail so to die. Not his death of the cross *per se,* therefore, but his death in obedience to his Father's will, and in the accomplishment of his mission of revealing God to men and so reconciling men to God, is the significant thing. Jesus died for the world in the same sense that he lived and taught

([1]) Heb. 9:13, 14, 22, 26; 10:10, 14.

for the world. His whole life was a sacrifice, an offering to his Father of a lowly and obedient heart, not his death merely.

It has already been asserted that no doctrine of atonement can be deduced from the words of Jesus, without doing inexcusable violence to them. It should be added that this does not necessarily involve the inference that no doctrine of atonement is possible or true. The thesis cannot possibly be maintained that Jesus taught all truth, and that nothing is to be accepted as true in the sphere of religion, if it cannot be found in his words. The thesis that can be maintained is, that Jesus taught all that is fundamental in religious truth, and therefore no doctrine can be accepted as true that is irreconcilable with his teaching. His promise of the Spirit of Truth, to lead his disciples into all the truth, warrants us in hoping and believing that continual progress in apprehension of truth is possible to us. But no later development of Christian ideas can set aside positive teaching of Jesus. Whatever contradicts Jesus is not a further increment of truth, but an increment of error.

Consequently, whatever ideas of atonement we hold, they must, to be worthy of even provisional acceptance as truth, be in full accord with the teaching of Jesus: that God freely forgives men their sins on condition of repentance solely; that he forgives men their sins, because he loves us as a Father. And furthermore, the main feature of a doctrine of atonement should be its capacity and tendency to promote that repentance, or change of attitude toward God and man, which alone procures the divine forgiveness.[1]

---

[1] "The first question to ask concerning any dogma of the Church is not whether it conforms, or does not conform, to orthodox standards, but whether it serves to reveal or obscure the Figure of the Living Christ. For thousands of willing souls Christ lies buried in a grave of theological subtleties. It is for us to roll away the stones, not to dispute about the inscriptions upon them." E. Herman, "Christianity in the New Age," p. 180. N. Y., 1919.

VI

Jesus taught, then, that the way of deliverance is by repentance, change of attitude toward God. God forgives the sinner because he is God, our Father. Jesus nowhere claims that he procures from God forgiveness of sins for man; he makes known to man God's love and consequent willingness to forgive sins. Paul taught that deliverance is by way of propitiation and expiation: God forgives because his Son has made a sacrifice for man, and by trust in that sacrifice the sinner is "justified." Are these two forms of teaching so mutually incompatible that if we choose one we must reject the other?

Not if we understand neither as giving us, or attempting to give us, a scientific definition of God's forgiveness of sins. Not if we understand both Jesus and Paul to be illustrating the character of God and his forgiveness through human relations. Not if we concede that all illustrations are not the truth, but the clothes of truth. Illustrations can give us only glimpses of underlying reality, helpful but not exhaustive. None separately, nor all together, can tell us the whole truth about God and his relation to men. Viewed as scientific definitions, the teaching of Jesus and Paul cannot be reconciled; viewed as illustrations, each may be regarded as exhibiting part of the truth.

Nevertheless, it seems to be open to us to say that one illustration discloses more of God's nature than another, that one conveys a better idea of the essential truth than another, that one conforms better than another to the ethics of to-day, that one is drawn from dead institutions while another is in accord with living experiences. So that the antithesis between Jesus and Paul is not necessarily that between absolute truth and absolute error, but that between higher truth and lower, between better methods of setting forth the character of God and his dealings with us and inferior methods. Will religion lose anything, will even theology be seriously damaged, by admission that Jesus understood God better than Paul? Shall we fear to say that the relation of Fatherhood helps our age to understand God better than the relation of Judge?

Truth—meaning our apprehension of truth—is relative not absolute, dynamic not static, progressive not final. Paul's teachings about justification and atonement were finer and higher ideas of God and his relations to men than had been previously known to those who first read his letters. They continued to be helpful ideas for many generations. We are fortunate enough now to have attained still better ideas, chiefly through fuller comprehension of what Jesus taught. Must Paul, once an inspiration to Christian thought, henceforth be an incubus, because we insist on valuing the form of his teaching more highly than the substance?

The essential content of Paul's doctrine of atonement, apart from the form in which it is conveyed, is capable of restatement in terms of individual ethical responsibility, to which the world has now advanced. The difficulty is more than half eliminated the moment we assent to the proposition that Paul does not give us rigid and precise scientific formulae, that he is not a systematic theologian in the sense that Augustine and Thomas Aquinas were such. We shall then attach no more than their proper meaning to words like "propitiation," "redemption," "justification" and the like. Regarding such terms as fluid, not rigid, without doing them violence we can reach an interpretation that will accord with modern ethical ideas. For example, when the apostle says that the death of Jesus was to establish the righteousness of God (not his justice, as Paul's interpreters say), did he necessarily mean anything more than this: that the death of Jesus was the supreme act of obedience in a life wholly ruled by the will of his Father?

So interpreted, the sacrificial or expiatory element in

Paul's atonement teaching is not fundamental, but the vicarious. And this Jesus teaches as clearly as Paul. He could not do less and be a teacher of truth. The father of the Prodigal suffered with and for his wayward son. In all human forgiveness there is an element of self-sacrifice, which justifies the numerous sayings to the effect that Jesus bore the sins of men and gave himself in their behalf. The error has been in pouring the emotional and highly figurative language of prophets and poets into the mould of hard, precise theologic definition.

Vicarious suffering cannot be questioned. It runs all through life. Everywhere the innocent suffers for the guilty, not as his substitute, but as his partner. This is the price that men pay for the great blessings of family and social relations. A man can no more escape suffering from the sins of others than he can prevent their suffering for his sins. This is the meaning of brotherhood, the indelible truth of the old clan ethics: we are one race, and the sins of each are the sins of all. By sharing our humanity, the Son of God obligated himself to bear our griefs and sorrows. The solidarity of the race compels such suffering, and Jesus could not have escaped if he would. By so much as his office as Messiah and Deliverer set him above other men, by so much was his burden of the sins and sorrows of mankind increased.

It follows, therefore, that Jesus bore the sins of the world in a sense unique and to a degree unexampled. Partaker of our nature, he was not actual partaker of our sins, yet he bore them. He bore our sins as a hater of sin and a lover of men—sin offended his moral purity, it debased those dear to him. He bore our sin as one who tries to put it away, to destroy it. He did this as our fellowman; he did it as the Man in whom God dwelt most richly of all men, so that he became an expression of God and what God did he did through him. This was "the joy set before him" that enabled him to endure the cross, despising shame: the noble gladness of knowing that his endurance of sin was the deliverance of others. His suffering was truly redemptive, because in all the ages it has led men to forsake evil and seek the noble life and the true. The voluntary suffering of love that we see in him makes all other suffering for sin appear poor and small.

How can the innocent suffer the penalty of others' guilt? Because of his purity of soul Jesus must have lived under the most powerful consciousness of the nature of moral wrong and its effects on life and character. In that was a far more acute suffering than the mere consciousness of personal ill desert could have caused. He bore our sins, therefore, because he lived under the crushing weight of the world's sinfulness, took upon his soul the burden of all human souls. His life and death were a solemn testimony, out of the depths of this bitter experience, to the hatefulness of everything evil; and equally solemn testimony to the excellence of all the good. It was a vindication of the divine character, of the divine standards of conduct. And that he, in whom God visibly dwelt, should undergo this experience, was the highest possible testimony to God's love for a lost world.

"God was in Christ reconciling the world to himself." In these words Paul has given us his highest conception of atonement. Other attempts to explain are on a distinctly lower ethical plane. Indeed we should do well to banish the word "atonement" from religious literature altogether, and use instead the word "reconciliation," which is both more Scriptural and more rational. It may be granted that there is no single, uniform explanation of the work of Christ in the New Testament, or even in the writings of Paul. There has already been too much "systematizing," that has been the root of many evils. Still, "reconciliation" is the best word, if not the exclusive word, to describe our loftiest ideal of Christ's work. Reconciliation is the bringing of God and men into moral unity and mutual fellowship. It is not a doctrine, but a fact of history and experience, that Jesus in his death has been the supreme means of reconciling men to God. All schools of theology will grant that. What they differ about is the process by which reconciliation has been accomplished. It is matter of comparative indifference how reconciliation is accounted for, provided we hold fast to the fundamental thing: this is not primarily a question of law and government, but of relation between persons.

One other word that Paul uses has been seriously misinterpreted, "propitiation." This has almost uniformly been seized upon and employed by theologians to support their ideas of sacrifice and substitution, which we have seen to be ethically untenable. In this they have done injustice to Paul. True, in the spoken Greek of apostolic times, it was not uncommon to describe propitiatory gifts to the gods as ἱλαστήρια (¹) and Paul may have been acquainted with this usage of the word. But he was certainly much better acquainted with its use in the Septuagint, where it invariably(²) denotes the *kapporeth,* or cover of the ark of the covenant in the Holy of Holies of the Tabernacle. Here, between the wings of the cherubim, was the *shekinah,* the radiance or glory of Jehovah, visible symbol of his presence with his people and his willingness to forgive sins. Since the time of Tyndale, the term "mercy-seat" has been found in all English versions as the equivalent of ἱλαστήριον. Paul(³) and the letter to the Hebrews(⁴) use this word metaphorically of Jesus. It is inconceivable that they should have had in mind the heathen sense of it, rather than the thought it would instantly suggest to every Jew. No, they intended to say of Jesus that he is our "mercy-seat," the meeting-place of

(¹) Deissmann, Biblical Studies, p. 131.
(²) Ex. 25:17, 22; 26:34; 40:20; Lev. 16:2, 13; Num. 7:89.
(³) Rom. 3:25.
(⁴) Heb. 9:5; 2:17.

God and man, the visible symbol of God's presence with his people and the surety of the divine forgiveness.([1])   In this sense, the only interpretation that accords with probability, the word is fully in accord with the ideal of reconciliation, and certainly suggests nothing of sacrifice or expiation or substitution.([2])

([1]) The kindred word ἱλασμός, found in 1 John 2:2, 4:10, will bear the same interpretation without violence.

([2]) For a full conspectus of the Scripture passages relating to atonement, see Appendix.

CHAPTER X

WHAT THEN IS CHRISTIANITY?

I

WHAT is Christianity? Is it chiefly a life or chiefly an institution? Is Christianity the Church, historic, present or possible?

According to Jesus, Christianity is the Kingdom of God. He cherished a social ideal, a vision of a reconstructed world, a new human society, composed of regenerated men, a society of which good will to others, mutual service and helpfulness, was to be the law. To be a member of the Kingdom was to undertake the Great Adventure of the spirit, which may involve much privation and pain, but leads to the heights of achievement and blessedness. The teaching of Jesus affords no hint of purpose to establish an organization, though he must have known (since any man of good sense would know it) that something of the sort would almost certainly grow out of his teaching. Indeed, he must have been sensible that without organized propaganda his words would be evanescent, and his influence as a teacher would prove no more than a ripple on the world's life. Yet he seemed utterly careless about organization; his to supply the spirit, others might provide the body, of his new society.

Paul occasionally mentions the Kingdom, but only occasionally and only mentions. He does not use the word in the gospel sense, but rather as something pertaining to the future life. Even in the fourth Gospel the ideal of Jesus has visibly faded from the consciousness of his disciple. Paul's idea of the "gospel," as we have seen, is not the immediate coming of the Kingdom, but a Message of forgiveness of sins through the death of the Christ, in consequence of which one is admitted to the heavenly Kingdom. And in Paul's mind organization is a most important thing. He spent his life in founding and extending the *ecclesia,* local organizations of believers in Jesus after the model of the Jewish synagogue, the chief function of which was to make known everywhere the Message he had delivered to them. So great importance did these groups assume in his eyes, that he declared that Christ died for the *ecclesia,* that the *ecclesia* was the body of Christ, the Temple of the Holy Spirit.

The rapid transformation of the "faith" of Jesus into the Faith, from a spirit and life into a creed, a cult and a Church, is one of the most interesting and fruitful of all historical studies; but this is not the place for even a brief outline of it. What we are just now interested to note is, that during the first stages of the transformation the continued influence of Jesus is indicated by the earliest and most persistent name for his religion, "the Way." By this name, the Church testified in word, even while denying it in deed, that the chief legacy of Jesus to the world was an ideal of life. And, however much overlaid by tradition and ritual, this truth has never been quite lost. "Throughout the whole history of the Church," says Weizsäcker very justly, "the imitation of Jesus, and the contemplation of the whole personality of that sincere and living human soul, has represented a distinct stream, a distinct form of Christianity, of peculiar simplicity and force, which holds the balance against the Pauline form."[1]

The colossal hypocrisy of embattled nations praying to the same God for power to kill each other has dealt the finishing blow to men's faith in the historic Christianity,

[1] "The Apostolic Age," I:173.

the religion embodied in institutions. If Christianity cannot be reinterpreted, if it cannot be reëmbodied, if it cannot be made to mean something it has never meant since apostolic times, it is doomed. The Church to-day is not an agent for establishing the Kingdom, but a competitor of the Kingdom. The first task of the Church— of any church—is to increase its own numbers, property, income and influence in its community. The success of any minister, of whatever badge or title, is measured by his efficiency in accomplishing this specific task. His one duty is "to build up the Church," and woe to him if he fails. He is the slave of institutionalism.

The new Christianity that we must have, if we are to have any, is simply a renewal of the Christianity of Jesus, so long overlaid by tradition as to be lost sight of, so long denied by the official teachers of religion as to become forgotten. In its zeal for things, historic Christianity has ignored men. And so far as it has concerned itself with men, it has held up to them a wrong ideal. Its conception of Christian character has long been mainly a series of negatives—a notion that was put into a quaint phrase by a late popular "evangelist," who described being a Christian as equivalent to "quit your meanness," give up your vicious practices and stop neglecting your business.

And so it has come to pass that the Church is giving to the world a distorted, inadequate, and therefore false, interpretation of Christianity. It is laying emphasis on the unessential things, the negative virtues, and slurring over the essential and positive, until the world no longer connects the essentials specifically with Christianity. Men who are learning to esteem unselfishness, generosity, helpfulness, as the great and fine things of life, do not commonly think of these as Christian virtues. In their view a Christian is a man who does not gamble or drink or swear or smoke or run after women, and especially one who carefully shuns the company of men who do these things, and cultivates a spirit of self-righteousness in consequence. That to be a Christian is something much finer and manlier than abstinence from personal vices ("these ought ye to have done and not to leave the other undone"), the man of the world has no idea whatever, and the "Christian" himself has little.

But the Church has often shown a marvellous power of recuperation. There have been times many before ours, when it seemed in the last agonies of dissolution, and it has nevertheless awakened to new life, much to the discomfiture of its foes and to the great delight of its friends. It may be that such an awakening of historic Christianity, such a refashioning of its institutions, is at hand. But nothing short of entire revolution in its ideals and methods, full recovery of the spirit of Jesus, will suffice. The Church must cease to be merely ameliorative and become regenerative. Undoubtedly there is a vast amount of human misery that, since it cannot be immediately cured, should be relieved; but this should be a mere by-product of Christianity, not its chief aim. If Jesus can do no more than

> make a dying bed
> Feel soft as downy pillows are,

he is out of date. It is help in life, not death, for which the hard beset man of to-day is looking and longing; and no religion that does not offer this has the slightest chance of acceptance with him. It is because Jesus is still in the world, as an energizing, creative Spirit, and because he can give help to struggling, despairing men, as no one else ever has given or can give, that there is still hope for Christianity. Let us who know of this power tell the world about it, and a new Christianity will be born out of men's new experience.

II

What is Christianity? Is it a form of worship, or a form of sound words, or a form of polity, or a form of ministering the sacraments? If it is none of these things, but the negation of forms, a thing of the spirit and not of the letter, where shall we look for Christianity to-day? Is it not true that those who "profess and call themselves Christians" are concerning themselves mainly with forms? It will do the reader good to answer these questions for himself, and he will be wise to think awhile before he speaks. The world is answering them now, and if men must choose between the dryness and anarchism that goes by the name of Protestantism and the paralyzing spiritual despotism called Catholicism, they will assuredly choose—neither!

That religion is an affair of the spirit is quite emphatically and unanimously affirmed by Christian teachers, however their practice may contradict their words. Thus they bear testimony to the truth that the power of Christianity lies in its capacity of development and recuperation—a power shown no less strikingly in its institutions than in individual lives. In other words, Christianity is and always has been what it was first proclaimed to be, a way of life, the power of God unto salvation. But deliverance of a soul is not a mechanical thing; it is a spiritual process that cannot be accomplished by sacrifices or sacraments. It is quite in accord with human indolence that men should look for a salvation to be accomplished in something done for them. It is very sweet—for some—to sing:

> Nothing either great or small
> Remains for me to do;
> Jesus died and paid it all,
> All the debt I owe.

But what if the theology of this is as poor as the poetry? What if there never was any "debt" and Jesus has there-

fore "paid" nothing? What if everything remains for
us to do? "But salvation is the gift of God; the Scriptures say so; and we have but to stretch out hands of faith
and receive." The premise is correct; the Scriptures "say
so"; yet the conclusion, while it appears to be logical, is
really a *non sequitur*. Salvation is as much a gift of God
as daily bread, but on the same condition: man must work
for it. The ideal of Jesus is a salvation accomplished by
men, not for them, from within, not from without. Jesus
does not deny God's grace; he tells us how God's grace
acts. God inspires the desire for deliverance, God sup-
plies the power, but the work must be done by the saved
man in his own soul, or he is never saved. Any other
deliverance of a free moral agent is inconceivable. Man
must be the captain of his own soul; God has so made
him; his final orders must come from himself.

In all our theology, our philosophizing about religion,
we must keep close to the facts of experience to ensure
validity to our results. Only the assured facts of the
Christian life can impart this element of reality to our
thinking. "The deepest and most precious faith," says a
recent writer, "the faith none can afford to lose, is the
faith that to discover the truth about reality and to follow
this truth loyally, will in the end lead to the highest good.
To live by error or illusion is costly."[1] Our deepest
conviction should be that it is best for us to know the
truth and adjust to it our thinking, our conduct and our
hope. And so, as religious experience has developed, as
it has advanced, as it has become richer, more complex,
as through it we are ever more approximating the ultimate spiritual reality, theology has been continually
changing. This is a necessity of the case, nothing less
than a spiritual law. The greatest error of historic Christianity, an error so grave in results as to be both tragic
and pathetic, has been its agelong effort to substitute for

---

[1] W. G. Everett, "Moral Values," p. 420. N. Y. 1918.

the ever ripening expression of the inner life of Christians of all ages the Christian experience of a single age, as an unchanging, authoritative, infallible norm of the Christian life for all time to come. Instead of something dynamic, the attempt has been to make theology static. The bane of religion is the dogmatist's search for authority, and his insistence that he has found authority where none exists. For, in the usual sense of the word, there is no authority in religion, nothing fixed, unalterable, infallible; because religion is life, and life is growth, and growth is change.

Therefore theology ought to be no bed of Procrustes, on which we place this New Testament document and that religious experience, chopping off a bit here, stretching out a bit there, until everything fits exactly into our preordained "system." That too nearly describes the method of all theology of the past, but such will not be the method of the future. A too ingenious exegesis, warranted to make all parts of the Bible agree to a hair's breadth, is impossible to reconcile with the profession that these words are Holy Writ, and therefore demand from us especially honest handling. A scientific exegesis will not press the word of one writer into artificial agreement with another, nor evacuate one part of all real meaning to "harmonize" it with something else, nor read into the text ideas that could never have entered the minds of the writers, in the vain hope of making all say the same things.

After all, the question comes to this: Is there any sound foundation for religion in the facts of life, interpreted according to our progressive knowledge of man and the world? Or is religion, as many to-day are telling us, nothing more than a synthesis of the dreams of enthusiasts and the babble of theologians? The sound conclusion seems to be that religion has to do with verifiable facts of experience; and that its mysteries, some of which may prove insoluble, are yet no greater than the mysteries that confront science. A difference of terminology has long hidden this even from men ordinarily keen-sighted: where religion says "faith" science says "hypothesis." Both involve the same mental process and the same spiritual attitude. The hypotheses of science are the response to the mind's demand for intellectual unity and completeness. They outrun full demonstration. That is scientific faith, and religious faith differs no whit. God is a hypothesis equally with gravitation, and one hypothesis is no more matter of faith than the other. Gravitation is a hypothesis that attempts to unify our knowledge of the heavenly bodies and explain their movements. All that we really know is that stars and planets behave *as if* they were mutually attracted in a certain way. Likewise the entire cosmos behaves *as if* there were a Being who includes and unifies all the phenomena of nature, all the elements of experience, into one organic life process, controlled by intelligence, will and goodness.

The problem of theology is not a question of knowing everything, or of fully comprehending anything; it is a question of unifying our knowledge and clarifying our ideas and refusing to pretend to believe contradictories. The essence of obscurantism is blind clinging to discredited facts and theories of religion, and it is the "theology" guilty of this unpardonable sin that is here held up to reprobation. A Christian theology will be a necessity so long as there is a Christian life; for religion must not consist of mere vague emotions and aspirations, but must be founded in a definite philosophy of life, corresponding to our scientific knowledge as well as to our inner experience, or it cannot successfully appeal to a world that more and more demands reality as a basis for its living. If such a theology as this is impossible, then religion is doomed to become the sole property of the "neurotic, the erotic and the tommyrotic."

III

What is Christianity? Who shall tell us, Paul or Jesus? Which teaches the truth that Christians should accept as fundamental and authoritative? And, if the answer to this is, "Both," then comes the further question, Are their teachings mutually in agreement, or are there elements in each that are mutually contradictory and exclusive? Is there a rational way of holding both teachings, as to substance at least? Have their words been misunderstood, distorted into semblance of contradiction that does not actually exist?

As to the teachings of Jesus, distortion is certain. The fact concerning his work that most moves our wonder and pity is that nobody understood him. The great tragedy of Jesus was not his death but his life. No human being has been so solitary. There were those who loved him, a few, but among them all he had not one real friend, not one to whom he could bare his inmost soul and be sure of sympathetic hearing. Weep over the dying Jesus, ye who will, while those who have eyes to see mourn the living Jesus, the man who had none to whom he could unlock his heart. Loneliness is the penalty of greatness, and none was ever so lonely as he, because among all the sons of men he was greatest.

Yet, in spite of mental impenetrability, a certain measure of the truth did percolate through the souls of those in the inner circle of disciples and became the possession of all his followers. The memory of his hearers, fortunately for us, was better than their insight, and they preserved with remarkable fidelity teachings that they neither believed nor comprehended. Do we lay ourselves open to a charge of complacent conceitedness by this assumption that our generation understands Jesus better than his own? Some may think so; some will certainly not lose the opportunity to say so. But others will reason thus: If nineteen centuries of divine Providence and Christian

experience have thrown no additional light on the significance of the Man and the Teaching, what are Providence
and Christian experience good for? One is content to
leave his critics to wrestle with that problem.

And if the teaching of Jesus has been misunderstood and
distorted, so has that of Paul. There is an element of philosophizing about the facts of religion in his letters that is
totally absent from the words of Jesus, but that of itself
constitutes no real difficulty. Paul could not help being
shaped by the school of Gamaliel, nor could he avoid the
powerful influence of the prevailing Greco-Roman civilization of Tarsus. These things imply differences between
him and Jesus, but not contradictions. It is to later
thinkers, taking shelter behind his name, that we are to
look for the contradictions. Historic Paulinism is as little
the creation of the apostle, as historic Christianity is the
creation of Jesus. Both are sheer perversions of their
original. The highly speculative element in Paulinism
was mainly the contribution of Greek philosophy through
the influence of the Fathers of Alexandria, of whom
Clement and Origen were most eminent. They, and not
Paul, are the real authors of Christian theology. Both
were Platonists. They made much use of Paul's writings,
but vastly transformed his ideas while most professing
to follow the great apostle.

Under this Greek influence, Christianity was made a
philosophy for the cultivated, while at the same time, under the spell of certain Asiatic cults, it was made a mystery
for the ignorant. The two tendencies combined in Catholicism, and Augustine put the capstone on the edifice.
His interpretation of Paul has passed current for the
original teaching of the apostle to our own day. If Augustine failed in any detail to complete the transformation of
Paul, Calvin supplied the defect.

No student of the early centuries, however, can avoid
the conclusion that, if Christianity means chiefly a scheme

of doctrine, Paul is its real source. That is to say, his writings furnish the primary materials out of which later theologians formulated that chain of doctrines that for centuries has been called the "gospel." Such, for example, as that "in Adam's fall we sinned all"; that the Son of God, who lived in the divine likeness and glory, but took upon himself human form, died as a propitiation for the sins of men; that faith in him justifies the sinner without works of law; that only those specially chosen by God believe and are saved; that Christ will come again to judge the world, and the bodies of men will be raised from their graves, and the saints will reign with Christ forever. This is historic Paulinism, and it is historically true that the religion of Jesus did not assimilate Paulinism, but succumbed to it.

The undeniable difference between Paul and Jesus was made an absolute antithesis by the early Church, and has remained an antithesis to this day. Wherever Jesus and Paul agree, the followers of Paul are comparatively silent. Wherever Jesus and Paul seem to differ, they not only follow Paul but exaggerate the difference. In every case where it is at all feasible, they substitute Paul for Jesus. Now if this antithesis is to be maintained, if we must choose between the Jesus of the Gospels and the Paul of the theologians, we must choose Jesus. Else, let us cease to call ourselves Christians and rename ourselves Paulicians, as certain heretical sects once frankly did. And surely of all possible heresies the least pardonable is to profess to follow Jesus and really to follow Paul.

But if Paul may be reasonably interpreted once more, as he has not been since the days of Augustine, we may keep both him and Jesus as the chief teachers of our faith. What the Christian world can no longer afford to do, is to let the theologians' Paul thrust Jesus into the background. It can no longer afford to permit the social gospel that was the essence of the original Christianity to be over-sloughed by a theology called Pauline, but really an un-Pauline Greek philosophy long since discarded by philosophers, but still held fast by theologians. The freedom that Paul once asserted from the law of works, we must now claim from the law of dogma. Such freedom is our birthright.

IV

What is Christianity? Is there place in it for Paulinism?

We have reached the conclusion that the divergence between Paul and Jesus would cease to appear serious, in any theologic sense, if a reasonable interpretation of the writings of Paul were substituted for the unreasonable perversion of them that has so long obtained. For it is essentially unreasonable not to distinguish things that plainly differ, to identify things that should be kept carefully separate in our thinking. The solution of our problem has already been foreshadowed. Most of our difficulties in relation to the apostle's teachings disappear when we adopt as the principle of interpretation the simple hypothesis that Paul is not stating "eternal truths," not formulating dogmas for all time, but illustrating permanent religious and ethical principles in terms of thought comprehensible by his own age.

It would be a reasonable corollary from this principle that analogies suggested by institutions then existing would be illuminating to Paul's contemporaries, but that now, when those institutions have ceased to exist, the ideas connected with them have also ceased to have force and significance. It is the identification of the passing show of his own age with the permanent in religion, that has made the great apostle the apparent leader of the blind into the ditch of unbelief. Once let us get it clearly in mind that the illustration is not to be identified with the truth illustrated, that the analogy is temporary but the principle permanent, and real antagonism between Jesus and Paul no longer exists. Differences remain, but not contradictions.

An instance of what is meant lies on the very surface of the Epistles. Paul's letters are full of assertions that believers are the "slaves" of Christ, and of illustrations founded on slavery.([1]) It was perfectly natural that he should choose slavery as an analogy of the new and intimate relation that exists between the believer and Christ, that the sense of obligation, strict and indissoluble, to him who had shown himself to be the Great Deliverer should so express itself. Slavery was a universal institution in the first century, as familiar in all its details as the family relation, and lending itself as easily to illustration of religious truth. But while the family still endures, slavery has gone. What was natural to Paul is unnatural to us.

We can no longer think in terms of slavery. The institution has so far passed away from our knowledge and experience that it has no more reality for us than the relations of feudalism. If Paul had lived in the Middle Ages he would undoubtedly have likened the believer's relation to Christ to that of vassal and overlord, and the illustration would then have been significant and helpful. But analogies drawn from slavery or feudalism or any past state of society are a hindrance rather than a help to men of our age. Before they are valid, they must be translated into terms of our own experience. Untranslated they do not give us any assistance in understanding our relation to Jesus, but function as a barrier between us and him. For he is not in reality an owner and we his chattel slaves, nor is he an overlord and we his vassals.

([1]) Three of his letters he begins by calling himself a slave of Christ (Romans, Philippians, Titus). He describes himself and Timothy to the Corinthians as "your slaves for Jesus' sake"; he calls the former state of unbelief "slaves of sin," and the new status of the believer as "slaves of righteousness," "Christ's slave," "slaves of the Lord" and the like. Gal. 1:10; 1 Cor. 7:22; Eph. 6:5; 2 Tim. 2:24; Col. 4:12.

It is not because we wish to deny the reality of the bond between us and him that no Christian of to-day can think of himself as slave or vassal to Jesus. We do not desire to make the bond less strait and enduring, but these analogies are impossible to us. "Slave" and "vassal" no longer illustrate truth; they only obscure truth.

What are called the "great doctrines" of Paul are of the same character precisely: illustrations of religious truth from contemporary thought, analogies from contemporary institutions. Paul and Calvin had one experience in common, a fundamental experience that conditioned all their thinking. Both had been brought up under the shadow of Roman imperialism; both had been indoctrinated with the principles of Roman law. The spirit of Roman institutions had made an ineradicable impression on their minds. They were one in conceiving the character and acts of God in the light of the greatest institution and the greatest personage known to their respective times, the Roman Empire and its Emperor. The sovereignty of God, his omnipotent power, his absolute rights over the world and the race he had created, seemed to them elemental truth about God, and so each made this the fundamental postulate of his theology.

Because of their familiarity with monarchs and trappings of royalty the Scripture writers generally, and Paul especially, put many of their truths in forms that are for us quite obsolete and meaningless. Or, so far as they have meaning for us, it is a wrong meaning, so wrong as often to be repulsive. The popular caricature of the Scriptural teachings about God, though a caricature, retains many of the features of the original: An absentee God, an Almighty King on a distant throne, with a court of angels ever about him singing his praises, flattered by the homage of men and constantly interfering with the affairs of the universe in response to the selfish pleas of sycophantic worshipers—this is the popular "God." These unworthy ideas defile a large part of our hymnology, and still supply the greater part of the phraseology of our prayers, yet no respectable Christian thinker to-day conceives God after this fashion.

On the contrary, we conceive God in a fashion very different. We look on Kaiser and imperialism, not with admiration, but with abhorrence; if God were such as he, we would as soon worship the devil. Emperors are an anachronism. Despotism, on earth or in the heavens, is unthinkable. To us God is not monarch, but Father, and the greatest thing in his personality is not sovereignty but love. He is not seated on a distant throne, but is the ever-present Power in whom we live and move. It is no longer true for us that

> God's in his heaven,
> All's right with the world.

If God were in his heaven, all would be most wrong with the world. All's right with the world, because God is not in some far-away heaven, but is here in the world he has made, in the struggle of his creatures, fighting with them to win greater victories over evil, toiling by their side to bring in a larger good than men have yet known. An autocratic God, despotically ruling the universe from the outside, sufficed the age of Calvin, as it did that of Paul; but we must have a democratic God, an immanent God, a God who dwells with us and in us, a God who is still in the throes of creation, a God who calls us to be his comrades and helpers in the enterprise of making a new earth wherein righteousness dwells.

According to the author of Genesis, God created man in his own image, but that statement suggests a much larger content to our minds that it did to his. We can no longer think, as that Hebrew writer did, of a God who made a world in six days and "finished the work that he had made," and because he had finished his work "rested on the seventh day from all his work which he had made," and inferentially has been resting ever since. To us the creation of the world does not seem a work begun some five thousand years ago and finished out of hand in six days, but a process begun uncounted ages ago and still going on. Not instantaneous creation, but continuous creation, is our idea of divine activity. God is not an idler in the heavens but is still a Maker. "My Father has been working hitherto and I am working," said Jesus.

Creating man in God's image is God's greatest work, as the writer of Genesis said, but it is a work by no means finished. We may well look for the coming, not of Nietzsche's Superman, a Gulliver amidst Lilliputians, but for a race of Supermen, as far greater than men now living as are the highest races of to-day greater than their savage ancestors—as far greater, perhaps, as those savages were greater than the brutes from which they sprang. Our confidence in the indefinite perfectibility of man rests on our belief in the continuous creative activity of God. He has something to make of man better and higher than we now know, or perhaps can now conceive. The "new creation" in Christ Jesus of which Paul speaks([1]) is now in process of creation, and in a deeper sense than that intended by the apostle John we may say, "Now are we children of God, and it is not yet made manifest what we shall be."([2])

A larger idea of salvation follows necessarily from this larger conception of God and his works. The epic of redemption is not the story of a single soul, striving against giants and angels and demons for a few years to attain a solitary holiness, but the struggle of a race through countless generations to realize an ideal of social righteousness, justice and love. So far as Paulinism can help in this struggle, it will be a welcome ally. By far the greater

([1]) 2 Cor. 5:17; Gal. 6:15.
([2]) 1 John 3:2.

part of what the world has hitherto called "saintliness"—
a cultivation of the personal virtues, with absolute disregard of duties to fellowmen—is mere evasion of duty and
far from the admirable thing it has long been conceived
to be.   Indeed, the world is nearly ready for the assertion
that the greater the "saint" the greater the sinner.   In
this warfare, the "slacker" will find little tolerance.   The
old Roman proverb, *Unus Christianus est nullus Christianus*—one Christian is no Christian at all—had a good
deal of truth wrapped up in its five terse words.   Quietism
is not, as Nietzsche declared, the logical development of
the gospel, but its antipodes.

Religion begins historically in clan ideas, in the totem
and taboo, and not in individual seekings after God.   It
is in its essence and inmost fiber social, and all its institutions have a social origin.   Hence redemption must be a
social process.   Regeneration is not individual, because
sin is not individual.   But a minute fraction of human
evil, if any fraction at all, concerns a single person only.
Sin is social; its consequences affect the entire social group,
as well as the erring individual.   The cure of sin must
therefore be as much social as individual.   We must learn
to think of sin as an offense against our fellows primarily,
an offense against God in our fellows.   This larger view
of sin will revolutionize Christianity, and make it once
more the social force its Founder designed it to be.

When we thus conceive God and his relations to us, religion takes on a richer meaning than we can find in the
writings of Paul.   His teaching is not false, but in large
part outgrown.   His appeal is too much to the individual
soul to secure salvation by individual faith.   This is a
gospel of selfishness, that falls below the best ethical standard of the world outside the Church—a world that has
come to acknowledge, if not to practice consistently, the
truth that there is in man an instinct higher than self-
interest, the instinct of love, altruism, thought for the

other man.   The Church can never win on its present
lines, which are the lines of Paulinism.   It needs a revival of true religion more sorely than those whom in its
complacency it calls "the unsaved."   Of course, those
within the pale of the Church cannot easily be persuaded
that they are not among the securely "saved," yet the
real fact is that their case is often more hopeless than that
of the "unsaved," because they are so steeped in religious
conceit and so ignorant of what real "salvation" is.

The revival that the Church needs is therefore one that
will lift it out of its present complacency and selfishness,
that will make it hear the call of God to the heroic in man,
that will appeal to that capacity for struggle and self-
sacrifice which is the true image of God in us.   The
Church needs a revival that will inspire it to put far away
the desire of glory and happiness and ease, that will make
it listen to the divine voice that holds out to us as our reward of service, not a lazy heaven, but the joy of creation,
the glory of bringing good out of evil, beauty out of ugli-
ness, order out of chaos—the stern joy that warriors feel,
not the allurements of pleasure and luxury.   For ours is
a warrior religion.   Let hedonism be our philosophy of
life, but let it be that exalted hedonism which values most
the joy of battle, the joy of struggle, the joy of toil.   After
all, religion is the Great Adventure.   It satisfies the deep
Wanderlust of the race, and affords full scope for the
red-blooded man's fighting instinct, his passion for achievement of the worth while.

V

What is Christianity?   Is it democracy?   The Church
of the Messiah in New York, to which men like Robert
Collyer and Minot J. Savage have ministered in the past,
which has honorable traditions as a Unitarian church, has
disclaimed Unitarianism as too narrow for its present

conceptions of religion and has transformed itself into "The Community Church of New York." Is it necessary or probable that Christian churches generally will repudiate their historic names and traditions for some democratic or socialistic title more expressive of their new ideals and aspirations? If religion is to be identified hereafter with democracy it behooves us to understand what is democracy and in what it differs from historic Christianity.

Beyond a doubt historic Christianity as a whole has been undemocratic. With few exceptions, all forms of organized religion have had an aristocratic basis. Oligarchies of ministers or bishops have ruled Protestantism, and at times Catholicism, while in these later centuries Roman Catholicism has become an absolute monarchy. There can be no permanent *modus vivendi* between such Christianity and democracy—one or the other must eventually hold the field. Only a democratic religion can survive among a democratic people.

Democracy and real Christianity have a common ethical basis, for democracy is the rule of right. Hegel was justified in his theory of the State as an organism, with a supreme claim on its members, but wrong in making force the living spirit of this body. Right, the common welfare, is the animating spirit of organic society.

Democracy and genuine Christianity have a common goal, for democracy is liberty and Christianity has always been proclaimed as deliverance. Professor Thomas H. Green once defined liberty as "positive power or capacity which each man exercises or holds through the help or security given him by his fellowmen, and which he in turn helps to secure for them." Liberty is not freedom from restraint, but power to do and enjoy. The few restraints necessary in a civilized society, to prevent any from trespassing on the equal liberty of all, are so far surpassed by the increment of privilege and capacity to do, as to be negligible. That is precisely the conception of

Christian freedom taught in the New Testament—not a surrender of anything worth while, but the acquisition of new power and privilege. Both democracy and Christianity mean that every man and woman shall enjoy a free personality in a world of equal opportunity. There will always be diversities of gifts and achievements, and these diversities should be presumed to be greater, not less, in a state of freedom than our present state of partial slavery. Social equality does not mean social identity, but it will always be better for the world that many should have silver in their pockets than that a few should have gold.

Both democracy and Christianity insist on the worth and dignity of the individual, as well as on the value of social institutions. Both demand that every human soul shall be treated as an end; the exploitation of the present order treats him as a means. Man should live for his own perfectibility, not as a machine for producing wealth for another man. The exploitation of human life and human liberties that has gone on for a century in America under the pretext of equal economic opportunity for all, is no more democracy than Russian autocracy was democracy.

All genuine ideas of democracy find powerful support in the teachings of Jesus; while the best that we can say of the writings of Paul is that they need not be construed as opposing democracy. But the teaching of Jesus cannot be harmonized with a materialistic democracy. Material prosperity was not his ideal, though he distinctly taught that all men might and should have a sufficiency. When we have won the means of living for all, we must still turn to Jesus to learn what to do with life. Let us not be surprised if for a time democracy does not fully comprehend which is the graver problem of the two, since all its energies are just now required for the solution of the first. Objectors to all proposals made for the material betterment of mankind are quick to point out that the present state of mind of the proletariat affords no bright prospect of the higher sort of progress. They argue that workingmen fail to use for self-improvement any leisure gained by shortened hours of labor, and that they therefore deserve no further concessions.

But what reason was there to expect any immediate enthusiasm for culture among workingmen? Was it to be rationally supposed that the deadening monotony of their grinding toil would give them an appetite for the higher things surpassing that of their employers? Is it not true that, with vastly greater opportunity and encouragement, the employers often have as little love of culture as their workmen, and use their leisure as badly, if a little differently? And if this be indisputably true, is it not absurd to blame the workingman for being no more high-minded than his present social betters? Give him time to become accustomed to some leisure, and opportunity to acquire a taste for literature and music and art by placing these things more easily within his reach, and after a generation or two if his mental grade is no higher than that of the present "tired business man," it may possibly be timely to criticise his low tastes and small achievement.

Our reproaches of the laborer for his lack of interest in the higher things are not so much hypercritical as hypocritical. We are not really surprised that he prefers his newspaper to poetry and philosophy, cheap fiction to Thackeray and Turgenieff; that he would rather hear ragtime than symphony; that he goes to a ball game rather than to an art gallery on a holiday. Is not the same true of ourselves, in spite of our pretense of superior "culture"? In our self-conceit, we say of the "lower classes," as we contemptuously call them, that they have no capacity of enjoyment, when the higher pursuits are in question. Perhaps we are right; but let us consider how little they have by comparison of surplus energy, of stimulus, of leisure, above all, of knowledge. If their tastes are crude and their pleasures unrefined, it is not for us to judge them, since we have for generations deprived them of opportunity to cultivate their spiritual natures.

The taunting challenge is often flung at the workers that they only envy the rich, and that at bottom their chief desire is to wear diamonds and dine at the Waldorf-Astoria. Even if that were true, what of it? If the so-called better class can find no higher use for its wealth than to spend it in vulgar display and the gratification of sense, is it so discreditable to the workers that they desire the same things that most please their supposed "betters"? The rich buy pictures—art is usually a good investment—but do not love them. The rich buy books—one must have a "library" in the house—but do not read them. The rich go to the opera—it is the best place to show off dress and jewels—and talk throughout the performance. One recalls Mark Twain's reply to a chattering hostess: "You really must come to our box again Friday night; they give Faust then." "Charmed," said Mark; "I don't think I have heard you in Faust."

Equally misplaced is that oft-heard bemoaning of democracy's contentment with mediocrity, its jealousy of genius and even of talent, its lack of graciousness and charm, its deadly monotony. All these things are true, more or less, of democracy thus far, as they have been true of aristocracy at times. They are true of democracy, not because they are inseparable from it, but because democracy has been engaged in a stern fight for existence and has therefore had little surplus of leisure or wealth to cultivate the fine art of living. Yet it might not be amiss for these mourners to recall that it was in the democratic cities of Greece that art and letters most highly flourished; and that the next most distinguished period of culture is found in the Italian democracies of the fifteenth century.

What are some of the other faults of democracy? Democracy is vicious? Yes, but democracy might lend its vices to serve as the virtues of aristocracy. Democracy is inefficient? So Germany said; but the Marne and Verdun were France's answer, and Château-Thierry, Saint-Mihiel and the Argonne were America's. It has not yet been demonstrated that democracy is inefficient, even for war; but better muddle than tyranny, if we really must choose between the two. It is not clear as yet that we must have either.

A distinguishing trait of Jesus is his trust in human nature. His unshakable faith in God included faith in man, as made in God's likeness. Pessimism was impossible to him. Many who profess to be his disciples lack his belief in the indefinite perfectibility of man; they profess as their faith that man has no possibilities save possibilities of evil. But Jesus saw in man capabilities of all good, and saw him realizing his wealth of future excellence. One who understands this attitude of Jesus, and makes it his own, comes at length to comprehend that democracy is an elemental force. To describe anyone as "a champion of democracy" or "a foe to democracy" is as ludicrous as to call anyone a friend or foe of gravitation. In the case of either force it is wholly a question of the individual's getting himself aligned with it and acting in accordance with it, or being crushed. When Mrs. Partington tried to sweep back the Atlantic, she did not undertake a more hopeless task than that of an opponent of democracy.

The remedy for the defects of democracy is more democracy; education—not in the narrower sense of instruction, but in the wider sense of the harmonious training of all human faculties, alike of body and mind. *Mens sana in corpore sano* will still do as a condensed formula, with a sufficiently liberal interpretation of *mens*. We have been making "education" too exclusively concerned with the acquirement of "all kinds of delightful and useless learning," and too little with character. Ruskin was on the right track when he said that the learner should be trained "not so much to know what he would otherwise not know, but to behave as he would not otherwise behave." With a large construction of "behave," as covering all human conduct, this would be an excellent ideal of education in a democracy.

Not the late war merely, but unseen influences of decades have been hastening the world's drift towards democracy. Royalty long ago disappeared in England, like the cat Alice saw in Wonderland, until nothing is left of it but the smile. The King is an imposing figure-head for great state functions, or in a more private way a gracious layer of corner-stones or a dignified opener of museums, but as to power—England's King is only a gown and a crown. Royalties that are not thus content to be reduced to ciphers will soon be wiped off the world's slate altogether.

Democracy is the result of a long process of evolution, in which the underlying Power of the universe has been expressing his character in man and society. So we are able to profess as our faith, "God is democracy" with quite as much confidence as when we say, "God is love." But democracy is just beginning to modify religious thought, so long cast in the molds of monarchy and aristocracy. The theologian has been saying for ages that the history of mankind is the awful record of continued and wilful rebellion against God. Democracy suggests a new reading of the history of the world. Written in rocks or books it is one story: the glorious record of a painful search after God, a sublime outreach of man towards a higher goodness. Man never "fell"—he has always been struggling upwards after the good and true, stumbling and tumbling often, but always up and on again.

From first to last we find the story of man to be a constructive process; a more and more perfect social organism has been the everlasting goal. All nature has travailed together to bring forth man—body, brain, intelligence, ethical perception, social institutions. If there had been an easier way to produce man and human society, it is rational to believe that God would have chosen it. If there were any less thorny path for man to climb the heights of being than by strife and bloodshed, would God not have taken it? The late dreadful war is of a piece with the whole development of this planet, as geology and history tell the story.

Thus far, it must be conceded, that while destructive forces have been always in existence, and at times have been so active that they seemed on the point of overwhelming humanity in one red ruin, out of apparent chaos and death have in the end always emerged life and order and beauty. Shall we not have faith that such will continue to be the event? Not only has the history of the world been a record of social progress, but religion has been the decisive factor in that progress. We may trace the stages of social melioration by the gradual elevation and purification of men's ideas regarding God and duty. The highest point in civilization yet reached is coincident with a clearer apprehension of the principle that the welfare of the individual, and even his very existence, is conditioned on the welfare of society.

Yet the pulpit still proclaims its old gospel of individualism, "Redemption is individual. You cannot get ahead one inch except on that basis."[1] But the experience of centuries assures us that you cannot get ahead more than an inch on that basis. Real, substantial progress is possible only on the basis of a redemption that is neither individual nor social exclusively, a redemption that is individual *and* social. The salvation that Jesus offers has

[1] Bishop William Fraser McDowell, "In the School of Christ," New York, 1910. He, however, soon qualifies this assertion, by saying of Christ, "His plan included a saved man, a saved society, a saved world." Lecture II.

been too narrowly conceived and proclaimed: as an individual process with incidental results on society. We are coming to conceive it as fundamentally a social enterprise, with incidental results on the individual. The individual and society mutually act and react. For this new conception of religion we go to Jesus, not to Paul.

VI

We see then that a final answer to the query, What is Christianity? is conditioned by our notion of the content of "Christianity." That content is large, for it includes a philosophy, a religion and a cult. The philosophy of Christianity, or Christian theology, is purely intellectual. As a religion, Christianity signifies a life, the means by which men try to form and maintain right relations with God and their fellows. As a cult, Christianity means the Church and its worship, rites and sacraments.

All these elements are necessary; each is indispensable in its place. The religious life must have a rational basis to make it permanently possible, and the cult is imperative to stimulate the emotional fervor without which the life languishes. Any form of religion that lacks either a theology or a cult, lacks vitality. Deism was a consistent philosophy and inculcated a high ideal of life, but it had no cult and so it died. Comte took warning from that failure and tried to provide a cult for his Positivism, but it was too fantastic for success. Frederic Harrison has, however, for more than a generation maintained at least a semblance of a positivist cult in London, but he has succeeded by virtue of making his Positivist society a feeble imitation of a Christian Church.

A philosophy of religion is possible only as it proceeds from belief that there is a God about whom we know something, and that we can come into satisfactory relations with him. Hence the controlling element in such a philosophy is the ideal of God with which we begin and from which we proceed through all our deductions. It has clearly appeared in the course of our discussions that Jesus and Paul give us quite different ideas of God. These ideas are so very different that inferences cannot be drawn from both of them combined, while inferences drawn from either taken by itself lead to conclusions so unlike that at times they can hardly be recognized as referring to the same God. The two philosophies that result from taking Jesus or Paul as fundamental authority regarding God are at variance almost as radically as any form of Christianity differs from Buddhism. Historic Christianity has followed Paul. It is the main object of this book to convince readers that the Christianity of the future must follow Jesus.

And therefore it cannot be admitted that Christianity is reducible to mere ethics, or even to "morality touched by emotion," as Matthew Arnold defined religion. Ethics may be said to be the science of values in their relation to conduct as a whole. It is the interpretation of the moral experience of the race, by discovery of the principles implicit in the experience. It thus becomes the evaluation of all values for the purpose of life. The only decisive test of ethical values is reality—"revelation" cannot override fact. What we seek is the unity of experience in the interest of truth.

But ethics is also the art of living, the application of the discovered principles to the events of daily life. Here ethics coincides with religion, without becoming identical with it. Religion and ethics agree that the ultimate value is the welfare and character of mankind. Good conduct is that which tends to promote human welfare or develop the highest type of character; bad conduct is the reverse. We call justice, truth, benevolence, chastity, virtues because experience proves that their practice has been promotive of general welfare and character. Polygamy was esteemed virtuous for centuries, but has become vicious because of observed social effects. Drunkenness and gambling, once uncondemned and then tolerated, are now universally stigmatized as vices, because they uniformly produce deterioration of character and increase human misery.

"Virtue" and "Vice" are fluid terms. The duty of almsgiving is extolled by Jesus and Mohammed and reckoned as a virtue in all religions. It was a virtue in a social condition where it was the only possible alleviation of human misery, but indiscriminate almsgiving is anything but virtuous in our day. The public and private provisions for systematic relief of suffering are now so numerous and so great, that the giving of alms without careful inquiry is merely offering a premium to professional beggary, the attempt of a certain class to live without work. A former virtue has become a vice, in which many people persist because their heads are even softer than their hearts. "Thou shalt love thy neighbor as thyself" has long been taken as warrant for handing the poor a small coin and leaving them to wallow in their riotous and sordid slums. It is now seen that we love our neighbor only if we try, not merely to relieve his immediate hunger and nakedness, but to extricate him from his poverty and make him share our prosperity. Society is beginning to apprehend that all enterprises for the mere relief of distress are vicious, and that what is demanded is a determined and intelligent campaign for its cure.

If it be objected to this analysis of conduct that its basis is the old discredited hedonism of Aristotle, it may be replied that "happiness" has been enlarged to include all those experiences of spiritual satisfaction that result from the noblest activities. It was sheer perversity that made Carlyle denounce hedonism as a "pig philosophy." Hedonism may be so narrowed as to become inadequate as an ethical theory, and like nearly everything it may be perverted, but Christian theologians should be slow to condemn it after proclaiming for centuries the happiness of Heaven as the goal of all Christian effort.

The discussion of the preceding pages has been little else than detailed exposition of three propositions, which together form a syllogism:

There has been progressive apprehension by man of the character of God, and of his purposes in the creation and maintenance of this universe.

This progressive knowledge of God is contained, in its highest form, in the Jewish and Christian collections of literature known as the Old and New Testaments, or the Bible; and it culminates in the words of Jesus, as preserved in the Gospels.

The teaching of Jesus is therefore Christianity—the norm of religious truth—and all other teaching must be compared with it and corrected by it. Whatever will not bear that test must be laid aside as part of the outworn and outgrown garments of religion.

These propositions are uncomplicated with any theological speculations regarding the person of Jesus. Obviously, if true at all, they are equally true whether Jesus was human or divine. It is for those who have followed the author patiently through these pages to say how satisfactorily the above propositions have been sustained.

APPENDIX

CONSPECTUS OF N. T. TEACHING ON ATONEMENT

Those who trust in themselves that they are orthodox, and set all others at naught, make great professions of close adherence to the Scriptures. They assert the teaching of the New Testament especially to be that Christ died as a substitute for sinners. All other teaching regarding Atonement they denounce as heresy and a denial of the supreme authority of the Bible. They have appealed to Caesar; to Caesar they shall go. Following is a list of the chief passages in the New Testament relating to Atonement, literally translated into current English, and classified according to their teaching. The list is believed to be approximately exhaustive; at any rate, it is fully representative of all the different types of teaching; and if any important passage has been omitted, it is by inadvertence, and not to evade any difficulty that it might present. It will be seen that only a single text (I Pet. 2:24) even *seems* to teach substitution; and that is a reminiscence of Old Testament poetry, the language of emotion, not of exact scientific definition.

1. ATONEMENT DUE TO DIVINE LOVE.

John 3:16, For God so loved the world that he gave his Only-Begotten Son, that every one who trusts in him may not perish but have eternal life.

Rom. 5:8, But God made known his own love unto us, in that while we were sinners Christ died in our behalf.

II Cor. 8:9, For you know the gift of our Lord Jesus Christ, that he became poor for your sakes, though he was rich, that you might be enriched by his poverty.

Eph. 5:25, Husbands, love your wives, just as Christ also loved the church and delivered himself up for her sake.

Tit. 3:4, But when the love toward man of our Saviour God appeared . . . which he poured out on us richly through Jesus Christ, our Saviour.

I Jn. 3:16, In this we know love, that he for our sakes laid down his life.

I Jn. 4:9, God's love was made evident in our case by this: God sent forth into the world his Son, the Only-Begotten, in order that we might live through him.

2. OBJECT OF ATONEMENT.

(a) to remove sin.

Rom. 5:6, Christ died in behalf of the ungodly.

Rom. 5:8, While we were yet sinners, Christ died in our behalf.

Rom. 5:19, For as, by means of the disobedience of the one man, the many were constituted sinners, so also by means of the obedience of the one, the many will be constituted righteous.

Rom. 5:21, Him who did not know sin, he made sin[1] for our sakes.

Rom. 6:10, For in that he died, he died to[2] sin, once for all.

Heb. 9:26, To put away sin he has been manifested.

I Pet. 2:24, Who himself bore our sins in his own body on the tree.

I. Pet. 3:18, Because also Christ suffered once for all in behalf of sin, the righteous in behalf of the unrighteous.

I. Jn. 3:5, And you know that he appeared to take away sins.

(b) to vindicate God's character.

Rom. 3:21, 26, Apart from law, a righteousness of God has been manifested . . . by means of trust in Jesus Christ

---

[1] That is, treated him as if he were a sinner.

[2] The probable meaning is, "He died with reference to sin," or "in relation to sin."

. . . for exhibition of his righteousness in the present time, to the end that he may be just and the justifier of him who is of trust in Jesus.

3. ATONEMENT, HOW EFFECTED.

(a) by the death of Christ.

John 3:14,15, As Moses lifted up the serpent in the wilderness, so must the Son of Man be lifted up, that every man who trusts in him may have eternal life.

II Cor. 5:14, For the love of Christ constrains us, who judge this: that one died in behalf of all; therefore they all died.

Heb. 2:9, That he by God's grace, in behalf of every one might taste death.

See also Rom. 5:8 and I Jn. 3:16 under (1); Rom. 5:6, 8; 6:10; and I Pet. 2:24, under (2); and Heb. 9:15 under (5).

All passages referring to "the cross" (such as Gal. 6:14; I Cor. 1:18; Heb. 12:2) or to being "crucified with Christ," (such as Gal. 2:20; 6:14) also belong to this phase of the teaching.

(b) through Christ's blood([1])

Matt. 26:28, For this is my blood of the [new]([2]) covenant, which is poured out for the sake of many [unto remissions of sins].

Mk. 14:24, This is my blood of the covenant, which is poured out for the sake of many.

[Lk. 22:20, This cup is the new covenant in my blood, which is poured out in your behalf.]

Jn. 6:53-55, Unless you eat the flesh of the Son of Man and drink his blood you have no life in yourselves. He that feeds upon my flesh and drinks my blood has eternal life . . . For my flesh is real food, and my blood is real drink.

([1]) "The blood is the life," Deut. 12:22; cf. Lev. 17-11.

([2]) Words in brackets are probably interpolations into the original text.

Eph. 2:13, You who were once far off, are now made near in Christ's blood.

Heb. 9:13, 14, For if the blood of goats and bulls . . . sanctifies to the purification of the flesh, how much more will Christ's blood.

Heb. 9:22, Apart from shedding of blood comes no remission.

Heb. 10:4, For it is impossible that the blood of bulls and goats should take away sin.

Heb. 10:29, The blood of the covenant; also 13:20.

Heb. 13:10, Jesus, that he might sanctify the people by means of his own blood.

I Jn. 1:7, And the blood of Jesus, his Son, purifies us from all sin.

Rev. 1:5, To him who loved us and freed us from our sins by means of his blood.

Rev. 7:14, These are they who came out of the Great Persecution; and they washed their robes and made them white in the blood of the Lamb.

4. ATONEMENT EFFECTS FORGIVENESS OF SINS.

Acts 5:30-32, Jesus, whom you killed . . . did God exalt . . . to give . . . remission of sins.

Acts 13:38, By means of this man, remission of sins is proclaimed.

Acts 26:18, The Gentiles, to whom I will send thee . . . that they may receive forgiveness of sins.

Eph. 1:7, In whom we have . . . the forgiveness of our trespasses.

Heb. 1:3, When he had made a purification of sins.

I Tim. 1:15, Jesus Christ came into the world to deliver sinners.

5. ATONEMENT DESCRIBED AS RANSOM.

Matt. 20:28, For the Son of Man came not to be served, but to serve, and to give his life as a ransom instead of many. Mk. 10:45 is a parallel passage.

Rom. 3:24, Justified freely by his gift, by means of the ransom that is in Christ Jesus.

I Cor. 1:30, But of him are you in Christ Jesus, who became wisdom to us from God, and righteousness, and sanctification, and ransom.

Gal. 3:13, Christ ransomed us from the law's curse, having become a curse in our behalf.

Gal. 4:5, God sent forth his Son . . . that he might ransom those under law.

Eph. 1:7, In whom we have the ransom by means of his blood.

Eph. 1:14, Who is the pledge (or first payment) of our inheritance until the ransom (payment in full) of the purchase.

Eph. 4:30, In whom you were sealed unto a day of ransom.

Col. 1:14, The Son of his love, in whom we have the ransom.([1])

I Tim. 2:16, For God is one; one also is a go-between of God and men, Christ Jesus, a man who gave himself as a ransom for the sake of all.

Tit. 2:14, Who gave himself in our behalf, that he might ransom us from all iniquity.

Heb. 9:11, Christ as a high priest . . . by means of his own blood entered once for all into the holy places, obtaining an eternal ransom.

Heb. 9:15, He is a go-between of a new covenant, in order that, death having occurred for a ransom of the transgressions under the first covenant, those that have been called might receive the eternal inheritance.

I Pet. 1:18, Not with perishable things . . . were you ransomed . . . but with precious blood of Christ, like a lamb blameless and spotless.

Rev. 5:9, Worthy art thou to take the roll, and open its seals. Because thou wast slain and didst purchase for God

([1]) The words following in the A. V., "through his blood," are almost certainly a later interpolation.

with thy blood, out of every tribe and tongue, and people, and nation, and made them a kingdom and priests to our God.

6. ATONEMENT DESCRIBED AS "MERCY-SEAT"([1])

Rom. 3:25, Whom God set forth as a mercy-seat, by means of trust in his blood.

I Jn. 2:2, And he is a mercy-seat with reference to our sins; and not for ours only, but for the whole world.

Heb. 2:17, That he might become a merciful and a faithful high priest in things pertaining to God, to be a mercy-seat for the sins of the people.

7. ATONEMENT DESCRIBED AS SACRIFICE.

I Cor. 5:8, For Christ, our passover, was sacrificed.

Heb. 5:1, Every high priest . . . is appointed . . . to offer both gifts and sacrifices in behalf of sins.

Heb. 5:7, Who is not under a daily necessity . . . of offering sacrifices, for this he did once for all, in offering himself.

Heb. 9:14, Christ . . . offered himself without blemish to God; also verses 26, 27.

Heb. 10:10, Through the offering of Jesus Christ's body once for all.

Heb. 10:12, But he, having offered one sacrifice in behalf of sins.

Heb. 10:14, For by one offering he has perfected forever those who are sanctified.

8. ATONEMENT DESCRIBED AS RECONCILIATION.

Jn. 12:32, And I, if I be lifted up, will draw all men to myself.

Rom. 5:9, 10, For if, while enemies we were reconciled to God by means of his Son's death, much more, being reconciled, we shall be delivered by his life. And not merely

---

([1]) A meeting-place, for reconciliation, of God and man. A. V. "to make reconciliation"; other translations "to make propitiation."

that, but [shall be] exulting in God through our Lord Jesus Christ, by whose means we have now received the reconciliation (cf. 11-15).

II Cor. 5::18-20, And all things are from God, who reconciled us to himself by means of Jesus Christ, and gave to us the service of reconciliation: namely, that God was in Christ reconciling a world to himself, not reckoning to them their trespasses and having committed to us the message of the reconciliation. On behalf of Christ therefore, we act as ambassadors, as though God were entreating through us: we beseech, on behalf of Christ, Be reconciled to God.

Eph. 2:16, That he might reconcile both [Jews and Gentiles] in one body to God by means of the cross.

Col. 1:20, 21, And by means of him to reconcile all things to himself, having made peace by means of the blood of his cross . . . And you he has reconciled by the body of his flesh by means of death.

INDEX